BLACK JACK BOUVIER:

THE LIFE AND TIMES OF JACKIE O'S FATHER

BOOK YOUR PLACE ON OUR WEBSITE AND MAKE THE READING CONNECTION!

We've created a customized website just for our very special readers, where you can get the inside scoop on everything that's going on with Zebra, Pinnacle and Kensington books.

When you come online, you'll have the exciting opportunity to:

- View covers of upcoming books
- Read sample chapters
- Learn about our future publishing schedule (listed by publication month *and author*)
- Find out when your favorite authors will be visiting a city near you
- Search for and order backlist books from our online catalog
- Check out author bios and background information
- Send e-mail to your favorite authors
- Meet the Kensington staff online
- Join us in weekly chats with authors, readers and other guests
- Get writing guidelines
- AND MUCH MORE!

Visit our website at
http://www.pinnaclebooks.com

BLACK JACK BOUVIER:

THE LIFE AND TIMES OF JACKIE O'S FATHER

KATHLEEN BOUVIER

PINNACLE BOOKS
KENSINGTON PUBLISHING CORP.

http://www.pinnaclebooks.com

PINNACLE BOOKS are published by

Kensington Publishing Corp.
850 Third Avenue
New York, NY 10022

Previously published as "To Jack, with Love"
First Zebra Printing: 1979
First Pinnacle Printing: April, 1999
10 9 8 7 6 5 4 3 2 1

Printed in the United States of America

Dedication

To my husband, Michel Bouvier; Jackie O and Black Jack Bouvier—always alive in my heart; and to my sons, Mich and John—with love.

INTRODUCTION

Jack Bouvier's niche in American history, as the father of Jacqueline Bouvier Kennedy, is admittedly not vast, nevertheless Jack possessed certain qualities that made him rather famous in certain circles in Manhattan and East Hampton, Long Island. And because of his daughter's eventual world-wide fame, some of that fame rubbed off on Jack so that he is now also known, via books on Jacqueline, even in remote corners of the earth. After I wrote *Jacqueline Bouvier: An Intimate Memoir* in 1996 I received a letter from Tasmania remarking on the poignancy of Jack's love for his daughter, and a letter in a similar vein from a reader in Singapore.

To call Jack Bouvier an unforgettable character is to belabor a cliché. But he was, nevertheless, a special figure on the American social scene. Recently he was mercilessly, and erroneously, caricatured in Gip Hoppe's play *Jackie: An American Life,* which had a modestly successful run in New York's Belasco Theater for six months in 1997 and 1998. The play, which was a relentless and unsparing farce, depicted Jack Bouvier as a wild, cheap, vulgar womanizer dashing in and out of East Hampton's Maidstone Beach Club cabanas in pursuit of young girls.

His niece (by marriage) Kathy Bouvier will tell you, in

this charming memoir, that there was nothing cheap or vulgar about Jack Bouvier.

As his nephew (he was my mother's older brother) I can vouch for the fact that Jack Bouvier possessed an un-matched sense of style, and a manly elegance that has since almost disappeared from American life.

Jack Bouvier was, first of all, devastatingly handsome, a debonair, and charismatic personality who often fooled people into believing he was a movie star. Frequently, in New York, people would come up to him in the street and ask him for his autograph, thinking that he was Clark Gable, who had recently made such a tremendous impression on the public portraying Rhett Butler in *Gone With the Wind*.

And there was something about Jack's looks that closely resembled the swashbuckling actor. He had a broad face with wide apart china blue eyes, a strong, decisive chin, jet black hair, and he wore a year-around tan. So dark was he during the months of July and August that he became known by a variety of nicknames alluding to his complex-ion: "The Black Prince," "Black Jack," "The Sheikh," and "The Black Orchid."

I remember how Uncle Jack's clothes mirrored and em-phasized the sobriquets by which he was known. A very for-mal man, he wore magnificently tailored double-breasted tan gabardine suits with shirt and tie even outdoors in the blazing heat of mid-August in East Hampton. Some of his sartorial eccentricities, evident in several photographs dis-played in this book, were rolling up the sleeves of his jacket just enough to reveal his gleaming white cuffs and sparkling jeweled cufflinks, and wearing evening pumps during the day with slightly rolled up trousers revealing no socks but an incredibly deep tan on his ankles.

I never saw Uncle Jack dressed informally. When he took his young daughters out to Central Park on a snowy winter day he never wore sports clothes or sweaters or boots. No, as you will observe from an illustration in this book, he would be dressed as he always was, in New York winters, in an immaculately tailored dark navy blue double-breasted overcoat with a white handkerchief in his breast pocket, white shirt, with tie, highly polished black leather shoes, and a black homburg.

Even on horseback, when he rode in East Hampton's summer horse shows with his wife, Janet, and daughter, Jacqueline, he would wear a beautifully tailored tweed jacket with shirt and tie, and the inevitable handkerchief exploding from his breast pocket.

It may be an exaggeration to suggest that Jacqueline developed her love of beauty and extraordinary sense of style from her father, but I think not. Jacqueline's mother dressed rather plainly, without any special flair. To see Jack and Janet together, Jack was clearly the rooster and Janet the hen. As their marriage wore on, Jack's influence over his daughters waxed whereas Janet's influence waned. That is, until Janet divorced Jack in 1940 and remarried in 1942. When she took her daughters up to the vast Auchincloss estate in Newport, Hammersmith Farm, to stay with her new husband, Hugh D. Auchincloss, Jr., known as "Hughdie," Jack's influence over his daughters inevitably suffered.

Now Jacqueline was compelled to divide her time between the Bouviers and the Auchinclosses. Mr. Auchincloss was a very wealthy man, much wealthier than Jack, and was therefore able to provide Jacqueline with certain advantages Jack could not afford. One of these was his vast estate overlooking the Potomac in McLean, Virginia, "Merrywood," where the Auchinclosses wintered, and which offered Jacqueline the opportunity to enjoy one of her favorite sports, fox hunting, in the open countryside.

However, as long as the Bouviers held on to their magnificent estate in East Hampton, "Lasata," Jacqueline would be inevitably drawn to her father. Jack maintained stables for Jackie's horses at "Lasata" and the estate boasted a riding ring where she could put her beloved horses through their paces in private. And, of course, not far away, was the Atlantic with its thundering surf, another delight for the Bouvier grandchildren.

Grandfather Bouvier died in 1948 and since none of his five children were left large enough inheritances to maintain "Lasata," the magnificent estate on Further Lane had to be sold. And when it was finally sold in 1950, for a small fraction of what it is worth today, Jack Bouvier lost one of the strongest holds he had left on Jacqueline's time and affections.

It would, however, be extremely misleading to insinuate that the loss of "Lasata" caused any lessening of Jacqueline's affection for her father. Jacqueline loved her father deeply and she, for him, became his reason for living.

Yes, as you will fully realize by the time you finish Kathy Bouvier's memoir, Jack's love for his daughters, Jacqueline and Lee, became, as he grew older, the only circumstance that gave meaning to his life. When he retired from the Stock Exchange in the early fifties, he had nothing more to live for than a phone call or an occasional visit from Jacqueline. Guests entering his modest apartment on East 74th Street would always be amazed by how many photographs of Jacqueline greeted them. They were everywhere: on the walls, the tables, bookcases, on top of the TV set.

It had always been that way. To behold Jack Bouvier and Jacqueline strolling arm in arm down Park Avenue on, let us say, a Sunday afternoon in the fall would be to encounter two people delighting in each other's company. Here was an affection between a father and a daughter that was intimate and, in the end, eminently constructive. For I believe Jack Bouvier created the woman Jacqueline eventually became. He was a modern-day Pygmalion and she was his masterpiece, Galatea. He had taught her how to dress and move and behave in public. He had endowed her with a unique sense of style and love of beauty. And he had supported her financially from her birth, through boarding school and college, to the day she married John F. Kennedy on September 12, 1953.

I do not think it is an exaggeration to say that the origin of the image of style and beauty Jacqueline would one day project to the entire world, as First Lady, was ultimately traceable to her father's influence. Kathy Bouvier's charming book memorializes Jack Bouvier, and thanks him for the incomparable gift he gave our country and the world.

John H. Davis
July 1998

FOREWORD

John Vernou Bouvier III, father of Jacqueline Bouvier Kennedy Onassis, died many years ago (in 1957), but he still seems to linger and to influence the memory of his beloved daughter. My husband, Michel Bouvier, was Jack Bouvier's nephew, Jackie's cousin.

When Jackie died, Michel, our son John, and I went to her funeral. Before the formal ceremony, which was to be held at the lovely church around the corner, we stopped at Jackie's apartment to view her coffin and to give her our last respects.

What I remember most clearly was the sight of a beautiful oak drawing table which stood in front of a large window overlooking Central Park. This was where I imagined Jackie did what she liked best. Where she painted, wrote, and possibly just sat, thinking of how to protect and nurture her beloved children.

In the living room, which was warm and comfortable, many little well-polished tables held photographs in similar silver frames. Most of them were of her handsome father looking at his best. Strangely, there were no photographs of Jack Kennedy. They might have been in the bedroom. I do not know.

As you will see after reading this book, a strong bond of respect and love existed between Jackie and her father. I was holding Jack Bouvier's hand when he died. He did not recognize me. As I held his hand, he called out for Jackie. She arrived just minutes after he died. She was devastated, but even then showed the courage and self-control she showed years later when Jack Kennedy died.

The one thing that touched the members of the Bouvier family most was that she made a point of having her father's grave covered with masses of blue bachelor button flowers as if to personify the spirit of the man who had lived life to the hilt.

Jackie was buried in Arlington National Cemetery next to Jack Kennedy. Jack Bouvier's remains are in East Hampton, Long Island, New York, in a large burial plot intended to hold members of the Bouvier clan. There was disappointment that Jackie had not chosen to be buried there. Black Jack is there, and so is my husband, Michel. Michel died just months after Jackie, possibly due in part to his insistence on attending Jackie's funeral even though he was desperately ill at the time.

I miss them all, as I believe does everyone whose lives they touched.

I hope this book will help keep them alive in our memories.

Kathleen Bouvier

PROLOGUE

1929

An endless plume of black smoke trailed from the smoke-stack of the locomotive as it chugged relentlessly across the nation.

Inside their compartment, few words passed between the two unlikely traveling companions huddled against the gathering October chill. They had given up their futile attempts at breaking the long, awkward silences with small talk.

Arms crossed on his massive chest, Charles Mattei watched restlessly as the train crossed the Great Divide. Years ago, as a young man, he had cut cross the mountains en route to California. Arriving at Los Olivos, he had set up the historic stagecoach tavern which bore his name.

At any other time, the rugged saloonkeeper might have reminisced about those days gone by or remarked on the beauty of the western terrain beyond the windows. Instead, he spoke about the tender, broken man he had come to love as a son during these last hopeful months.

His companion nodded grimly. He was the image of elegance in his perfectly tailored double-breasted black suit and high, starched collar, and his swarthy face and deep blue eyes seemed to have been drained of their usual aura of vitality. Though his face revealed a character filled with strength and optimism, he seemed overwhelmed by grief.

But even in mourning, he presented a striking figure to all of those who wandered down the narrow train corridor past the compartment. Everything about him spoke of breeding, wealth and power.

Beneath his prominent nose, a pencil-line moustache arched over a pair of full, sensuous lips. But for the deep, almost black hue of his skin, John Vernou Bouvier III— "Black Jack" Bouvier—was a dead ringer for Clark Gable. And throughout his life, in the far corners of the world, Black Jack would be cornered by autograph hounds who were convinced they were at last face to face with Rhett Butler.

But on Park Avenue or Wall Street, or in the radiant never-never land of East Hampton, there could be no mistake. Jack Bouvier was the notoriously glamorous multimillionaire whose name appeared in the society columns almost every day. Heir of the illustrious New York Bouvier clan, his daring gambles in the stock market and his unbroken line of amorous conquests had carved a reputation Clark Gable would have envied.

For all his magnetism and charm, Jack was by nature a man of few words. Not shy or violent by any stretch of the imagination. But laconic. His quick, sharp tongue, with a hint of New York City and more than a suspicion of worldliness, was compelling.

People were drawn to his silences as well. Behind his flashing cerulean eyes, Black Jack Bouvier's brain was always moving—focusing, analyzing, shifting from one object to the next. He was a man who could and did make others' fortunes. Strangers sensed that, and hung on his every word.

But now, he had a haunted, foreboding look. As the train

made its way across the western third of the continent, he sat staring at the empty space in their traveling compartment. His mind was like some blank screen, on which talking pictures of his childhood were projected.

For a day and a half, Jack sat there silently, lost in memories of his younger brother. Then, as the train pulled out of the shadow of the mountains and began picking up speed across the Great Plains, he grew more animated. Although his mourning was far from over, it was time for Jack to dive back into the world of Wall Street.

For four days, he had been isolated, and heard no steady reports from the floor of the New York Stock Exchange, other than the brief long distance calls he was able to place during the train's frequent stops. Now, in the second week of October, 1929, there was strong reason for concern, as the Great Bull Market just kept soaring higher and higher.

Publicly, specialists like Black Jack Bouvier were all smiles as they announced "General Motors will go to a thousand!" and "Radio Corporation—you can't go wrong!" All across the nation, washerwomen and bankers, busboys and industrialists alike were riding the great wave of prosperity. The stock prices, defying the laws of gravity, seemed to know only one direction—up!

But in recent months, there were signs that the market, like dress hemlines, which had soared to midway between the knee and perdition in the last year of the decade, could not float above reason forever.

Indeed, the past few weeks had seen prices rising and falling erratically, as the heat and pressure of trading reached record intensity. It was only a matter of time before it exploded.

But in outposts of civilization like the sleepy Middle Western cities where the transcontinental express pulled into stations, the boiling New York Stock Exchange seemed a million miles away. Determined as he was, John Bouvier failed in his efforts to get the latest stock reports. The communications network, jammed by the intense flurry of activity, was hours behind the times.

Bud, Jack's younger brother, had argued strongly for liquidating his personal assets and preparing himself to fall short—if necessary, making a market in his specialties—an often costly operation. Ultimately, Jack was so impressed by Bud's advice that he sold all of his holdings. He stood to make another fortune, or lose everything, during the next few days.

Now, at the height of his concern, Black Jack had dropped it all and gone to California to bring his little brother home.

Only five nights before, Bud had called up his estranged wife in New York City from Mattei's Tavern, pleading for one last chance. If he could really stop drinking this time—completely—would she consider taking him back?

She had said yes. Wearily. But she had said yes.

Several hours later, Bud collapsed at the bar.

Now he was lying in a coffin, traveling homeward by train with his brother Jack and his last good friend. It was a lonely vigil for Jack Bouvier, one he would never forget.

Inexorably, "Bud," William Sergeant Bouvier, had come to the end everyone had dreaded. The commander who had fought with distinction in the trenches of Saint-Mihiel and the Meuse-Argonne, and received the World War I Victory Medal, had lost his battle against alcoholism.

Bud was gone. Bud, the beautiful, the graceful athlete of the Bouvier dynasty. The vivacious and sensitive youth who had thrilled everyone with his flawless horsemanship, magnificent tenor voice and tap dancing and soft-shoe. He had died an ugly, pitiful death.

The tragedy was the first assault on the Bouviers. It struck their perfect world with the force of a hand grenade. And in many ways, they never fully recovered from it.

When the train at last pulled into Grand Central Station, Jack was on the verge of nervous exhaustion. Weary as he was, he would not be separated from the corpse of his younger brother. Supervising the whole, sad ordeal, he arranged to have the coffin transported to his Park Avenue apartment. There William Sergeant Bouvier lay in state until the funeral the following morning.

A small family service was held at the chapel of the Helpers of the Holy Soul on East Eighty-sixth Street. Afterwards, the intimate gathering made its way in solemn procession to the Gate of Heaven Cemetery in Westchester County.

The scene at the graveside was painfully brutal. Maude Sergeant Bouvier, Jack and Bud's mother, was so smitten by the death of her son that she was literally incapable of attending his funeral. Also absent was Jack's wife, who remained at home caring for their newborn daughter, Jacqueline Lee—the baby who would grow up to be "the greatest woman in the world."

Kneeling by the graveside were Bud's former wife, Emma Louise, and his nine-year-old son, Michel Bouvier III. Young Miche carried himself with a comportment beyond his years as he struggled to make sense of what had happened. Although he understood that he would never again see his father, it would be years before Michel gave up looking for that beautifully sculpted familiar form in every crowd, or stopped expecting to find him waiting outside their apartment in a sporty new coupe, or in the garden of the family estate in East Hampton.

Behind the thick black rim of his pince-nez, John Vernou Bouvier, Jr., Bud and Jack's father, fought back tears. Though Bud was gone, the family and its interests remained. The odds were now almost certain that young Michel would remain the only heir to the Bouvier name. Jack, at thirty-eight, was not a young man by any stretch of wishful imagination. So far, he had only produced a single child, the infant Jacqueline.

In his own generation, John Vernou Bouvier, Jr. had been the only recipient of the Bouvier legacy. From the time of his birth, that fact had always been impressed upon him. It was a situation which the Bouviers had already faced twice since their rise from anonymity to aristocracy in the early nineteenth century.

As the mourners drew away from the muddy grave, Jack threw a fatherly arm around Michel's shoulders. With Bud gone, Jack, and to a lesser degree the child's grandfather, would take on the responsibility of raising him—to the extent that the boy's mother would allow. From now on, Michel would be regarded as the carrier of the family name.

The finely tended lawns of the cemetery, the brightly colored flowers on the well-kept graves, the sumptuous tombstones and statuary all bespoke the fact that America in mid-October, 1929, was witnessing a prosperity never dreamed of. Every day, it seemed, a new technological marvel brought heaven one step closer to earth. Overnight, horse-drawn carriages were replaced with cars, people began tuning in to "music in the air"—the radio. Lindbergh had flown across the Atlantic, becoming a celebrity and setting a standard of heroism for all young men to emulate.

At the hub of the nation's grinding wheels of fortune, specialists like Black Jack Bouvier were wheeling and dealing, engineering excitement, creating an atmosphere of confidence and power which drew investors magnetically to their stocks.

For Jack, his infant Jackie and his new young ward were two more reasons for concern about the market. Anxiously, he pumped more and more into his rising specialty stocks. Then, as the stagnant economy halted the rise of the market and loomed menacingly over the heads of so many brokers on Wall Street, Jack got out at the last instant by selling short—selling stocks which he was then obligated to replace within a period of weeks.

Following Bud's advice to the letter, Jack's gambler's sense of timing was perfect. As the market suddenly plummeted like a dirigible on fire, deflating the economy and the extravagant hopes born of the twenties, Jack Bouvier was actually raking in a profit.

Unfortunately, no one suspected that Bud had been too ill in his final days to implement his own ideas. When the market crashed fourteen days after his death, the estate of William Sergeant Bouvier was reduced to ashes.

ONE

The New Bouvier

I was brought into the Bouvier family when I married young Michel. Immediately after our wedding reception in Guayaquil, Ecuador, Miche and I boarded an old DC-3 and wended our roundabout way up to the States, and New York.

In 1946, I was a new and rather frightened bride. An English girl raised in Ecuador, where my father was the director of the Bank of London in South America, I had been young and possibly even wild before meeting Miche, but that was only relative to the rigid standards of our small international enclave. Miche's reference to good times back home, however, were always imbued with the faintest hint of out-and-out debauchery.

Insofar as the Bouviers were concerned, I was not sure what sort of family I was marrying into. Miche was a towering man and quite devastatingly handsome, and he took pride in both traits with a typical Bouvier vanity which was quite unseemly by British standards. I might add that his self-assurance also went beyond the bounds of British decency.

Nonetheless, he was a gentleman born and bred. We were

very much in love, and we set about the business of marrying. There would be time to worry about his family later.

By the time of our wedding night, I had become vaguely aware that the Bouviers were hardly an average fun-loving American family. I was prepared for almost anything when we touched down in New York and were immediately driven to Jack's apartment on East Seventy-fourth Street. Of course, we would stay with him until we could find a suitable apartment in the city. Jack would have it no other way.

Nothing in this world, or any other, could have prepared me for meeting that vivid and complex being. John Vernou Bouvier III, father of Jacqueline Bouvier Kennedy Onassis and Princess Lee Radziwill, had been anything but modest. He simply had no reason to be. He knew he had everything a man could ever want. And he enjoyed it!

His familial dignity and strict code of honor always remained beyond reproach. Jack felt toward my husband as he would toward a son of his own—particularly after the divorce from Janet Lee left him with two daughters and no great promise of a legitimate heir of his own. There was never a second when Jack did not treat me as a daughter—this in spite of the fact that we were living in his apartment, and Miche, on occasion, would be gone for several nights.

Of course, I was new in the country, and felt not the slightest bit of peril. I found Jack charismatic, irresistibly handsome and debonair. But I had not the slightest knowledge of his reputation as a lover.

In Guayaquil, we had never heard of Black Jack, or the Black Orchid, as he was sometimes called. Nor did I have any inkling that he had cut a wide swath across the entire breadth of the fashionable female population, from New York City to the tip of Gatsby territory: The Hamptons.

The revelation was not long in coming. Even in my innocence, living in the apartment, overhearing the telephone calls and meeting some of Jack's companions, I soon became aware of how the land lay.

The repercussions of Jack's infamous and legendary courtships continue into the present. Just recently, I came across a grey-haired dowager whose face was animated by a radiant glow as soon as his name was mentioned. Whatever her memories of their liaison, she clearly had not one regret. Nor did she have any need to divulge such a time-honored secret.

Of course, there have been a few elderly matrons whose mouths pursed unattractively at the mention of Jack Bouvier, and who disparaged his manifestly inexhaustible capacity to seduce any of their friends and acquaintances who struck his fancy. Intuition tells me that those were the distinguished few who had not been invited to share his bed.

At Jack's funeral mass, the back pew of St. Patrick's was an unbroken line of women of all ages—most of whom we couldn't identify—in black mourning veils; a fitting tribute to Jack's lifelong pursuit.

Inevitably, women were always at the center of Jack's life. To some extent, it was almost preordained. Devoted as he was to his beautiful mother, Maude, Jack was off to a strong start as a ladies' man. Nature helped. Blessed as he was with the good looks of a Gable, the Latin swarthiness of a Valentino and the disarmingly cheerful charm of a Lindbergh, Jack took to women like a duck to water.

Glancing at the photographs of Jack which are scattered throughout our house, I am always reminded that a director once asked him to try out for the part of Rhett Butler in *Gone with the Wind*. There could never have been a more perfect choice for the role, but Jack refused it. No doubt the kidding it would have occasioned on the floor of the stock exchange had something to do with his decision.

As it was, he received more than his share of the limelight there. "Hey, Jack," the call would frequently echo across the hall, "I hear you're trading Ethel!" At other times, it would be, "Tell me Bouvier, is Sandra really at $38 1/2$?" And always, they would fall back on calling him Black Jack, the Black Orchid of Wall Street.

He had the swarthiness of a Pakistani, and all of the hauteur of an Arabian sheikh. Surprisingly, his soulful eyes were a very dark, hyacinth blue. His strong physique and his phenomenal complexion were of singular importance to Jack. The duplex apartment at 740 Park Avenue had one maid's room which was transformed into a miniature gymnasium, complete with a professional sun lamp. Jack worked out there religiously, as well as at the Yale Club on Vanderbilt Avenue.

When the weather permitted—time was never an issue where such essential matters were concerned—Jack would sunbathe. At home, he would haul one of the enormous easy chairs out of his dressing room and put it in front of the oversized window, open to the strong easterly sun. Then, without the least show of modesty vis-a-vis the neighbors—and in a period when strict decorum was observed— he would strip down to nothing and sprawl out beneath the sun.

While skirts were crawling shockingly up to mid-calf, and ladies still wore stockings in the water—to say nothing of cover-up bathing dresses—Jack was sunning as naked as he was born in a very big window facing Park Avenue.

I marvel at the fact that there was never a complaint. Perhaps any outrage was mitigated by the sight of his physique, which was nothing if not magnificent. He was tall and broad-shouldered. Not an ounce of fat softened his tight dark skin.

The only comments about Jack's nude sunbathing came, curiously enough, from the men's quarter. At the Maidstone Club in East Hampton, he would regularly abandon his cabana and all modesty to soak up the sensuous warmth of the sun in unabashed delight in the courtyard amid the men's lockers. Apparently, all of his cohorts did not share

Jack's enthusiasm for freedom. But that fact never fazed him one bit.

Black Jack never saw any reason to conceal what the good Lord had given him. And by his own reckoning, He had given him just about everything.

Even his one imperfection—a tiny mole above the right corner of his lip—seemed only to add to his beauty. Beyond impeccable physical attractiveness, fine style and tremendous wealth, Jack's seductiveness lay in his aura of unquestionable masculinity. He looked like the concrete realization of a young girl's dreamy fantasy—the glamorous sheikh who would whisk her off to his tent in Araby.

In fact, if she was indeed chosen, the young fortunate was more than likely to find herself at the Canoe Place Inn, being wined and dined by candlelight. At the appropriate moment, the headwaiter would appear with a flaming silver platter of pressed duck—the very duck which Jack had shot for her at dawn.

Also at just the right moment, every staff member of the elegant old country inn would vanish, so that Jack's *coup d'amour* could be achieved with the utmost discretion.

It's a pity that the code of dress dictated that no turbans or flowing robes be worn by men; Jack would have looked perfect in such regalia. However, he did his best to look impeccable in tailored gabardines and pin stripes, buttoned down blue or white Brooks Brothers shirts and striped F. R. Tripler club ties.

Jack was a rake in the most glorious way a man could be. In the end, when he had decided to terminate a bedtime partnership—he was not always exceedingly kind. Yet no one could ever claim that he had done anything to disguise his dishonorable intentions. From the start, he let it be known that he was "playing the field." After hours, there was a constant barrage of phone calls from eager young women. Jack would answer them, discreetly stepping into another room, regardless of his momentary companion.

Nobody could accuse him of trying to conceal, or even play down, the extent of his philandering.

People today get righteously indignant when they hear of Jack Bouvier's amours, but the women he dated didn't. They knew just where they fit in in the scope of his life. He would never have tried to fool them on that score. Each of Jack's ladies was one in many, and had to know from the start what she was letting herself in for. Jack was an old-fashioned bachelor or man-about-town, and gave her the treatment which was expected of that sort of man.

Why then did they flock to him in droves? Perhaps it was the insatiability of the frenetic age in which they lived. Or maybe it was just the radiance of Black Jack Bouvier's animal magnetism. As long as a girl could maintain his interest, Jack Bouvier saw to it that her every dream came true—unless it was a dream of somehow monopolizing him and the outpouring of his generous affection.

Jack wooed his thoroughly modern women with wine and roses every day, and with total and devoted obsession. Until he broke it all off, Jack would take his young loves to Jack and Charlie's "21" and later to the Polo Bar of the Westbury, to all of the most glamorous Broadway openings as well as to cozy and romantic hideaways in the country.

Illogically, his old-fashioned woo-pitching never failed. Never but once, that is—when he met his match—but that's getting far ahead of our story.

During his twenties and thirties, Jack lived the Great American Dream: he was a Yale man; the most eligible bachelor in New York; handsome to a fault; and fabulously wealthy.

His chauffeur-driven cars went from a Nash touring car, to a Lincoln Zephyr, to a custom-built Stutz touring car designed in part by himself.

By the time Jack was thirty-five, his stock market profits alone were well over three quarters of a million dollars. At the same time, he was earning in excess of $75,000 a year as a specialist broker—earnings that would be the equivalent of $200,000 today. His specialist stocks included, among others, Texas Gulf & Sulphur, Baldwin Locomotive, and Firth Carpet.

And even when his personal finances were not entirely in order, no one could ever have guessed it from the elements of his sumptuous life style. He lived on New York's fashionable East Side, summered at large country houses in East Hampton, maintained a stable of thoroughbred horses, and belonged to the Maidstone Club, the Yale Club and the New York Racquet Club. He was even listed as one of Mrs. Jacob Astor's golden "400."

It was a time when, to paraphrase the great voice of the era, Emil Coué, every day in every way, things just kept getting better and better. Jack's unbounded optimism was raging and infectious. His habit of optimism seemed to preclude the possibility of any day failing to be grander than the one which had gone before.

It was a golden light which tinted and falsified any serious reflection upon the times. Even the dim prospects of Bud Bouvier's life were somehow lightened by the fact that he, too, was a millionaire by virtue of his stock holdings.

Of course, that was on paper. Like so many other images, it was a rose-colored, two-dimensional still life. And beneath the surface of their fortunes—and most aspects of American life in the first quarter of this century—far less savory realities were preparing to pierce through the tinsel of illusion.

For the present, though, Jack could ignore all of the problems. He was more than content to glide across the unmarred, glossy surface of life. Never introspective, he ran roughshod over his own anxieties, refusing to recognize them. While he was an exceedingly kind and warm person, Jack could at times seem cruel and totally indifferent to the sensitivities of others. Perhaps it was the only way he found to defend against emotional pain.

As a gambler, Jack had the uncanny intelligence to make a fortune on Wall Street. Yet he was often extravagantly stupid in spending it. He was generous to a fault, yet put far too much emphasis on money. Considering the responsibilities he had to a wife, two daughters, and his nephew, Miche, and the demands put upon him by his own standard of living, and by his considerable margin account with his brokerage firm, this was not at all surprising.

In short, Jack was the quintessential man of fortune during an era when life was an endless series of happy escapades. And he lived it to the hilt.

Or so it seemed. No life can be exempt from suffering, and ultimately Jack's was no exception. In the end, he did suffer—and suffer greatly.

But for the present, America was riding on the tide of a prosperity so great that it seemed it would never be threatened. There was just too much—of everything!

And there, riding on the crest of the wave, with an embarrassment of riches, was Jack Bouvier.

It was the Age of Opulence. And he was having a very good time, indeed.

TWO

To Be A Bouvier

Today, the Bouvier name is immediately associated with Jacqueline Bouvier Kennedy Onassis. Perhaps then one thinks of her sister, Princess Lee Radziwill. But certainly, the Bouviers were a distinguished and powerful clan long before Jack's two magnificent daughters had even made it out of rompers.

This is a book about Jack Bouvier, one of the most charismatic and fascinating men the world has ever known; a man whose inimitable style and lust for life dazzled New York society and brought him to the pinnacle of the Great American Dream. But it is also the story of an era and a family which, destined for greatness, achieved it and strove for even more. The Bouviers figured so prominently in Jack's life that to omit his family would be to tell only half his story.

Today, the only members of his family who retain the family surname are myself, our first son Miche, along with his wife Pauline, son Mischa, and daughters Suzanne, Theres and Darcie and our second son John and his wife Lulu and daughter Jassica. Somehow, curiously, even when *we* speak of the Bouviers we find ourselves thinking of that great family of the past. The legacy has always been that strong.

Rare as it is in America, the name Bouvier is as common as Smith or Jones in some parts of France. At the time of the American Revolution, there were many French emigrés of that name who fought for the colonists. Family legend notwithstanding, none of those men appears to have been an ancestor of Jack.

The founder of the Bouvier fortune in America was the original Michel Bouvier. Not terribly long after he managed to escape with his life from Waterloo, Michel picked up stakes in the tiny picturesque village of Pont Saint-Esprit, located on the Rhone River.

Arriving as an immigrant at New York Harbor, the young man immediately found work as a cabinet maker, just as his father and his father's father had done. Hand-crafting furniture was a time-consuming art, a source of tremendous pride to the young man—and it was also his meal ticket. Michel devoted himself wholeheartedly to his work, and at the end of two years had managed to save just over five hundred dollars—sufficient money for him to relocate to Philadelphia and open up shop.

At the time, the nation's capital had already shifted from Philadelphia to the District of Columbia. But the City of Brotherly Love remained the bastion of culture in the American wilderness, and French emigrés migrated there in droves. Once they had arrived in the formidable banking and commercial center of the former colonies, they discovered a stone wall blocking their assimilation.

It had always been chic to derive from the French aristocracy, but for the immigrant artisan or laborer, French Catholicism unlocked no doors of opportunity in the New World. Like every other minority group, the French banded together in tight-knit enclaves to resist the effects of prejudice. It was the natural place for Michel Bouvier to make a new start.

Of course, there was no more mixing between classes for the French in Philadelphia than there had been in Paris. But in a world apart, many French aristocrats insisted upon hiring their own as domestics or artisans.

It was in the capacity of a cabinetmaker that Michel Bouvier first came to serve His Royal Highness, the King of Spain.

Napoleon Bonaparte, always respectful of familial duty, had given Spain to his older brother, Joseph, who had worked himself up from the position of Emperor of the Two Sicilies. Like the young Bouvier, Joseph I had managed to escape defeat at Waterloo, carrying with him not only an aristocratic title, but also no small share of the imperial treasure, both gifts from young Napoleon.

Arriving in Philadelphia, Joseph Bonaparte established a home in the palatial estate known as Point Breeze. In time, after Michel Bouvier had constructed furniture and performed a thousand less rewarding tasks there, he advanced to supervising house carpentry at the estate. Then he was given charge of all construction projects.

Soon, Michel was working for many of Philadelphia's top French citizens. Included among his regular employers was Stephen Girard, the legendary self-made millionaire. The banker, who wore a mysterious black eye patch, had begun in obscurity in Bordeaux. Arriving in America, he set about making his fortune. A felicitous marriage had brought Stephen Girard one trading clipper as part of the dowry.

A decade later, he owned over twenty.

Michel Bouvier's good fortune was a bit more average. He married well to Sarah Ann Pierson. She presented him with an heir, Eustache, the following year. Two years later, in 1826, Sarah died in childbirth with Thérèse.

In 1828, Michel married well once again, choosing for the mother of his children a hearty and well-educated

woman of seventeen whose family had no small suspicion
of aristocratic roots.

Louise C. Vernou came with no dowry, but she encouraged Michel in all ways to rise in society and fortune, and
laid out the framework for building a dynasty by increasing
his heirs from two to a dozen, adding Elizabeth, Louise,
Emma, Zenaide, Alexine, Mary, John Vernou, Josephine,
Michel C. (known as MC). And last came Joseph, Jr., who
was born in 1852 and, like his sister Josephine, died in early
childhood.

Throughout the years in which his issue increased,
Michel Bouvier continued to perform all manner of skilled
and unskilled tasks for the gentry. He made and repaired
furniture, provided a moving service, even delivered firewood. He worked furiously, and with devotion and skill. His
wealthy patrons recommended him to their acquaintances,
who then became regular customers. Michel redoubled his
efforts, hired assistants, took on more work, worked even
longer hours. His earnest dedication was rewarded with
some degree of financial comfort.

But he was hardly sitting pretty. In fact, if fortune was a
carriage, he was still very much at the wrong end of the
harness.

So Michel gave up crafting cabinets by hand and went
into mass production. He began importing veneers and
marble, producing table tops by employing factory methods. As profits arrived, he began investing them in property.

It was the land and construction speculations that really
paid off. On his lots in the city, Michel began developing
brownstones, then turning them around at a huge profit.

Fortune struck when his extensive West Virginia holdings, which he had purchased at three acres to the dollar,
turned out to be coal-bearing. Overnight, the firewood de-
liveries ended; Michel delivered bituminous instead.

When Michel Bouvier finally did sell the coal lands, he

made an astronomical profit. His family was, at last, launched in style.

His children were educated at private schools to benefit from the advantages he had always been denied. In time, the family moved into a luxurious brownstone mansion on North Broad Street, the most elegant address permitted a man of new means in exclusive Philadelphia. They hired maids, a cook, even a coachman, and began to live in a style of elegance and luxury.

Upon coming of age, Eustache, Michel's eldest son, declined to settle down. Spurred on by his father's success, 'Stache, barely in his twenties, left home to find his fortune. Profligate by nature, he quickly disgraced himself in the eyes of his father.

Supported by Michel for the next twenty years, Eustache alternated his time between prospecting for gold and prospecting for women in California. He clearly had no success to show from the former, although his prowess as a ladies' man is well-documented.

The next generation of Bouviers, when they chose to marry, married well. Elizabeth wed a wealthy businessman named Joseph Dixon, and Thérèse married into the Pattersons of Philadelphia. Emma Bouvier married Francis A. Drexel who had just joined his father's prominent and influential bank in Philadelphia. Frank and his brother opened up international investment houses on Wall Street and in Paris. Among the dozens of institutions they controlled were several in which they were in partnership with an ambitious young man named John Pierpont Morgan.

Of all the marriages, the best social alliance was made by the first John Vernou. Returning home from the Civil War—in which he had been wounded at Bull Run and at Gettysburg—John fell in love with and married Caroline Maslin Ewing. Carrie's father, Robert Ewing, was the dean of Philadelphia Main Line society. The respectably wealthy descendant of a colonial family, he befriended many of the

great statesmen of his day, had his portrait painted by
Thomas Scully, and held court for the most elegant circle
in America.

Carrie and John moved at once to New York, where Frank
Drexel arranged a clerkship for him at the subsidiary Wall
Street brokerage firm of Drexel, Winthrop and Co. Even
with his brother-in-law's help, John did not immediately
thrive in the booming jungle of New York. Their first years
there were marked by repeated letters home, requesting
money.

Soon they were joined in Manhattan by John's younger
brother, "MC." Michel Sr. loaned each of them sufficient
money to buy seats on the Stock Exchange.

When the Panic of 1873 struck, it took its toll on the
Bouvier fortunes, lowering Michel's assets to just under one
million dollars. At the time of his death several years later,
he left each of his eight remaining children $85,000 or
about half a million dollars by today's standards.

Eustache returned home to make a final peace with his
father, and to collect his share of the estate. While two-thirds
of it was held out of harm's way in an inviolable trust fund,
'Stache took what he could and set sail for Australia, with
the announced intentions of pursuing the same goals there
as he had in California—women and gold.

John Vernou Bouvier never did augment his principal.
Nonetheless, he and Carrie lived quite well between what
he earned as a broker's broker—known in the trade as a
"two dollar man"—and the dividends on his own holdings
in the market.

MC Bouvier, however, basing his whole life on the market,
was soon on his way to amassing a wealthy man's fortune.
Beginning with the management of the Vanderbilt account
at Morgan & Drexel, the younger brother then went on to
form the Wall Street firm of MC Bouvier & Co. Even before
Michel, Sr. died, MC was worth well over half a million dollars.

In time, MC became the managing executor of his father's estate. With his mother also gone, he inherited the responsibility of caring for his older sisters as well. Louise, early in life, had fled home and, against her father's wishes, joined a convent. But there remained three other maiden sisters—Zenaide, Alexine and Mary. In addition to his own legacy, MC managed the investment of the three "house nuns' " inheritances.

He bought an elegant four-story brownstone on West Forty-sixth Street, just off of Fifth Avenue, and after selling the North Broad Street residence, the foursome settled in the New York townhouse where they would spend the rest of their lives.

With the Philadelphia mansion gone, the Bouviers set out to establish themselves among the elite of Manhattan. The three sisters at once made their bid for entry into the world of the Astors and the Vanderbilts. In a town which did not exhibit the social snobbery of the Philadelphia Main Line, nor its begrudging attitude toward fortunes made through applied brilliance and hard work, they were quickly assimilated into the highest echelons of society. At long last, the Bouviers had truly arrived.

Money and health exhausted at the age of fifty-nine, Eustache, the lone black sheep of the family, sailed back into New York City on a clipper ship. Arriving as a pronounced failure, he took up residence with his brother and three sisters in the house on West Forty-sixth Street, where he died three years later.

The three sisters boasted that they would die one and all of them virgins. MC made no such declaration. But he *did* die a bachelor.

At the final tally, the sole heir to the Bouvier name would be John Vernou Bouvier and Carrie's only child, John Vernou Bouvier, Jr. Throughout his childhood—and beyond—it was a weighty responsibility he was never allowed to forget.

After receiving his LL.B. from Columbia in 1888, John

Vernou Bouvier, Jr. entered upon a career as a trial lawyer
which, by all accounts, was brilliant. He worked his way up
through several law firms until, at the turn of the century,
he set up his own trial practice. Soon he would be charging
clients upwards of a thousand dollars a day for his legal
services. Not one of them ever quibbled with the price.

His gift for oratory was truly astounding. In a thundering
voice brimming with self-assurance and dignity, he would
mix lofty thoughts and impossible words—the latter culled
from his privately printed pocket lexicon—with an assort-
ment of simple home truths guaranteed to wring a nod of
agreement from the most recalcitrant listener.

Longwinded? But of course he was! It was both part of
his grandiloquent style and also a strategic technique. Making a point before a doubting jury, John, Jr. was at his best,
artfully twirling the waxed tips of his moustaches as he laid
out his case. He would draw out his subjects and verbs, em-
bellishing them with such laudatory adverbs and rousingly
patriotic modifying clauses that the ladies and gentlemen
of the jury had to be restrained from leaping out of their
seats in their fervor to help him protect the American way.

In jumping to that defense, the jurors would incidentally
discover that the object of their protection was more than
likely John, Jr.'s client, about whom they'd forgotten their
misgivings.

As the years passed, John, Jr. devoted more and more
time to public speaking, often on the behalf of organizations like the New York Bar Association or the Sons of the
American Revolution.

Nowhere was he more eloquent than at the ribbon-cut-
ting ceremony for the George Washington Bridge. As his
speech was carried over the radio to millions of listeners
throughout the country, he held a rapt audience in his
thrall. Even his youngest grandchildren stood at attention,
trying hard to seize each multi-syllabic, multi-faceted word!

How much they understood then cannot be known. But

for years after, Miche, Jackie and the rest of them referred to the structure as Granddad's Bridge.

John, Jr. was the first Bouvier to look beyond the world of finance and power to evince a serious interest in culture. Among his papers there remain dozens of essays on the role of women in society, on celibacy and contraception, and on the other heated topics of the century. He was an avid reader, knowing the classics well, and devoting his later years in particular to Shakespeare and Macaulay. He took his position as heir to the family name with great seriousness, and went to many pains to chronicle the family history, trace its genealogy, and pass it all down to posterity.

At the turn of the century, America was still fully testing out the notion of aristocracy. With the number of dynasties increasing, family name and money became increasingly important as a barometer of social prominence.

Two generations removed from the humble wellspring of their wealth, the Bouviers were prepared to mix with the best of them.

Never a retiring sort, John, Jr. threw himself into the heart of the fashionable society his aunts had first entered. Naturally, he married well—the beautiful Maude Sergeant, a well-connected woman of considerable reputation and charm, whom he met at a romantic old inn at Westhampton Beach, the Howell House.

Beyond that, the young lawyer found his way into all of the exclusive clubs: The Sons of the American Revolution and the Society of the Cincinnati (both by virtue of the Ewing branch of the family); the New York Athletic Club; the prestigious Union Club. At all of these, he was a frequent, and powerful, voice.

On May 19, 1891, Maude Sergeant Bouvier gave birth to a son. The entire family sighed with relief once an heir to the Bouvier name, John Vernou III, was born. His father had a country home built at Nutley, New Jersey, and the following year, the family moved there. In 1893, Jack was joined by a baby brother, Bud. The following year a girl, Edith, was born.

As the Gay Nineties galloped to a close, America caught its first glimpses of the twentieth century, the modern era. Gathering the Great White fleet, America set out to become a world power. Heroic old war songs rang out as weary Spain buckled beneath the pummeling fists of the new and belligerent nation. Throughout the country, night turned to day as electric lighting spread like wildfire. The telephone was all the rage!

John, Jr. spent those years in a daily commute to Manhattan, building up his reputation and his monetary resources toward the time when he and his family could return triumphant, and in style.

For six years, Sacony, the trusted Italian coachman, would drive the young lawyer to the train station. Boarding the New York Express, John would take his customary window seat in the elegant lavender-velvet panelled dining car. Like every respectable dining car of its day, this one was equipped with a jovial black waiter, immaculately dressed in white.

Ignoring the clearly printed menu in front of his eyes, John, Jr. would ask the ritual question every morning. "Well, George, what have you got for breakfast this morning?"

"Yessuh, Mr. Bouvier," the waiter would reply, regardless of whatever the kitchen held, laughing and making a little song out of his answer, "We got fresh fish on a dish, ham and eggs, and po'k chops."

Joining in the laughter, every day without fail Jack's father would order his usual boiled eggs on protein toast and coffee. Of course, cholesterol had not yet been invented.

For six long years, the ritual was reenacted daily while the young father waited restlessly for the chance to step into the shoes of senior partners at Hoadley, Lauterbach and Johnson.

Then came the brisk winter dawn when Sacony came racing into the house at six in the morning, his breath escaping from between chattering teeth in tiny wisps of smoke. "Mister Boovah!" he hollered in his broken Italian accent. "Mister Boovah. I seena de horse—itsa falla down."

Through sleepy eyes, young Jack watched his father's face flush with alarm as he began racing about the living room in a flurry of activity. Oblivious to the effect of his words, Sacony continued with a full discourse on the sad state of the horse while his master's face grew paler and paler with concern.

Only when he noticed that John, Jr. was telephoning the veterinarian did Sacony pause for breath. After listening for a second, he cut off the worried lawyer. "Ohhh, no!" Sacony exclaimed cheerfully. "Not *you* horse! Itsa Mr. Bergah horse!" With that, he shrugged and headed back outside.

When the sleepy master of the house recovered from the shock, everyone burst into uncontrolled laughter. The story of the day the horse fell down quickly became a family favorite.

During his first five years as a law office clerk, John, Jr. learned that senior partners never retired. After five years as a junior lawyer at Hoadley, he sadly realized that it seemed unlikely that any of them were within a decade of death—his one means of advancement.

Just prior to the turn of the century, he formed the firm of Bouvier & Warren, with offices at 31 Nassau Street.

In 1905, Maude gave birth to twin daughters, Michelle and Maude. Soon afterward, John, Jr. set to work on his magnum opus, *Our Forebears*, a privately published volume detailing the rise of the Bouviers.

He spent many years compiling the family history, which documented the aristocratic French origins of the family, and presented their coat of arms—the lion rampant on a gold field which he bore on his signet ring—as well as that of the Vernou branch. *Our Forebears* was riddled with inaccuracies, not the least of which was associating the Vernou name with the aristocratic family of de Vernoux, and the Bouvier clan with the aristocratic family of that name which lived in Grenoble—some distance from the sleepy little village of Pont Saint-Esprit.

The first edition was presented to his children, and each of the three subsequently revised and expanded versions was presented to his grandchildren, as well as to the Library of Congress, the New York Public Library, the Library of Columbia University, and the New York and Pennsylvania historical societies.

By the time his granddaughter was in the White House, John Vernou Bouvier, Jr. had been dead thirteen years. Jackie, like the rest of us, had long since accepted his illustrious tales of the Bouviers as gospel. So had the hundreds of other prominent Americans who having read the private edition, passed along its information—fact as well as fiction.

Jackie's grandfather wrote the book not for the public, but ostensibly for his descendants. In view of that, it is hard to fault the man. Writing for the sole edification of his own kin, John Vernou Bouvier, Jr. decorated the facts with a bit of fancy. Perhaps he did rearrange the truth a little here and there—but wasn't it his stated purpose in *Our Forebears* "to arouse no unbecoming pride of birth, but rather to excite a worthy spirit of emulation"? His children and grandchildren did carry over to their families that sense of greatness and of destiny. And in that, his purpose has been achieved admirably.

Later, some sort of nobility was linked with the Bouvier family tree, manifested, some said, in Jackie's exemplary comportment as First Lady during Jack Kennedy's tenure in the White House and also in Lee's marriage to a deposed prince of Poland. It hardly seems a crime if their grandfather, like so many others of his day, wished to pretend there was some aristocratic blood in the Bouvier veins.

In fact, there wasn't. There was something much better. A long line of hard-working, courageous men who managed to make a place for themselves and their families, without the aid of others. Or of noble blood.

THREE

The Clan

Jack's immediate family, as I knew them, consisted of his daughters, Jackie and Lee; his father; his twin sisters, Maude Davis and Michelle Putnam; and their other sister, Edith Beale. During the First World War, John Vernou Bouvier, Jr. had been commissioned as a major in the Judge Advocate's office. The title stuck to him, and Jack's father was known to us as "the Major."

The Bouviers at home were, to say the least, *overwhelming!* While the Major did belong to many terribly conservative organizations in his time, he was nonetheless a bit of a rebel by nature. Perhaps by genetic inheritance, Jack and Edith were also quite difficult as children. They had learned from their father the subtle art of smiling politely at pompous social dictates, then doing exactly as they pleased. But while Jack's father did pay lip service to his peers and in many ways bowed to convention, Jack and Edith simply "did not care to" as they grew older.

This was a source of increasing friction between the generations. To make things worse, they always believed in expressing themselves *positively* and *loudly*. From adolescence on, the Major's eldest son was continually being cut out of his will with the admonition to either mend his ways or not get a penny of his father's money. Once Jack had amassed a considerable fortune on the stock exchange, his ways would clearly never change for anyone. But even earlier, the threats never mattered much. Sooner or later, he was sure to be reinstated.

Generally, none of the Bouviers took being told what to do very seriously. Trying to run their lives was a total waste of time. And still is.

Jack and Edith fought like cat and dog, gaining tremendous pleasure out of egging one another on. Christmas dinners were particularly memorable for the traditional arguments between the siblings. Once one began, it was sure to flare into marvellous fireworks of quick wits and impassioned speeches.

The displays were short-lived. It seemed they never stayed mad at one another for long. Possibly they weren't angry at all, but enjoyed the furor they inevitably caused.

Jack's relationship with Edith was a strange one. I never could figure out whether they liked each other or not. There was no question that she needed him: Edith telephoned her older brother constantly, frequently to his annoyance. No matter how often he shouted, *"HANG UP THE DAMNED PHONE!"* Edith still persisted in keeping up a constant conversational barrage.

It's possible that Jack was the one member of the family who truly understood Edith. That was no easy matter. There were no guidelines to follow in analyzing her personality because Edith was simply unlike anyone else.

Beginning in early childhood, Edith developed character traits that would later develop into true eccentricity. She was oblivious to social pressure from the start, having absolutely no need for public approval except where it concerned appreciation of her singing voice.

And in truth, it was a beautiful voice, though Edith

tended to use it more often than the ear could take. Warbling incessantly, even a Marian Anderson might rapidly
become a bore, but Edith constantly performed on a daily
basis, spurred on to her full repertoire at the drop of a hat.

She should have been an actress. She might have been a
great one, in the tradition of Lynn Fontanne or Tallulah
Bankhead. Instead, she spent the early years in East Hampton on the fringe of respectability as a bohemian. Her latter
years were spent in seclusion, living as a recluse in the genteel squalor of her house, Grey Gardens.

Certainly, some of the flair for theatrics was handed down
to Edith and Jack from the Major. With his dramatic sword-
tip moustaches, his *pince-nez* and his full-throated, booming
voice, the Major would argue with all the artfulness of a
Clarence Darrow and the visual panache of a Barrymore.
Perhaps, like so many successful lawyers, the Major was in
reality a frustrated actor.

Maude and Michelle, the red-headed twins, were less theatrical but no less adamant about matters close to home.
Of course, a Bouvier was expected to have opinions about
all matters touching upon the lives of family members. And
they always did.

For the sheltered and quite shy young woman that I was
when first brought into the family, it was quite a harrowing
experience. There was no room for reticence in their lives,
and I had that deeply ingrained reserve thought proper for
the well-brought-up English girl.

I found it extremely difficult to show my feelings and
took offense easily, but silently. The Bouviers took *nothing*
silently. If something bothered them, the whole world
would know it! In addition to his prolific verse writing and
speechmaking about town, the children grew up exposed
to a constant bellow of *"GOD DAMN IT TO HELL!"* which
the Major would roar at the least provocation.

At the height of some of their mightier verbal battles, I
was positive they would kill one another. But I soon learned

that the arguments lasted only until the victor in the war of
words had been established—then it was all summarily
dropped. Unless, of course, the loser could contrive some
further point which might settle the matter in his or her
favor. In which case the whole thing would flare up all over
again.

They were all such powerful personalities, and the clashes
confused and terrified me more than a little. The only members of the family who seemed to understand my predicament were my husband, Miche, and Jack. Actually, I think
Jackie also understood. She was younger than the rest of
us, and given to a quietude of spirit; the opposite of her
grandfather.

Between her frequent absences while at school and vacations spent at her mother's home, Jackie's exposure to the
family squabbles was limited. While, as a newcomer, I didn't
know her feelings all that well, there were quiet smiles of
commiseration across the battlefield.

I suppose that having two daughters so close to my own
age gave Jack the needed insight into my dilemma. I felt
completely out of my element. Somehow, he sensed that
and sympathized with my plight. For that alone, I will be
eternally grateful.

Looking back on it now, I realize the Bouvier habit of
unadulterated openness was a healthy thing. It trained
them to have quick minds and even quicker tongues. Beyond their home, they were known as masters of repartee.
All of the Bouviers were more persuasive than was perhaps
good for them.

The love and pride they felt for one another was in no
way touched by their vehement arguments. But as one was
staring down into the heart of a boiling quarrel, it was hard
to remember it was only the Bouvier method of letting off
steam. And at those times, they simply petrified me.

The one strong unifying bond in the family was Maude.
Without exception, every member of the clan adored her.

With Jack, her firstborn, Maude shared a very special relationship. During even the most bustling of family get-togethers, they always found time for a quiet stroll *à deux,* or else a half hour of gentle chatting in some far removed corner.

Maude was a striking woman. She had soft, translucent skin, a mane of copper-colored hair, and a matchless figure. On her English father's side, Maude represented the first generation of Americans. But her mother's grandfather had already been prospering in New York when Michel Bouvier founded the American branch of his family.

After the birth of the twins, Maude developed severe physiological complications. Her magnificently turned ankles swelled with phlebitis, and dropsy set in. Her appearance was still graceful, but now quite full. Nonetheless, Maude was determined to keep up her beauty for the Major and their brood.

Her hands and feet and neck remained fine and thin. To accentuate them, Maude took to wearing long, flowing gowns, in lavender or diaphanous pale blue crepe. That old style suited her so well that many were unaware of the painful swelling of her once-slender legs. In time, she brought the fashion of elegant flowing robes back to East Hampton.

Maude Sergeant Bouvier was a matriarch in the most positive sense of the word, herding her flock of Bouviers with a strong if overindulgent hand. She was fiercely protective and possessive of her family. And as her affluence and social authority increased, she used both to pave over the difficulties of life for her brood.

Maude died before I had the opportunity to meet her. But so strongly has she continued to be the focus of family conversation that her presence to this day is almost tangible.

No lesser woman could ever have held together so many diverse offshoots of the family tree for so long. By the time of her death, they included Jack Davis, Maudie's son who later wrote *The Bouviers: Portrait of an American Family;* his

sister Little Maudie, who dedicated her life to teaching re-
medial reading at the Brearley School in New York; Bouvie
Beale—a lawyer and charming *bon vivant* whose enthusiasm
for good foods and knowledge of wine has always seemed
to turn the family dinners into an adventure; Little Edie,
who remained with her mother out at East Hampton; and
of course, Miche, Jackie and Lee. Which is not to mention
Shella—Jackie's most contemporary cousin and school
companion at Miss Porter's; Scottie, Michelle's other child;
and Phelan Beale, Jr., who for years made an annual pil-
grimage home from Oklahoma.

Bound as they were by familial love, Jack liked these people to varying degrees. The aura of Maude's memory
floated above them all, and long after she was gone, they
were still somehow fighting for her affection. There was
always too much competition among them, and the tendency to form cliques within the family was not always attractive.

But woe betide the outsider who dared to criticize a family
member. In the spirit of Maude, the whole clan would come
down on that unfortunate's head. And descending as a
united force, they would often leave scars.

Of course, there was always one other unseen presence
at all Bouvier gatherings. A far darker cloud than the rose-
ate memory of Maude, Bud and the tragedy of his death
seemed always to hang overhead. Sometimes, without a
word being spoken, they would be painfully reminded.
Some gesture of Jack's, or a view of Miche's evocative resemblance to him, would dredge up the past. Once more,
each member of the clan would be caught up in a wave of
guilt, as they tried to make sense of it. How could it ever
happen?

If life was a Garden of Eden for the Bouviers, how had
tragedy reared its head in their midst? Immediately after
Bud's death, their lives still seemed lush and full. Life was
perfect in fact—in full and glorious bloom. But somewhere

there was something unseen and unspoken, a gnawing suspicion. A worm in the bud.

Because of the obvious similarities between himself and his brother, Jack was most stricken by the sheer power of Bud's death. Secure in his knowledge that Maude could absolve them of any responsibility for their actions, and protect them from all harm, young Jack had lived his life to the hilt. His great enthusiasms, his appetites, even in their most extreme forms, had always gone unchecked.

In her own loving way, Maude Sergeant Bouvier became a destructive force in the lives of her children. In addition to her infinite capacity for love, she also had a great need to be needed. With her fledglings in tow she led as a natural leader: relentlessly. Even when her followers tripped and fell over her line.

She smoothed over all obstacles in their path. It never seemed to occur to Maude that they would one day have to do without her, pull their own weight in the world. In dominating the objects of her affection, she protected them far too much.

There was little in the world which they wanted and could not get. Developing their charm, her children would use their smiles like shields or talismans to ward off unpleasant things. Naturally, the world was obliged to accept behavior from them which would have been insufferable from any other source.

Her children were always to be center stage. With such strong physical assets, their appearance was always stressed. The roots of their self-image were too shallow, never truly breaking below the surface.

As for the more important qualities—warmth, sensitivity, intelligence—they were all herded out of sight along with other problems, festering unseen in the backstairs of their lives. As adults, the flaws of each of her three oldest children grew to tragic proportions, leading them one by one to total dissolution.

By the time Bud's death first filled Jack's mind with feverish thoughts and endless explorations of the past, it was already too late. Not only for them, but for an entire way of life in America, the seeds of destruction had been fully sown.

The harvest of ruin would come a generation later though its first signs had not yet surfaced. And as far as the Bouviers could see, the rich would get richer and the poor would get poorer.

In the meantime—the in-between time—it was all one big, happy chorus of "Let's Have Fun."

FOUR

Bud and Jack

John Vernou Bouvier III and William Sergeant Bouvier had everything two young men could possibly want. They were fabulously good-looking, wealthy in their own right, good at practically everything they tried—except schoolwork. And full of the devil.

The younger brother was finer featured, while Jack in his earliest years looked almost like a caricature, or an unskilled first attempt at carving those same features. He was born particularly masculine-looking, which was not entirely becoming to a child. His features were much too massive. The huge eyes, dominating nose and wide mouth were out of proportion to his tiny face.

In short, unlike Bud, Jack was by no stretch of the imagination a pretty baby. Although by the time he reached puberty, it became evident that he was to become a strikingly good-looking man.

The differences in the duo's personalities followed the same basic lines. Bud was artistic, graceful and extremely sensitive. Jack was wildly exuberant in everything he did, brash, bold and prepossessing.

From the start, the two were locked in a fierce rivalry, competing for approval from everyone around—a propensity all too pronounced throughout the Bouvier clan. Although their love for one another was always apparent, hostility would flare up bitterly between them. Despite his more artistic and sensitive disposition, his finer features and superior agility, Bud invariably was humbled by his brother in the social arena, where he was forced to stand in Jack's burgeoning shadow.

Conflict between Jack and his father was also inevitable. The greatest difficulty between them was that old bugaboo—the generation gap. The Major was a true product of his times, and Jack insisted upon being a man of his own, coming of age at the freewheeling turn of the century. Despite their occasional bouts of mutual affection, the two never did come to understand each other in the slightest degree.

The Major was a stickler for etiquette and obedience, but with Maude calling the shots, the children could ignore all of that. Even when their transgressions were serious, Maude would ignore the detours from proper behavior; whenever necessary she would cover their tracks to divert the Major. A repentant Jack, tears in his eyes and a seductive little smile on his lips, was sure to hear her say, "Very well, I won't tell your father, this time."

As was so often the case in his era, Jack ultimately became as close to the permanent servants of the Bouviers' household as he was to many of his kin. At an early age, he knew how to summon and manipulate authority, and it is not improbable that he made life almost intolerable for them.

Time after time, they would scowl at the boy and blame his bad French blood for his naughtiness. As far as anyone was concerned, he was oblivious to criticism. But one day Maude found the lad alone in a corner of the house; he had pricked his finger and was making it bleed in an attempt to "drain out all that bad French blood."

Of course, such repentant phases were the exception, and rather short-lived. Soon after the bloodletting incident he retaliated against the Nutley staff for some irksome thing or another. In the best tradition of his father, young Jack immortalized his emotions in verse. That artistic expression, as aired within easy earshot of the kitchen, went like this:

> *Barbara has a face like an ash can,*
> *Katherine has a face like a shoe,*
> *Sacony has a face like a monkey,*
> *And Antoinette has a face like a canoe.*

As intended, more than one of the immortalized overheard the quatrain. Failing to appreciate the similes, they complained bitterly to Maude.

Jack was lightly punished, but sufficiently to discourage him from ever again attempting a poem. His interest in all things literary ended at age nine. It's a pity. For unlike so many of the Major's poems which have been handed down, Jack's at least rhymed well.

While his early childhood was overflowing with such light-hearted pranks, they had no serious or lasting effects. His defiance began to blossom, however, once he was sent off to prep school. Jack was an indifferent pupil at best, and Maude could no longer conceal all of his antics. At the Morristown School in New Jersey, Jack thoroughly disgraced himself in the Major's eyes by conducting his academic life with mediocrity.

From there, the Major routed his eldest son to Philips Exeter, a great bastion of preparatory training. Of course, a Bouvier was supposed to excel at everything.

Jack tried to lead his classmates. He did succeed, but it was on the wrong playing field. He majored in poker. This was the reason provided for expelling him from Exeter, though there were undoubtedly others.

Today, to be expelled from school for playing cards would be considered the ludicrous height of injustice, but in those days, flagrant gambling just was not done. Particularly if, as in Jack's case, the offender played for high stakes and always won. In all events, Jack was asked to leave Exeter.

He did nonetheless manage to scrape into Yale, via Princeton Prep and Harstrom's Tutoring Academy. And once enrolled in college, Jack thrived in his own element.

He studied sufficiently, though without great enthusiasm. No one in his right mind would ever have fancied Jack an intellectual. Nor did he ever pretend to be one. He had not the least interest in living through books—Jack Bouvier was much too interested in living things out in the flesh. Not for him the vicarious pleasure of experiences found in the writings of other men.

Jack simply never found time to find out how other people lived. Anything which interfered with his own exciting pleasures was boring. And boredom Jack Bouvier would not tolerate.

Instead of studying, he threw parties. Wild, extravagant parties—including people from all walks of life. Presiding over them all, Jack shone at his brightest.

Holding court above the blaring of a nine-piece band or the scratchy rumblings of an Edison phonograph, Jack was superb. He would always dress in white flannel or gabardine pants, his blazer the latest tailored cut. In the center of the room, a Bloody Mary in his hand, Jack cut a figure too dashing for any girl to resist.

Jack's ballroom technique was adequate. As might be expected, his shimmy had a special flare to it. But his specialty, known as the "Why Dance?" was exquisite. At the right time, with the girl he had chosen, Jack would slowly, ineffably, dance her into the darkest corner. There, they would wind down to a pulsating motion, with their feet stationary—and their hips working overtime.

Jack's fetes were always popular with his classmates, although many of them developed a more than passing dislike of him. He had just too much going for him and was too flamboyant about it. At times, he could run roughshod over the sensibilities of the less fortunate. In his element, Jack Bouvier did have *everything* going for him, and he just couldn't see any harm in enjoying that fact. If, in the process he trod on other men's toes, he was only briefly sorry.

Life was one grand ball, and he was just too busy dancing.

Those who became Jack's pals, like the frat members of Book and Snake, Jack's coveted society, were in for a great time. As long as they remained willing to ride in on his coattails and be content with the sumptuous spoils of his glory.

Even the Yale men who privately detested Jack made a show of friendship to gain entree to his parties. They knew that few women resisted his charms, or a fighting chance to rebuff them. Any party of Jack's was guaranteed to line all the corridors in the house with beautiful women. Few men would carry their dislike of Jack so far as to miss the fun.

In the meantime, Bud, despite his clear intellectual gifts, was floundering. Although he had followed his older brother through Morristown, then actually made it through Exeter, he was not accepted at a college. Instead, the Major put him through another year at a special school.

When Bud was finally ready for college, the Major decided to enroll him at the one institution where a Bouvier could never fail—his own beloved alma mater, Columbia. As a freshman there, Bud majored in rowing and passed his academic courses.

The following year, Bud left Columbia and transferred to Yale, joining Jack's college, Sheffield Scientific. The competition between the two brothers, spurred on by proximity, grew fiercer. Bud, being a superb athlete and a horseman in particular, quickly made a name for himself on the polo and boxing teams.

Jack, although he fancied himself an athlete, won no trophies on the track team. But his success with the ladies was unmatched.

At the parties, Bud all too often found himself playing second fiddle to Jack. Unlike the older brother, Bud did not make the pursuit of women a compulsion. Nonetheless, constantly following in his brother's wake was bound to have its effects.

For those eligible young ladies who had failed to win Jack's heart, his younger brother was clearly second-best. By no means a carbon copy, Bud bore enough physical resemblance to Jack to be irrefutably from the same mold.

Jack had always known how to benefit from that likeness. As a matter of course, when he had tired of the lavish affections of a beautiful young lady, he would graciously get off the hook by bringing in Bud as a proxy. And Bud, puzzled by the resentment he felt when presented to a stunning young debutante as "My brother, the greatest old guy in the world," would take over where Jack left off.

But the one arena where Bud always bested Jack was drinking. Even when Jack would not submit to a contest, or was forced to bow out in time to save the evening's pursuits, Bud would continue to down liquor furiously. All too often, instead of shimmying or tap-dancing or clogging—where he always stole the show—he drank himself under the table.

It was a serious problem. Like so many other young men of his era, Bud Bouvier was drinking too much by the time he reached college. His earliest bouts, disgraceful as they were, had to be carefully concealed from the Major by the rest of the family. While the problem was glaringly clear to all of them, the Bouviers recognized only that such a topic was not suitable for conversation. Alcoholism was far too scandalous to mention, and Bud's father never learned of the earliest prep school episodes.

It was while the brothers were both at Sheffield that Jack became engaged to a young and wealthy socialite. Certainly, he had been engaged numerous times before, but this time, it was different. While she had a lovely sense of humor about many things, she insisted upon taking their betrothal dead seriously.

Jack went along with the announcement against his better judgment. Of course, he had suggested marriage in the first place, and could hardly back out now. At the time he first brought up the topic, Jack had quite naturally been sold on the idea.

Not for the world would he ever mislead a lady. It was just that sometimes, in the heat of passion, his singlemindedness would lead his tongue to overzealous declarations.

And this time, Jack realized—as his fiancée strode with fierce pride and elegant beauty into the Bouvier house on her first weekend visit—that this was no laughing matter.

From the first, Maude and Michelle were in awe of their brother's new-found treasure. She was haughty and beautiful and rich as Croesus. The opulence of her life was apparent as soon as she began to unpack her matched, monogrammed, Mark Cross ostrich-leather luggage.

The twins, renowned for their curiosity, sat at the foot of the bed unabashedly staring as the lovely young woman proceeded to unpack three seasons' worth of designer fashions for all occasions. They were glorious—fine aquamarine silks, cotton lace camisoles, even dainty little jackets with maribou collars!

Twin heads of red curls bobbed in astonishment as the contents of the suitcases poured out. It seemed to them that Jack's beautiful fiancée was planning to stay forever!

She was the youngest daughter of a powerful industrialist, a man who had made millions by prodigiously guarding his corporate assets. He was no less cautious with his youngest daughter. Like virtually all of Jack's girls, though he claimed that he couldn't care less, she happened to be a devout Catholic, and hell-bent on marriage.

Maude took one look and realized the seriousness of the

girl's intent, and of Jack's ambivalence. Apparently, he had an advanced case of cold feet. He waited until the last moment, then broke down and blurted out all of his painful confusion to the one woman he knew would understand him.

"Ma," he agonized. "I can't do it. I just can't marry the girl. Tell me what to do!"

To such pained and delicate pleadings, Maude had always come up with the right answer for Jack. The right answer consisting of whatever Jack wanted to hear.

This time was no exception. "Well, Sonny, shouldn't you tell her *something* before it's too late."

Taking heart, the beloved son thrust his hands into his pockets and bolted out of the door. He returned late that same afternoon. By the time evening had fallen, so had another sandcastle named love. Jack had said what needed to be said and called it its proper name.

By midnight, the woman for all seasons had fled and was riding the homeward train. She had scarcely even had time to change her clothes.

To celebrate, Jack went out riding the next day. Togged out to the teeth, his brown Irish tweed jacket with the cuffs rolled up, his college tie flapped over his shoulder as he galloped into freedom. He breathed deeply as he bounded over the rolling Long Island hills, exuberantly flashing his million-dollar smile. This time had been a little too close for comfort.

During Jack's college and early Wall Street days the scenario was replayed many times, with only slight variations in the script. Jack escaped the altar just in the nick of time with the same dramatic timing as Tom Jones from the gallows. Just when the floor fell out from under his feet and the collar tightened around his deep bronze neck, Jack would somehow make good his escape. The next day would once again find him galloping free.

Often, the great escape was staged with Bud arriving from

the wings. A common ploy included introducing the young
hopeful to the younger Bouvier. Bud would launch into
courting the utterly confused creature as Jack subtly inched
away. By the time the young lady figured out that she was
being dumped, she would generally be more astonished at
the tactic than annoyed. But more importantly, Bud would
cushion her fall, so that hitting *terra firma* would not bruise
her pride.

Throughout college, there was a standing bet between
the brothers concerning which of the two would make it
through first. Bud, the heavy favorite in spite of Jack's head
start, made the mistake of giving Jack long odds. When the
older brother was finally able to collect on that wager, picking up his Yale diploma in the process, amazement rippled
through the entire Bouvier clan. The most surprised of all
was probably Jack.

It also left him with a problem in hand. What to do next?

Jack's grades were not even within sight of the top of his
class. One of the comments in his graduating yearbook
summed it up concisely, "Jack," it said, "took his senior
year in doses."

In fact, he had taken all of his schooling in doses. Swallowing only as much of the bitter pill as he needed to pull
through and leaving the rest where it belonged—moulder-
ing away in some dusty academic file.

Nonetheless, his years at Yale had not been wasted. Un-
erringly, his gambler's nose had led him down the right
track. Perhaps even more than for their brains and good
looks, the brothers of Book and Snake were notorious for
their gobs of money—even far more conspicuous than
Jack's.

When Jack considered his options after graduation, all
signs seemed to point in the one direction where his skill
for gambling could be put to respectable use, utilizing his
friends' substantial capital. Following in the footsteps of his
great-uncle MC, Jack chose Wall Street.

Through his sister Edith's husband, Phelan Beale, Jack secured a job with Henry Hentz and Co., beginning as a clerk.

Working with Hentz's partner, Hartwig Baruch, brother of the legendary financial whiz, Bernard Baruch, Jack quickly ingratiated himself. He had good betting instincts, just the right amount of boldness, an ability with numbers, and an overload of youthful enthusiasm for the market. Of course, Jack also possessed that award-winning smile. Baruch became his guardian angel.

It was upon first arriving on Wall Street that Jack picked up the various nicknames which tickled his vanity. He became know as the Black Orchid, the Black Prince . . . and of course, as Black Jack. The names, no reflection on his morality, played on his dark complexion, perhaps the greatest wellspring of all of his sources of vanity. Never one to pass up a good thing, Jack enhanced his tan seasonally with endless bouts of sunbathing. At other times, with no less fervor, he took sun treatments at the barber's.

Undoubtedly, he was also called names not nearly so inspiring. Or flattering. Jack was not universally loved by the legions of less successful stockbrokers *cum* ladies' men. But all other names were consistently forgotten, or at least ignored by Jack and the rest of the Bouviers. While I have never heard Jack referred to by any less ennobling name than Black Jack, I have no doubt he was. Perhaps frequently.

Naturally, Jack made enemies on the floor of the exchange. His cavalier and freewheeling style would not be slowed down for anyone's sake. For those who felt the moral obligation to try to force him into low gear, Jack could undoubtedly be a real pain in the neck—if not in a region somewhat lower than that.

There is no way to puncture and deflate his image. The image represented the man precisely. Quite simply, Jack was authentic. Jack was what he was.

It is not surprising that Jack had only a small circle of

close male friends. Men all too suddenly felt themselves
paling in his bigger-than-life shadow. Unintentionally, he
would end up filching the affections of their wives and girl-
friends. To have a buddy like Jack around was not always
convenient. And for most men, Jack's likeable charac-
teristics did not seem worth pursuing when exposure to
him could so easily undermine a thriving relationship.

Jack could never have avoided other men's jealousies.
Anyone could envy his life on Wall Street. He loved his job,
and impressed the right people by doing exceedingly well.
He took his pick of all of the celebrated young ladies who
danced around New York, and spent the summers with his
family in exclusive East Hampton.

Together with another young Wall Street figure, Julian
Noyes, Jack established a bachelor apartment at 375 Park
Avenue, one of the finest residential buildings, with a sweep-
ing horseshoe car entry, tended by a valet and a doorman.

When the two young men grew tired of pursuing love
and fortune in the Empire State, or bored with wild binges
of drinking or gambling, they would pull up stakes for several weeks and go to Europe. Returning from that continent
renewed by their excesses, the pair would pursue their interests in New York with increased vigor.

In the meantime, Bud continued plodding through Yale,
with increasingly disappointing results. He saw only disapproval in his father's eyes. Until an opportunity for distinction in a different arena presented itself—the battlefields
of World War I.

For Bud, it represented a chance to retreat from New
Haven honorably—to regain his self-respect, and find dignity in his family's eyes. Already, his French blood was boiling to rout the Germans from his ancestral homeland,
crying out for a cause, for the chance to be a hero at last.

The family had embraced a long line of warriors. His
mother's great-grandfather had been an officer at George
Washington's side. His father's father had fought at Water-

loo and in the next generation, John Vernou Bouvier, Sr.
had been pierced through the lung in the Battle of Bull
Run. Now, with everyone else in the family cheering, the
young patriot abandoned his studies at Yale and volun-
teered for the army.

While Bud trained as a Captain in the Infantry Officers'
Reserve Corps at Camp Dix, New Jersey and then graduated
as the youngest Captain of Infantry in the army from the
Madison Barracks in Plattsburgh, New York, Jack was more
than delighted to remain at his job on Wall Street. However,
Uncle Sam soon descended upon him and dragged him
into conscription. He was put in the ignoble position of a
common soldier.

However, that incongruous tour of duty was short-lived.
With the help of a few powerful Wall Street friends, Jack
managed to transfer to the more exciting Aviation and Signal Corps, where he made second lieutenant.

For the time being, Jack was stationed at Scott Field, St.
Louis. Missouri was not his idea of a glamorous and exotic
place, but his attempts to become a fighter pilot failed, and
he never did manage to get shipped out of there. Stuck in
the Middle West, Jack had to content himself with exploring
the female species of the region, unhampered by threat to
his life or limb.

In the meantime, Bud was packing up his old kit bag. His
preparatory training at an end, the new doughboy was catapulted across an ocean and dropped in the midst of a raging
war.

FIVE

In War, In Love, At Peace

The early war years were very good to the Bouviers, particularly to Maude and the Major, whose new military title coincided with a sharp rise in his social prominence and financial fortunes.

In 1914, John Vernou Bouvier, Jr. was earning upwards of a thousand dollars a day as a lawyer. In addition, his military position brought him into contact with many of the leading power brokers of the day, broadening his distinguished clientele enormously. At the same time, Maude had come into a significant inheritance.

They were at last ready to move back to New York City, and do it in style. After spending a year at the Hotel Renaissance, they selected a posh duplex apartment at 247 Fifth Avenue, just around the corner from the Major's favorite watering hole and bridge haunt—the Union Club. The apartment—the first duplex to be built in New York—was chic by anyone's standards, and in the one location they found suitable.

During those days, no vendor would dare clutter the sidewalks of Fifth Avenue. Pushcarts and sidewalk sales were the invention of other times and locations. Fifth Avenue was built for people of means, and tolerated only the finest clubs and shops of New York.

Of a Sunday, anyone who was anyone would be seen strolling up and down the broad Avenue, doffing his top hat or demurely bowing to other passers-by of wealth and breeding.

For the Major, a Sunday stroll with his two young and beautiful twins was part of an unbroken ritual. After break-fast with Maude, they would dress in twin apricot-married-with-peach frocks and set off beside their proudly strutting father.

Midway through the promenade, the twins would pause in front of the entryway to the Union Club, not daring to join the Major as he popped in there briefly. Twin manes of red hair stirring gently in the breeze, they would graciously accept a stream of compliments from passers-by, allowing small clusters of admirers to form. Then, at the height of their glory, their stately father would appear at the head of the stairway, then proceed down with slow, proud steps.

Nonchalantly returning greetings, he would offer each of the twins an arm, and the three would drift triumphantly toward home.

In time, the scene would shift *in toto* to Long Island summer communities stretching from Quogue to the exclusive enclave at East Hampton where the Bouviers would rent a cottage. On weekends, the Major would motor out to join them, his brimmed hat turned backwards on his head to make him look a bit more sporting.

Where her children were concerned, there was nothing that Maude did not consider of utmost importance. So the twins had to be dressed identically in brown and orange, their red curls spiralled just so. Even special bathing caps, like sun bonnets, were designed in the mother's attempt to keep the sun from violating their fair complexions. Maude detested freckles.

However, when the Major's massive Duesenberg appeared on the horizon, Maude's carefully twirled coiffures were flung to the wind. Spotting the brass carriage lamps in the distance, the twins would race down to the road.

With its winter top removed, the limousine was transformed into a touring car. The twins would vault inside for a hug, then climb into the red leather rumble seat and take off, clutching the bonnets in their hands, and letting the elements do their worst.

Maude had inherited sufficient money to purchase a summer home there. After much searching, they decided upon Wildmoor, a beautiful, rambling white clapboard house ringed with sun porches on two stories.

There on Apaquogue Road, the Bouviers spent much of their time socializing with their neighbors, bathing, riding at the East Hampton Riding Club and, of course, golfing at the Maidstone and sailing at the Devon Yacht Club.

For the twins, the sun porches provided an excellent open air theater from which they could watch an endless stream of diversions. Escorted by sporty men in gabardine jackets and ascots, elegant young ladies would trickle by in exotic open town cars or coupés as they made their way to the beach or to town.

Of all of the motoring beauties, their favorite was a stunning young woman with pale, ice-blue eyes. She was always careful to raise a gloved hand and return their waves of admiration as she glided by with any one of several dozen beaux.

Of course, every eligible young East Hampton bachelor was at her beck and call. She was, quite simply, the most beautiful woman the twins had ever seen. She was elegant and terribly chic with her casually pinned-up honey blond hair, tiny ringlets sweeping down and framing her heart-shaped face. She had absolutely perfect, gleaming white teeth and a long, graceful throat. As she motored past, her cool dignity, her breathtaking beauty and natural grace compelled all who saw her to instant awe and admiration. Her name was Emma-Louise Stone of the Chicago Stones and that, if not her beauty, was enough to commend her.

East Hampton society, in those days, was rigidly circumscribed but it had welcomed the Chicago Stones as unreservedly as it had the Bouviers before them.

The founder of the Stone dynasty was one Ebenezer Stone, a soldier in the War of 1812, and an Indian fighter. His son, Horatio Odell Stone, had worked as an itinerant merchant, a boatman on the Erie Canal, and a farmer, before being drafted as a soldier in the Black Hawk Indian War—and marching to the front. Once there he determined that the war was over, turned around and marched home again.

Soon growing restless down on the farm, Horatio sold it and settled in the village of Chicago. Working as a lumberjack, he saved up enough money to open Stone's Grain and Grocery on North Water Street. As Michel Bouvier had done in Philadelphia, Horatio Stone began investing in land.

While he never found coal, the railroads found Chicago. As the city exploded into a livestock capital, Horatio sold land for stockyards.

By Emmy's generation, the Stones were legendary Middle Western philanthropists. In addition to owning land in numerous suburbs, the family still owned much of Chicago's South Side, with several dozen of them living quite comfortably on trust funds. Her father, a leading physician, had married Madeleine Masters, a sculptress of note, and a lesser poet. Her brother, however, had recently sprung into literary notoriety with his *Spoon River Anthology.* At the time, of course, Edgar Lee Master's classic was scandalous.

As far as East Hampton society was concerned, Chicago was at the edge of the civilized world. Europe, however,

where Emmy had been educated and which she knew like
the palm of her hand, was the matrix. In addition to her
beauty, she spoke fluent French and German and was well-
versed in the arts. It does not seem surprising that she was
the most celebrated young woman in town where beautiful
and wealthy debutantes were ubiquitous.

Black Jack, on leave from St. Louis, picked up her scent
as soon as he had unpacked at his parents' summer home.
Having once caught sight of the exquisite face beneath the
wide-brimmed straw bonnet, and the Dresden China figure
which followed on down, Jack immediately set out to court
Emmy in her mansion in the dunes, just a bit down the
road—overlooking the sea and Geogica Pond.

Deceived by her fragile looks, he had counted upon a
quick victory. Instead, he found himself cooly rebuffed at
every turn. Emmy had her uncle's dexterity in the weaponry
of words, and more than a helping of her mother's fiery
artistic temperament.

She also had the stubbornness and the hardy resilience
of her pioneer ancestors. Many years after Dr. Carl Stone's
death, Emmy's mother remarried. About Nils Grön, her
stepfather, the less said the better. But he had brought a
great deal of misery and the experience had helped to forge
Emmy's iron will. She was not about to be bowled over by
an average-intensity lightning-bolt hurled by one Jack Bouvier.

Emmy's unapproachable calm only fed the flames of
Jack's passion for her. Resistance was the one factor he
found irresistible in a woman. Grinning his most disarming
grin, Jack struggled harder and harder for her affections,
his every failure to overcome her merely increasing the ar-
dor of his suit.

He zeroed in on Emmy with every bit of charm in his
considerable arsenal. He took her dancing, but could not
persuade her to snuggle against his broad chest, not even
on the ride home, careening around a corner with the two

right wheels off the ground. Stopped by the side of an isolated country road at dusk, Emmy would not disengage her
hand from the door handle of Jack's elegant coupé nor
disengage her gaze from the beauty of the Island landscape.

Jack refused to withdraw. Like a moth circling a candle,
he became more and more desperate for the flame. Strutting regally like a peacock in his most tightly tailored gabardine suit—the ultimate ploy which had never failed to
win the admiration of any young women in East Hampton—Jack found Emmy unimpressed to the point of being
bored.

Ruefully, he admitted that he had met his match. The
delicate girl parried his every thrust with her own devastating charms. Amused and beguiled, Jack still intensified his
efforts beyond all reason, only to be met by disturbing
truths.

His ultimate failure came the day he appeared at her
doorstep, togged out at his considerable best, after an ex-
hausting morning of hunting with a party from the East
Hampton Riding Club. He never made it past the front
door.

"Hello, Jack," she breathed in a quite blasé voice. Then,
after a pause, "Please go home and bathe. You smell of
horses."

He was crushed.

At other times, it was, "No, I simply can't go out with you
today." Or, "Please forgive me, but I *do* have other plans."

That he accepted these and so many other rebuffs and
kept coming back for more was a testament to the irresistible hold she had over him. And also to Jack's single-minded
persistence.

Long after Jack had run out of methods to win her admiration and traps to ensnare her heart, he was still far
from losing hope. For Jack, that would have been out of
character. He clung furiously to his goal until at last she
resigned herself long enough for them to become engaged.

Jack, at the apex of the most stubborn mountain he had ever climbed, paused at last. Radiant in his achievement, he surveyed life from the perspective of his crowning success.

The engagement lasted two whole weeks. It was a disaster. Their characters were not in the least compatible; their standards too diverse for harmony.

Emmy thrived on art and music and beautiful, esoteric things. Jack's pleasures were horses and gambling and beautiful women. There was no way the two could ever be happy as one. Realizing that, Emmy broke off the engagement.

It was a devastating blow to Jack's pride. And though he would never openly admit it, I suspect a great blow to his heart as well.

A week later, Bud arrived at Wildmoor on a four-day furlough, roaring into the driveway on a Motorcycle Corps issue Harley Davidson. He badly needed a rest, and firmly announced his intention to spend the next four days sleeping.

Jack, however, would simply not hear of it. He immediately roused his younger brother to take him to meet "the most beautiful girl in the world." An exhausted and slightly annoyed Bud acquiesced. He knew Jack would give him no peace until the girl in question was met.

He also knew Jack's discerning eye for women. Countless other young ladies had disappeared into the night after being heralded as "a peach" or "a real beauty," of "by far the best-looking gal in New York."

But "the most beautiful girl in the world!" It was a new phrase in Jack's vocabulary. And while the elder brother was always known for his optimism, there was a limit to his powers of exaggeration.

Having his young man's priorities in the right place, the younger brother vaulted out of bed, splashed cold water on his face, and replenished the pomade on his neatly slicked-down hair. With Jack spurring him on, the soldier set out on the brief hike to the Stone house.

He was not disappointed. She was every bit as lovely as could be imagined. In fact, Bud took one look at Emmy and fell head over heels in love.

So many times before, Jack had brought in his little brother to make good his escape from an increasingly diminishing female interest. This time, to his amazement, *Jack* had been given the brushoff and was, even now increasingly wedged out of the encounter. Somehow unbeknownst to him, Bud had suddenly acquired the Major's gift of gab, and an incredible interest and knowledge of all sorts of cultural minutiae. On her part, Emmy was visibly enchanted.

The next morning, the Bouviers were collectively amazed to find Bud dressed to the nines in his captain's uniform, alert and at his debonair best, at the crack of dawn. Emma-Louise Stone, it was quietly announced, had consented to go riding with him.

They saw little of him that day. After riding, Bud and Emmy shared a quiet lunch together. Then they played golf. Then they went bathing in the sea.

By noon, it had become a whirlwind romance. By all reports, the evening had raised their relationship to a tropical torrent of love. There could have been no more perfect setting. Dances at the club, the sand and the sea, long walks on the beach, holding hands beneath a full moon as their toes were lapped by the waves.

Bud's refined features, set off by his khaki officer's uniform, Emmy with her stunning beauty finally aglow with an inner fire . . . every element contributed its magic to the spell.

By the time three days and evenings had ended, the moonstruck couple could no longer bear to live apart.

Mighty Jack had struck out. To make matters worse, the pinch-hitter who won the game was his own little brother.

The same Bud who for years had been trained to join the rest of the players on the bench while Jack played the entire field. There was surely no joy in Jack's Mudville that weekend. It took him a long time to get over it, if indeed he ever did.

On his fourth morning in East Hampton, Bud called up the Major to inform him that there would be a wedding ceremony that afternoon.

The Major was filled with consternation, and the rest of the clan soon joined in his railing. It was a mere two weeks since Jack's engagement had been nipped in the bud. That was unseemly enough. But to make matters worse, Emma-Louise Stone had one very great strike against her. It wasn't that they disapproved of her personally—no one could have! But she was a Protestant. And in the Bouvier family, that was tantamount to being a heretic, if not a heathen.

Of course, in the heat of his impassioned protestations, the Major forgot that the center of the family, Bud's beloved mother, was herself Episcopalian. But that was another matter, entirely. That Bud, the son and brother they cherished, should betray the faith of their fathers—it was not to be believed!

The youngest son listened patiently to his father's most severe denouncements. When the Major finally paused to suck in some more air, Bud cut in with a suggestion. If any members of the family found the prospect of this wedding unpleasurable, he could feel free to stay at home. But he and Emmy would be married before the family altar at Saint Patrick's Cathedral at two o'clock.

In the end, love won out. As Bud and Emma-Louise took their sacred vows before the ornate marble and brass spiraling altar—erected by Uncle MC in honor of his father and mother—the rest of the clan bore witness. Emmy even wore a khaki bridal gown to match Bud's army fatigues.

After the ceremony, Jack waited his turn before planting

a chaste, cordial kiss on his sister-in-law's cheek. He was a wonderful sport.

Within a week after the marriage, Bud was sent overseas. His letters home, when he found time to write, did not dwell upon the horrors of war faced by the 78th Division, the "White Lightnings." Most of all he discussed the men he commanded—the 250 members of the 303rd Ammunition Train of the 153rd Infantry.

He was constantly aware of the danger to all of their lives. When they were summoned up to the front lines at the Meuse-Argonne, his doughboys were still wet behind the ears. Surveying the carnage all around, yelling out orders while atop a truck packed with explosives and ammunition, Bud led them forward.

Suddenly, just in front of him, a gas grenade exploded. Within seconds, all of the pack animals lay dead on the battlefield. In their midst, Bud lay paralyzed, staring blankly at the mottled hides and gripping his stomach.

After the battle, he was rushed to an overcrowded casualty hospital set up in an ancient chateau. He was badly gassed, and recovery would require a long time. A week later, the General Armistice declared an end to World War I.

While the family hero lay recovering in France, the war ground to a halt. Jack finally surrendered his attempts to get overseas. He had struggled to play as vital a role as possible from the American dugout. He resigned himself to an honorable discharge without the battle medals and citations for bravery which would adorn Bud's chest.

When news of Bud's injury reached Emmy, she could bear to be away from him no longer. She prevailed upon the Major, who was working with the top brass in Washington in the Adjutant General's office, to get her into France. Since officers' wives were not permitted overseas, a cavalier general arranged for her appointment as an ambulance driver under the title "Miss Bouvier." In order to be accepted for overseas duty, Emmy had to roll up her silken sleeves. Bending her delicate, utterly feminine frame to her iron will, she demonstrated her ability to drive massive trucks and ambulances, repair them when they broke down, and change their tires on a simulated battlefield.

She left America for France aboard an army transport, the only woman among hundreds of lonely servicemen.

When the radiant "Miss Bouvier" was first announced at Bud's infirmary, he tried to imagine how or why his sister Edith had pulled this off.

But across the ward floor, his questions—and his prayers—were answered. His delight at seeing his beautiful "sister" was noteworthy. The second he held her in an extremely warm brotherly embrace, his recovery took a leap forward. And his devotion to her was so strong that all but the most foolhardy and lovestruck soldiers immediately gave up asking Bud to set up dates with her.

As the machinery of war receded from the picturesque landscape, Bud and Emmy grew increasingly indiscreet. On weekends, they would disappear to quiet little country inns, enjoying to the fullest their idyllic love in sleepy and peaceful villages in the river region.

Bud was finally ordered home, and Emmy followed him on the transport ship, alone this time among a thousand jubilant soldiers, eager to return home to their people.

Disembarking in New York, Emmy and Bud shared the limelight. In the family's eyes, the spunky wife was every bit as much a heroine as Bud was a hero. The couple was cheered with endless admiration and delight.

The war was over. And it was time to return to the quieter pleasures of a normal life.

It was not really as easy as that. Bud had been very seriously gassed, and the damage to his health, above all to his heart, became more evident as the years passed.

For many thousands of American families, there was no homecoming at all. In addition to the war overseas, the influenza epidemic in 1918 had cost almost half a million Americans their lives. While the people of New York City danced in the streets and jubilation prevailed, the private mourning was no less intense.

There is a certain crassness in passing over these war years as cavalierly as I have done. But it would be perhaps worse to pretend to really know the horror and the pain, the fierce struggles to survive—or even, for that matter, the joy of amnesty—of an era which occurred before I was born.

For every man, the heavenly public peace still left a private hell of memories to conquer. For all that has been written about the agonies of that war, I can best imagine what it must have been like by remembering my father's sweet, pink, staunchly British face turning a horrible shade of deathly grey when, with insensitive stupidity we led him back, without any warning, to the scene of his victory in the trenches of northern France. His anguish had not diminished, only been set in the back of his mind through time and distance.

No one was ever told all of the traumas that Bud lived through in command of his band of soldiers. In addition to bearing the responsibility for 250 other lives, he rode into battle on an ammunition wagon. It takes very little imagination to picture the strain of sitting on a powder keg while bullets are continually spraying you and shells are exploding all around as far as the eye can see.

The war years affected Bud greatly. It may be more than surmise to assume that his later heavy dependence on alcohol was a form of deadening the memories of things too vivid to forget.

Unlike his grandfather before him, Captain William Sergeant Bouvier did not enjoy showing his war wounds or recounting time and again the story of his injury on the battlefield. I suppose there were some men who enjoyed reliving World War I. But Bud and the shell-shocked soldiers who fought in the trenches were not among them.

Upon returning home, Bud found himself ill-at-east, restless. The family paths to follow—leading to the bar association or the stock exchange—no longer made sense to him. He needed excitement. To keep moving, and room to do it in.

His opportunity for both came in the form of a job as field assistant with a small concern, the Morton Oil Company of Kisco, Texas. It was a far cry from the glamor of New York City and East Hampton.

Emmy found the sparse town of Kisco unbearably oppressive. When it was discovered that she was pregnant, Bud and Emmy decided for the sake of her health—as well as for the unborn baby—that she should return to New York.

Michel Bouvier III, the man who became my husband, was born in the Hotel Seville, in the heart of fashionable New York. It's remarkable that he was born at all! Emma-Louise, perilously ill with double pneumonia, gave birth to a four-pound baby. Not only did the infant survive, but he grew to be a strapping man six feet two inches tall. By the time he was six or seven, the heir to the Bouvier name was already known as "Big Boy."

Bud began commuting between Kisco, New York City and East Hampton, keeping his eye open for any move Lady Luck might provide.

At the right moment, he seized the opportunity to jump into a rising oil syndicate—one which later bore the name "Independent Oil." Rising to the vice-presidency, he manipulated his capital well. By age thirty-three he was, by virtue of his holdings, a millionaire. But success also meant constant travel, and Bud continued to see precious little of the family which meant all the world to him.

Jack's business fortunes fared equally well. His uncle Miche, who had founded MC Bouvier & Co., the second oldest firm on Wall Street, loaned Jack money to buy a seat on the New York Stock Exchange. He founded his own Wall Street firm, and proceeded to collect big money by the barrelful. Of course, he spent it with as much ease as he earned it.

Increasingly, Jack would tour the town in his new jet black Lincoln motorcar. For that extra romantic touch, Jack would leave the chauffeur at home, and personally drive his current girl. As the car sped down Fifth Avenue, lurching to a halt just behind a braking horse and carriage, or careening around the corner onto an unsuspecting side street, he would be guaranteed at least one strong clinch—if not from the thrill of it, then as a matter of holding on for dear life.

While Jack was still fervently sowing his wild oats, the small, dark-haired girl who was to become his wife—and Jackie and Lee's mother—was blossoming under his prominent and unsuspecting nose, there in his own backyard. It was hardly something you would expect Black Jack to miss.

But he did, and for an exceedingly long time. Jack's twin sisters were considerably younger than he. He paid little or no attention to their playmates.

To all of the little girls and young women, Jack was the ultimate fantasy. The stuff of which their dreams were made. He was powerful, wealthy, exotic and undeniably, darkly attractive. They watched him come and go abruptly through Maude's Fifth Avenue apartment, stop off to recharge his batteries at the Apaquogue House, and through the twins or the society columns, they heard of his latest glorious escapades.

He was always rushing off. To some meeting of importance, or the Yale game, or the Dempsey fight, or the horse show at the Garden. Most of the time, he was just dropping off some stunning young lady, or about to pick one up. If the twins' friend was particularly lucky, he would pause in the doorway, flash his heart-melting smile, and whisper the word, "Hullo." Then he would vanish.

He was dashing out of the house one day when he stopped dead in his tracks. However long it had been since he had last seen Janet Norton Lee, it had been time enough for biological magic to have turned her into full and deliciously admirable womanhood. There, across the room she stood, in all of her glory. The broad grin of her childhood had changed to a red-lipped and disarming smile.

Frozen, Jack eyed her, then leapt into the breach of courtship without another moment's hesitation. As he proceeded along familiar lines with his usual earnestness, the twins looked at one another in bewilderment. It must have been overwhelming for the girl as well. Certainly she collected beaux as easily as any other debutante, but they were not in a class with the Casanova of Wall Street.

Black Jack ritually showered her with attention from that moment on. If she resisted, it was to no avail. Janet simply did not have the sophisticated defenses to ward off Jack's considerable and practiced advances. Nor the desire to.

It didn't take long before they became engaged. The family, while very fond of Janet, was cautiously optimistic about the prospects of marriage.

Not that they didn't believe Jack's attraction was real. Janet had, after all, become quite an enticing young lady. And of course, there was no doubt about Jack's serious intentions.

They were just as serious as they had always been in such cases. It was just that there had been so many mature and equally attractive fiancées before. One by one, they had failed to maintain his attention and enthusiasm.

Jack's attention span where love was concerned was notoriously limited. As soon as he had reached the summit, it seemed that Black Jack always caught a glimpse of at least five other peaks which he had to mount and conquer immediately.

It seemed inconceivable that this naïve young girl could succeed where so many before her had failed.

As an escape artist, Harry Houdini's reputation was hardly greater than Jack Bouvier's. Not content with having captivated him, Janet Lee was determined to haul that slippery number all the way to the altar of marital bliss.

SIX

Lasata

As the twenties roared in, the gulf between the Major and his three oldest children widened. While he was steadily moving his way up the genteel and proper social ladder set before him as a youth, his son Bud was desperately scaling a cliff of self-destruction. Jack and Edith, it seemed to him, were plunging headlong into the vulgarity and chaos of modern life.

Edith had married Phelan Beale, a renowned attorney and friend of her father who was twenty years her senior. Soon afterward, they bought Grey Gardens, a beautiful gabled house down the road from Wildmoor. With the free lifestyles growing bolder every day, Edith turned her home into a miniature colony for artists, painters and futurist poets, violinists and jazz sax players. Individuals from all walks of life and all social strata were in regular attendance.

Holding court in the middle of bedlam was Edith. Always known for her artistic temperament, Edith, with her outlandish displays, both of garb and behavior, now grew legendary.

Eventually, the family turned their backs to her antics.

With two exceptions. The first was Maude who, every morning without exception, would answer the soft bell of the telephone in the central hall, and ask her eldest daughter the fateful question:

"How are you doing, dear?"

With the proliferation of popular psychology after Freud, "coping" with life—coming to blows with all of its minor obstacles—had come fully into mode. And Edith, punctual as clockwork, would relate every catastrophe and struggle of the day, from the static which made her superheterodyne radio unbearable, to the cough which was threatening her voice. They could design a technological marvel like the *Spirit of St. Louis,* and fly a man across the Atlantic, but the automatic starter on her auto had never once worked properly.

On and on the description went, until every last drop of Edith's modern blasé life had been poured out. It drove all of her siblings up the wall. Yet Maude would listen and nod patiently into the black receiver, offering conciliatory murmurs on cue.

The other glad recipients of Edith were her increasing numbers of nephews and nieces. Miche, and later Shella, Scotty, Jackie and Lee, adored her. When Edith threw open the front door and stormed inside the house, she was immediately dragged to the grand piano to play her favorite baggy tunes and sing in her rich operatic soprano voice. They never tired of her renditions of "Together" and "Blue Moon," although the older members of the clan had been sated with those tunes, having heard Edith sing them for the better part of a decade. If no intermission was forthcoming, the other adults would eventually lift up their children and bodily carry them off to end the concert.

Edith's frequent lateness was always a cause for uproar. When the Major had done with *that* tirade, there was always her indecent dress. Her skirts had now risen well above her calves; even the knees were being allowed to show. What with her lipstick and circles of scarlet rouge on her cheeks, he felt that she looked altogether shocking.

Not content with even the flimsy dresses of the flappers, which looked like barely disguised camisoles, Edith had now taken to abandoning all corsets and draping her torso in loose-fitting and exotic clothing, often with no more than a large safety-pin between her and stark nudity.

Then there was always the topic of "the type of life" she was leading and its dubious effects upon young Phelan, Bouvie, and Little Edie.

The Major was growing increasingly censorious in his attitude toward Jack, as well. In the spring of 1927, he was scheduled to marry Janet. But in spite of that—and the fact that he was already thirty-six—Jack showed no signs of abandoning his infamous lifestyle.

As his wealth increased, so did the size and frequency of his parties at 375 Park Avenue. With total disregard for the unevenly enforced Eighteenth Amendment, gin, Scotch and champagne flowed like tap water from every corner of the rooms. It was no different away from home. As a well-appointed man-about-town, Jack would sooner dip into capital than leave his solid gold hip-flask home.

On a regular basis, the Major would berate Jack for his extravagant and profligate ways, threatening to cut him out of the will. With repeated applications, the ultimate punishment, which had at first elicited some lip service of very limited duration, lost its efficacy entirely.

With the arrival of his first million, Jack became his own incorrigible man. He would whistle on the street, stuff his hands into his pockets, wear black dancing pumps to the beach, and do whatever else he pleased. At length, Jack faced up to the Major and refused point blank to accept any self-improvement plan or amend his ways for any reason whatsoever.

Of course, Jack did not go so far as to tell his father to

"Go jump in a lake." Nonetheless, he had come within an inch of impudence. And such disrespect was an outrage.

And then there was Bud. As the twenties bubbled along, he couldn't have been further from "bee's knees" or "twenty-three skiddoo." At the speakeasies which he frequented, Bud was generally too far gone to attempt the Charleston.

His health was in serious decline, and his million had rapidly evaporated between poor investments and outright swindles. His drinking excesses could no longer be hidden, and at least once Captain Bouvier had been brought to a clinic to "dry out." Because of his erratic behavior, Emma-Louise finally had to ask for a divorce. Then as Bud's finances dwindled, he began missing support and alimony payments.

The embarrassment of his younger son's inability to care for his family, which he had already exposed to the public eye with a scandalous break-up, was bad enough in the Major's eyes. But when Emma-Louise felt compelled to bring him to court for back payments, it could not be contained within the family, nor even in the smug and cheap tabloids of the day.

The Major had no notion of it until one morning over coffee where his eye fell upon a telling article in the heart of the *New York Times*. Not only had Bud placed a blot on the family escutcheon, but he did it in the one place where every social and business acquaintance of the family would be sure to see it.

For John Bouvier, Jr., the only mystery greater than the bleary drifting of the twenties was the role his children played in the mainstream, at the heart of the sumptuous decline of values.

In the meantime he and Maude had moved out of, but not sold, the Apaquogue house, and bought a fourteen-acre estate on Further Lane. For reasons which have been lost in time, they christened the new summer family seat "Lasata," an Indian word for peace.

Every May would see a mass exodus of Bouviers from Manhattan. Out of each of the Park Avenue apartments an entire family and household would move out to East Hampton. Together with her staff of maids, chauffeurs and cooks, Maude would transplant the family into the sprawling stucco mansion.

Lasata, built along the lines of an English country manor, had all of the easy charm of gracious homes of an earlier era. A more idyllic setting would be difficult to imagine. Further Lane was a sleepy road running parallel to the sea. The potato and cabbage fields lying alongside were broken only by the occasional outline of stately summer homes set back from the road.

Among them, the members of the extended family used every square foot of land. In front of the ivy-covered house, an expansive horseshoe-shaped driveway ringed the spacious lawn used for major family gatherings. Paul Yuska, the gardener and only permanent year 'round resident, employed a gang lawnmower with five sets of blades on each side, cutting a thirty-five foot swath with each sweep.

Within easy walking distance from the house, the glorious and exclusive Maidstone Club stretched out. As the saying went, "If you're not in the Maidstone, you're out of it." Of course, the Bouviers were founding members, and it formed one more center of activity for them.

To the west of the house, a tennis court stood enclosed within an impeccably manicured blackthorn hedge. Once there had been a game there during which someone tripped over the net and brought it down. With club courts so close at hand, no one saw any great tragedy in that event. In fact, it was so insignificant no one ever bothered to mention the fact to Maude. Consequently, it was years before she made it out to that part of the property and, seeing the tattered net lying on the badly worn clay surface, had them both refurbished. In the meantime, no one seemed to notice.

At the north half of the property, Jack had his own set of stables built with box stalls for eight horses. Although he was never an outstanding horseman, no one loved his horses more than he did, or found greater pleasure in coaching a superb rider like Janet—or his nephew, Miche and his daughter, Jackie, who might as well have been born on the back of her favorite mare, Danseuse.

Above each stall, its occupant would have his or her name displayed on a little carved sign with gilded letters: Danseuse, Portlight, Ghandi, Bas d' Or and Stepaside—Jack loved each of the animals dearly. Beside them was one additional unmarked stall for guest horses. In addition to a small, L-shaped pavilion which housed the feed and tack rooms, Jack created a jumping ring and a large paddock.

To get from the stables to the house one passed first through a long grape arbor. In autumn, the heavy green foliage would be upstaged by dangling, luscious purple grapes dripping down along the entire length of the passage.

Next came a special plot of land reserved for endless rows of tall, golden corn. Then the path homeward led through several acres of garden planted with every conceivable kind of vegetable, and all in overabundance.

Finally, the path gave out onto Maude's celebrated Italian garden. People came from many miles around to view that spectacle. To Maude, raising flowers was every bit as demanding an art as raising children. Her plants were nurtured not one iota less carefully. The resulting growths were, perhaps, equally temperamental, but they were without a doubt the most magnificent spectacle in the region.

Between expertly manicured boxwood and blackthorn hedges, flowers were alternated so that they would be in constant bloom throughout the garden for the duration of the summer months. Maude particularly loved delphiniums, and they grew in beauty and profusion all along the little brick paths zigzagging throughout the garden. Amid a host of classical statues in marble and bronze stood a small fountain in which a little naked cherub relieved himself into a tiny pool.

The house itself was no less pleasantly informal. West of the main entry, with its telephone room, powder room and stately central staircase, massive stuffed chairs covered in gaily flowered chintz spread out throughout the living room. Above the great central hearth hung a portrait of the beautiful, fiery-haired twins at twenty, painted by Albert Herter. Whenever weather permitted, a blazing hickory fire was lit, perfuming the air and warming the exposed beam ceiling and mahogany-panelled walls with an inviting glow.

At the back of the living room an enclosed sun porch was installed in the shade of an ancient linden tree.

At the head of the stairs and over the front door of the house was the Major's study. There he kept a desk and did the household accounts. But his library was downstairs in the living room and he liked to read near the open fireplace. His favorite wing chair sat next to an end table filled with current magazines and newspapers. Since this was also the site of Edith's grand piano, a natural terrain for conflict was established.

East of the central stairway, a thirty-foot formal dining room framed by exposed beams immediately caught the eye. Around a sparsely simple oak great hall table, up to fourteen elaborately carved chairs stood in a row waiting for their dinner-hour inhabitants. Like the rest of the house, the dining room was always festooned with flowers from Maude's garden. The conspicuous covering of every table with a carefully arranged bouquet was a detail Maude personally attended to daily for each of the rooms.

Upstairs, the master suite, comprised of a large bedroom and bath, plus the Major's study, took up the west end of the house. The remainder of the family bedrooms, some seven in all, were traded off regularly, with the exception of the twins' bedroom. When married couples arrived at Lasata, they would be given the largest bedrooms as a matter of course. If, after Jack's divorce, he on more than one occasion deferred and bunked with Miche, the only sentiment felt was delight that the family had turned out in such numbers.

For all of the children and grandchildren, as for Maude and John, Lasata came to represent the heart of the family. And though children might be berated, or even cut out of the will, no one was ever disinvited from Lasata. Everyone, without exception, considered the country seat as his own true home.

Sharing it was looked upon as an honor. Or in the most cramped conditions—which hardly constituted deprivation—at least as *noblesse oblige.*

Paul Yuska, the gardener and caretaker, lived in East Hampton and came to work daily. Nearby, a three-and-a-half car garage housed the Bouvier's assorted vehicles, as well as the chauffeur in an apartment with bedroom, bath and a small sitting room.

The rest of the servants lived in the east wing of the house, in a series of bedrooms arranged on the second floor, directly above the kitchen, pantry and walk-in refrigerator. At all hours, they could be seen flying tirelessly about the house.

It was an era when, even within the privileged class, the Bouviers were truly blessed. Today, even for America's most prominent families, the division between servants and masters is, at best, awkward. The injustice of such a double standard is now apparent, even when servants are well paid. But for those employed by the Bouvier family, it was clearly a matter of pride to contribute to the general luxuriousness of the home.

The servants were highly respected members of the household. Pauline, the nursemaid, governess and house *menagere* who had been with the family back at Nutley, had all of the influence of a parent on the children, and throughout Jack's life, she remained one of his closest confidantes.

All in all, she had raised Jack, his twin sisters, their children and Miche. In her latter years, the frail old German nanny, fierce in her demand for excellence from her charges, stayed on as a privileged family member, becoming a friend and confidante to every one of the Bouviers.

Pauline's standards could not have been more puritanical. To this day, her ghost hovers over the dinner table, intoning, "Willful waste makes woeful want. And you will rue the day you threw away that piece of bread." Other admirable dictates of hers included, "Never waste your time"; "Never look in the mirror"; "Always be neat and clean"; etc.

Strange and complicated man that Jack Bouvier became, up to the day he died Pauline occupied a special place in his heart. In his final delirium, he asked to see her once more. However, Jack's total devotion to Pauline is not really that difficult to fathom. While Jack refused to have anything to do with stolid virtue, he could nonetheless admire it in others.

Miche loved Pauline, too. Returning to Lasata after a long absence, he always rushed to greet the delicate woman and press her to him with all of his might. As he grew, Big Boy Michel substituted a strong and loving handshake for an embrace. After one particularly extended absence, the child—still years away from long pants—rushed to her and passionately grabbed her frail arm with delight. The next instant, a terrible cracking sound resonated through the hallway as her delicate wrist was broken. Ever after, Miche was to approach her with infinite caution, if undiminished love.

Although the Bouviers' favorite servants were always treated with love and respect, it would have been unthinkable for them to meddle in family affairs directly—particularly to enter into direct contradiction with the Major when he was railing against one of the younger members who had momentarily plummeted from grace.

With that one exception, they were part and parcel of the extended family. Brought in to the grand lives to make valuable contributions, to be amused at the endless antics and predicaments of the children, and also to be turned to in times of need.

In their earliest years, the servants gave the children the run of the pantry and kept them from upsetting Maude with antics like standing beneath her wire cage elevator as it descended, allowing it to sink down onto their heads till it triggered the emergency stop. As the children grew to adolescence and beyond, they could always turn to Pauline or Esther for solace or advice in painful matters of family politics or unrequited love.

With the great bull market stampeding, the Bouvier servants, like working class folk throughout America during the first quarter of the twentieth century, cashed in. At every opportunity, they invested. With Jack's advice and brokerage services many of them eventually retired with enough to live comfortably for the rest of their lives.

In the case of Esther, it went a step further. Not only did she use Jack as a broker, but she also learned from him the priceless skill of reading the racing form. As they grew older, all of the children and grandchildren came to rely on her for loans. Esther was the only member of the family who never ran out of money.

Throughout the summer months, Jack would always arrive in East Hampton on Friday evening and leave early Monday morning. Accompanied by young Michel—whose father was increasingly absent—Jack would board the train to East Hampton and begin the fast crawl out to the fork in Long Island where the Hamptons begin.

At the turn of the century, the shiny steel locomotive

which made the run was christened "the Cannonball." Now, twenty years later, the filthy black hulk belched smoke and perpetually bordered on planned obsolescence. As far as Jack was concerned, Cannonball was an early and brilliant public relations coup. Undoubtedly, a more apt name like the Wounded Tortoise Local might have chased off customers.

Nonetheless, it was always a joyous ride for the man and the boy. Sitting in the lounge car—which doubled as a bar—Miche would down endless Nehis while Jack preferred ice water with a twist of lime, which he would then refill with vodka from his hip flask.

To begin, Jack would virtually recite the story of his father's daily dialogue about breakfast with George, the waiter on the Nutley-New York line. When he got to the chorus of "Fresh fish/ On a dish/ Ham and eggs/ And pork chops," Jack and Miche would alternate lines to the rhythm of the train, working up to a little three-part harmony, with the third part droned by the basso rumble of the train.

Jack was a magnificent storyteller. Miche would listen spellbound as tales of high adventure on the stock market, hot air dirigibles, cutthroat encounters with bootleggers and successful conquests of unapproachable women poured forth. The more excited Miche got, the more emotive Jack would get. The stories grew in intensity, straining even the child's imagination with their spellbinding real life plots.

Then, when Jack finally danced her into that dark corner he had chosen at the beginning of the evening, or just as he finally got up the courage to spin the snake at the base of the Casa Basso restaurant in Westhampton where the smuggler's secret cache was located . . . the conductor would call out "Eeeeeeeast Hampton! This station stop is Eeeeeeeeeast Hampton!" The pair would scramble to the parlor car door, waiting to jump down until the last possible second before the train had pulled to a stop.

As soon as his little feet plunked down on *terra firma*, Miche would wait to hear the punch line of the story. But Jack, knowing a captive audience is the best audience, would save the denouement for the next trip they'd take on the Cannonball Express.

When Jack drove down, he followed the only highway which existed in those days, along the North Shore, past endless magnificent estates and grim little service stations. Between the long flat salt marshes and rows of neat potato fields, new communities were popping up, in imitation of the Florida developments which had rewarded so many speculators with millions. For some of the developers no style was too kitsch. Long Island offered the height of splendor, neo-Renaissance homes overlooking miniature canals modeled after Venice—complete with gondoliers.

Others, vaguely colonial in style, offered the miracle twentieth century material . . . pre-stressed concrete. And there was a rapid proliferation of brick garden apartments on tracts carved into the woodlands, which were convenient to Long Island Sound, New York City, and the race tracks. And on to the "Motor Parkway."

Zooming past the opulent twin Egg Harbors so immortalized by F. Scott Fitzgerald, Jack soon came to a winding country highway leading south to the inviolable Hamptons.

On the home stretch, Jack would open up the throttle and really start to fly. The East Hampton speed limits were actually enforced by several policemen on motorcycles with sidecars, but Jack had no need to worry. Bouviers were exempt from any prohibitions, including the speed limits, age restrictions, and sanctions against drunken driving.

Early on at Apaquogue, Maude had caught her first gardener trying a little too hard to get ahead by stealing a small arsenal of gardening equipment. Sweet, gentle Maude could never have turned the thief in to the police. Instead, after confronting him, she gracefully let the matter drop, even giving the offender enough severance pay to start all over again.

That act of Christian goodwill was the best investment she ever made. The unfortunate ex-gardener sought employment in the local police force, and rapidly rose to the top. He never forgot the break that Maude had given him. And ever after, any motorcycle patrolman who had the misfortune to nab an erring Bouvier on wheels would be summarily dressed down for his troubles.

For the children and grandchildren who reaped the windfall profits from Maude's investment, the situation just convinced them further that they were invincible. Perhaps untouchable as well. And no matter how thoroughly and consistently they tested the limits, everything in their lives seemed to prove them right.

As Jack pulled to a halt in front of Lasata's massive ivy-covered main house, dusk was just falling. In East Hampton, a party would always be in the making somewhere. Frequently, Jack had called ahead to have a lavish affair set up at the Devon Yacht Club.

The Bouviers were great golfers, and all of them serious—if not gifted—equestrians. There was nothing approaching a true sailor in the family. But the Devon Yacht Club was, in addition to the Maidstone, the other pillar supporting the weighty truss of East Hampton society. Naturally then, the Bouviers were in frequent attendance there.

Typically, an unspoken law granted the farthest corner of the compact hall—the one touched by only the faintest golden glow of candlelight—to Jack. Although there was no separation of generations in those days, the grandparents as well as the tots attending Jack's wild big-band dances would know and respect his private territory on the dance floor.

Jack's nieces and nephews would stare in wonder and delight, unabashedly toeing the boundary line of his domain as Jack landed his choice for the night. Ineluctably, the couple shimmied and fox-trotted, soft-shoed and Charlestoned their way into that corner. Once there, Jack would educate his partner in the latest dance step—the notorious one in which the foot motions trailed off and were replaced by a more than gently persuasive swiveling of the hips.

Outside the club, all of the members' sailboats were moored just off the shore, rocking gently in the bay. On a star-filled night, the dock was irresistibly inviting. It was also uncommonly narrow, and there was always at least one rather inebriated guest who would totter over the edge and have to be hauled out of the brackish water before he went down, dancing pumps up. It was always a moment of severe embarrassment for a couple just succumbing to the sweet perfume of romance who had slipped out to the end of the pier for a little necking.

Until crude reality splashed in their faces, they labored under the slightly tipsy delusion that they were isolated in place and time. Acting with total discretion. Of course, they had forgotten that everyone at the parties would sooner or later find themselves in the same delightfully compromising position. The Devon Yacht Club pier was, after all, the most celebrated lover's lane in that neck of the woods.

It wa an era which saw young and beautiful couples in their Gatsbyish best indulging in endless frolics as well as some outright debauchery. But even that, while risqué, never proved fatal.

The same can be said for gambling. In Jimmy Walker's New York, houses devoted to that vice, as well as others, thrived. On Long Island, gambling was centered pretty much in Montauk. And surely, Montauk Point provided an ideal setting for the activity. The tip of Long Island, it has a jagged and wild coast, one broken only by the occasional outlines of fishing boats and trawlers. Protected by the rugged rocks on three sides, the casino Jack frequented was approachable by land and by sea.

There, underneath a glittering cut glass chandelier, with a cigarette in hand, Jack would stand in impeccable dress, listening to the pounding surf as he placed his bets.

Jack would bet on anything. Horses, baseball, football, roulette, craps. But never blackjack; the name threw him.

There was no attempt to hide the gambling. It was flagrant, and attracted most of New York's top politicians, among many other celebrities. In terms of clientele, Monte Carlo had nothing over Montauk. All night long, an endless stream of Rolls Royces, Lincolns, Stutzes and Locomobiles would line the parking lot, where the chauffeurs got up their own poker games in less formal surroundings, peering every few moments for a familiar silhouette to appear beneath the mammoth green canopy proclaiming the "Angler's Club."

Not everyone bought the operation's front, hook, line and sinker. And one night, the impossible happened.

Inside the casino, Jack was playing roulette with confidence. And winning mightily. Beside him stood a no less illustrious New Yorker—Jimmy Walker, the mayor himself. The two were chatting—and betting—as the doors of the casino burst open.

As chips scattered and screams echoed throughout the hall, ten figures in double-breasted pinstripe suits and fedoras burst in and pulled out their guns.

Mobsters or gangland lords? Of course not! To them Jimmy Walker was one of the boys. And obviously one who enjoyed a good time at the tables as much as the next guy. No, it was worse than that. This was a bust! A political enemy of Walker had decided to do Jimmy in; the gentlemen smugly waving their handguns were none other than the vice squad.

It was a decision someone would live to regret. But in the meantime, as the feds crashed through the door, they just managed to make out two pairs of shoe soles as Jack and the mayor leapt together through the great bay window overlooking the Sound.

The escapade built a bond of friendship between the unlikely pair. Jimmy Walker had the intruders "taken care of." Then he made sure that there would always be proper protection guarding the driveway so that another leap through the window would not be necessary. That accomplished, the two men spent many a pleasant night rubbing shoulders at the roulette table as they bet fortunes on the turn of a wheel.

Filled as it is with so many coves and natural harbors, Long Island was the unofficial capital of the rumrunning and bootlegging trade. During the Prohibition years, the shoreline was pitted with shallow holes which were dug in a hurry and filled with bottles brought in by small launches in the night.

Grey Goose, Phelan Beale's shooting stand on the North Shore, was a drop-off point. More than once, wandering around bleary-eyed in the hours of dawn—after standing at attention and singing "The Battle Hymn of the Republic" while the crusty old Southerner hoisted up a confederate flag—Miche, and his cousins Bouvie and Phelan, Jr. would stumble across a cache of bottles. It was an exciting find, and one which was hard to keep concealed—and untouched.

But the village was very tiny, and always on the lookout for such indiscretions. The owners were not likely to take kindly to any bragging or filching. Nor were they noted for their gentle understanding. Nonetheless, with a bit of friendly persuasion, they could ascertain the names of any offenders from village locals in a matter of seconds.

Rumrunners were not merely tolerated by Long Island residents. In many ways, they were like doctors or priests, filling a deep and painful void in the lives of their clients.

Not just that alcohol was one central foundation of everyone's life. More than that, the cynical, jaded population of the Maidstone and the Devon Yacht Clubs had grown so unshockable, so utterly comfortable, that boredom set in. Women could go about nearly nude—get drunk, smoke endless cigarettes, make love to their gardeners—anything. There was simply no room in the modern age for any sort of moral indignation.

As they refused to get exercised about anything, fashionable people soon found *all* excitement gone out of life. They had their motor cars, their phonographs, their radios, their blue chip stocks. They could go where they wanted and do what they wanted. And they were miserable. They couldn't think of *anything* they really felt like doing!

The Wartime Prohibition act came to the rescue. Speakeasies sprang up overnight. Sitting in the sultry, dingy cabarets, sipping illegal booze while listening to frenzied jazz bands, the lost generation found all of the excitement to drown out the staleness, or the memories of the Great War. Liquor flowed as never before.

For so many elegant and highly placed gentlemen, the greatest thrill of the month was slipping out of the top hat and tails, leaving the wife and children back at the stultifying mansion, and crawling off with the chauffeur to some dive or backwoods rendezvous, to find a colorful and dangerous connection—the bootlegger.

The secret passwords, the moonlight meetings, the suspicions and safeguards—all of them had a thrilling exotic touch. And, as always, when the government tries to meddle in private morality, defying it is suddenly elevated to a revolutionary political statement!

To be "tight" was a bold and challenging condition to be in. Those who got "a good head start" on the evening, then carried it to the limits, were looked upon with admiration, rather than scorn. Even for women, the bigger hangover was the better one—a healthy nose thumbed at society. A sign that, in small measure, one could beat so many Big Daddies sitting down in Washington.

By the time Prohibition was repealed, it was too late for many young people. Even as the glamor and admiration for alcoholism continued to ebb, they were so "hooked," they intensified their drinking. Sooner or later, the Bud Bouviers would all find themselves lagging on a treadmill, and slowly being dragged down the path of no return.

In the meantime, with every F. Scott Fitzgerald story, people grew more and more determined to emulate the most blasé lifestyle imaginable. The good life included wild orgiastic parties and plenty of booze.

In East Hampton, it was the height of the Gatsby era. Great mansions. Sporting, elegant cars.

And destructive self-indulgence.

SEVEN

Of A Sunday

For the Bouviers, Sundays had always been a special day of intimacy. When in New York City, they would spend the day visiting other members of the clan throughout the town. For years, Miche was brought to his great-grandparents' house by Bud, who stayed there while in New York. Otherwise, Jack would bring Miche, Jackie and little Lee to their grandparents' apartment.

That, or to the maiden great-aunts. Particularly Aunt Mary's. There, in that magnificent brownstone, the children would each be announced by the butler before they came tumbling in. In the parlor Uncle Miche and Aunt Mary would be waiting, smiling loving approval from their straight-backed thrones. As the liveried footman hurried off to fetch cookies and milk, each child in his turn would be asked to tell what he or she had done with the week just past, whether or not they went to church that morning, and then many other less troublesome questions.

The only person in the world more impressive than the dapper old MC was his sister. Aunt Mary had the longest, shiniest, most beautiful red tresses Miche had ever seen.

Putting even the twins to shame. Throughout her declining days, she maintained that stunning head of hair. Ten years of Miche's life had gone by before he entered that brownstone early one weekday morning—sent by Emmy who heard that Aunt Mary had fallen seriously ill. Miche had been sent for at school for the occasion and he fully expected to find the beautiful wasp-waisted old lady waiting for him appreciatively—perhaps with a bonbon—at the top of the stairs that led to her bedroom. She wasn't there but he found an old lady lying dozing in her bed, almost translucent and absolutely bald! And there beside her— mounted on a wig-stand—brushed to perfection, healthy and glowing, was Aunt Mary's magnificent dark red hair!

Perhaps it was a final indignity. Aunt Mary, beloved, marvelous Aunt Mary died that very night.

At Lasata, the ritual was more intimate still. One by one, the male members of the clan would make their way to Maude and the Major's boudoir, to have breakfast in turn. For Miche and the other young grandsons, the most convenient route to the bedroom was via a branch of the ancient linden tree, and through the window. At irregular intervals throughout the morning, the changing of the guard would occur as a new presence clambered up the tree and tiptoed over to Maude's bed, where his predecessor would reluctantly abdicate the best breakfast seat in the house.

Awaiting the stream of morning visitors, Maude would awaken at dawn and have Esther draw a luxuriously steaming bath. By the time the first son or grandson had arrived, she was sitting up in the newly made bed, leaning back on lacy, sweet-smelling pillows propped against the massive carved oak headboard. Beneath the frilly bedjacket covering her pale white shoulders Maude would be wearing a particularly elegant, freshly ironed nightgown.

Each young man, entering the back or the front way as he chose, would find her waiting fresh and alert, a little breakfast tray sitting perched on her lap. After a good-morning kiss, she would ask him what he desired for breakfast, then ring one of the housemaids to have it brought upstairs.

Over the years, Maude grew to become a rather large lady, but her face and skin always remained truly lovely. In her soft, fluffy bedding, she reigned rosy and cool, like a strawberry atop a frothy mound of whipped cream. More than anything else, she appeared always to have awoken fresh and sweet-smelling. Ignorant of the elaborate preparations which preceded the breakfast ritual, the Bouviers were doomed to be disappointed in lesser women who failed to awaken as fresh and perfumed as their fair Maude.

The largest bedroom in the house was cozy and informal. Maude had decorated it—for intimacy and shared confidences—in warm, pastel colors. On every available surface were photographs of every member of the family at almost every stage of life. In the twin bed, the Major slept spreadeagled and more often than not snored like a trumpeting elephant. But awakening, he would complain bitterly about not having slept a wink all night—despite all evidence to the contrary.

Jack seldom missed Sunday breakfast with his mother, no matter how late and drunken the revels of the previous night. These were times which cemented the special bond between them—a bond which never weakened as long as either of them remained alive. No other woman ever took Maude's place in Jack's life, though many tried and failed. Jack's heart always remained the exclusive possession of his beloved "Ma," and later on, of his two equally precious daughters, Jackie and Lee.

At whatever time the Major awoke, he would immediately spring out of bed. After his morning exercises, the Major would massage the sides of his neck with vigor—"to promote healthy drainage of the eustachian tubes and maintain aural acuity." Years after he had gone all but stone deaf, he would ritually continue the painful massage daily.

In the meantime, his steaming hot bath was drawn. After finishing his exercises, the Major abruptly stripped out of his bathrobe and lowered himself into the almost boiling-hot tub. After several moments of grunts and groans of pain, the splasher would simmer down to a quiet, relaxed bath.

In actuality, it was merely the calm before the storm. As the Major was contentedly crooning "In the Good Old Summertime," the tub was emptying, before being refilled with ice cold water. As if he had not a care in the world, he ceased his tune and began lowering his powerful frame into the frigid pool.

Suddenly, the entire house would be filled with shrieks and bellows as the cold reached his *gluteus maximus*. The howls increased as—with water splashing in great waves all over the room—the Major thrashed about in agony, like a great walrus in its death throes. However great his suffering was in actuality, the daily chorus of pain was enough to keep any other Bouvier from entering the morning fitness ritual.

At the age of eighty, the Major still possessed the stunning physique and faultless complexion of a man half that age. When asked how he had accomplished that miracle, he would always point with pride to the diurnal trial by ice.

The last thing the Major did before calling for his coffee and *New York Times* was the daily grooming of the moustachio. Individually, every hair was brushed and manicured impeccably. Then the tight, long-haired strands were laced with Pinaud's wax and combed out, then curled until the sharp points extended beyond the edge of his cheeks. The resulting perfect handlebars were a point of pride for everyone—although for the grandchild who came too close, they could provide a rather ticklish lesson in diplomacy.

The Major was always the soul of discretion and caution—

with the exception of Sunday mornings, when bumping into him could well prove fatal.

After the breakfasts were over, the entire clan would begin to assemble in the living room. Dressed in their most elegant gowns and suits, the flowers of East Hampton society would pile randomly into assorted automobiles to make the brief journey to church for mass. One after one, the Locomobile—a special gift from Jack to Maude—the Lincoln, and any number of a dozen or so other town cars would circle out of the great driveway and form a procession leading to the church.

The Major, however, was always late. And at any rate, he would insist upon driving his own convertible Nash. Never greatly mechanically inclined, the Major had never once "converted" the car. His gear shifting technique was also stop and start at best.

As the years progressed, his persistence remained, although he had gone stone deaf and perilously nearsighted. Hopping into the bulbous vehicle, he would floor the accelerator and kick over the engine. Without the aid of hearing, the only way the Major could be assured that it was running was by the substantial vibration which came from a revved-up, roaring engine. As soon as he felt that surge through the floorboards, he would let out the clutch with a bang, and lurch off in a screaming rush down the driveway.

Gravel would fly all over the lawn. Invariably, Paul Yuska would report the following morning that the big gang lawn mower he needed to keep up the property once again required sharpening across all of its blades. The gravel had done it once again!

Try as Paul might to bring up the matter tactfully with Maude—if the Major was within earshot, it was all to no avail. As soon as the topic was broached, the Major would snap off his hearing aid and immediately immerse himself in reading. So, together with the death-defying journey of the Nash, sharpening the mower blades became an accepted weekly ritual as well.

All attempts on the part of his wife and children to caution John Bouvier, Jr. about racing the engine were met with equally deaf ears. The old man was not in the least mechanically inclined; could never have heard the racing of the engine; and most important of all, he didn't give a damn, anyway.

Ignoring the havoc always strewn in his wake, the Major on Sunday mornings would be preoccupied with the all-consuming fear of being late for Mass. He would barrel down winding, dusty Further Lane to Dunmere Lane, which led through the main street of town. There, at the major intersection of several roads, the Major remained oblivious to anything but his objective.

Without even a token downshift, he would run the stop sign, race into the center of the traffic triangle, swerve left, veer right, then speed down Buell Lane, where St. Philomena's awaited. Looking only straight ahead, with his foot pressed to the floor for the entire journey, the Major managed to keep his pince-nez in place and the car's paint inviolate.

For the sake of historical honesty, I must add that more than Lady Luck worked to keep the Major from disaster. Early on, the village learned to stay out of his trajectory on Sunday mornings. Not a child or dog would be permitted out of doors until he had passed. And when drivers saw his familiar Nash barreling down the road in a cloud of dust, they slammed on their brakes immediately, discretion being the better part of valor.

Since his driving record remained perfect, the Major refused to understand why the rest of the family would not set foot in any vehicle when he was behind the wheel. The sole exception was the intrepid Miche, who would brave the journey with his grandfather on occasion for quite questionable motives.

In point of fact, Miche adored the little Nash convertible almost as much as his grandfather. And he found that by being particularly attentive to the old man, and assuming an attitude of total obedience and grimly nodding agreement with whatever the latter said, he could often get permission to drive the former home. Perhaps even to take it out on a solo flight that evening, once Miche got within the ballpark figure of the New York State driving age.

Apparently, Miche considered that possibility a sufficient enticement to warrant near-death.

Once arrived at the doors of the church, however, the grandson's trials had just begun. For the Major, in keeping with his independent spirit, saw no reason to follow the commonly practiced ritual of the Mass. He had his own notions about when to kneel and when to stand, and followed his own inclinations. Of course, these did not in the slightest correspond with the times when the rest of the congregation and the liturgy felt those actions were called for.

The spectacle was so embarrassing to Miche that he tried whenever possible to ditch the Major at the church entrance and install himself in the farthest pew. But he couldn't always get away with such evasions, and there were many occasions where he suffered excruciating embarrassment at his grandfather's side. But apparently, the car was still worth it.

Following the introduction of his own small contribution into the collection plate, the Major would exit, leaving the rest of the congregation to see the service through to its conclusion. Behind his grandfather, the mortified Miche would slink furtively toward the door, threading between the scowling late arrivals who blocked the escape route.

With the Major at the wheel, they would roar blindly

home, joined soon afterward by the rest of the family, gathering for the Sunday feast.

As a rule, the Sunday menu featured a massive standing rib roast—reserved weekly for the Bouviers by the town butcher, and fresh vegetables just picked by Paul Yuska. Particularly the subject of raves were the baby lima beans, succulent and fresh, and golden corn dripping with fresh churned creamery butter from the neighborhood dairy farmer.

After cocktails on the terrace with fantastic, chopped liver canapés, a famous Maude-concoction, the Bouvier family at table was bursting with energy. The noise was deafening, and confusion reigned as every family member was busy riding his or her own cloud, talking at length about the latest pitfalls or triumphs of his or her life—drifting obliviously in and out of the conversations starting up simultaneously all around the table.

It was all innocuous enough at the beginning. Then, somewhere along the eighteen-foot length of table, some remark, vaguely registered at first in the back of the mind, would grow to demand an immediate challenge. In a second, the entire Bouvier clan would be embroiled in a contest of wits and volume. Everyone had a clearly stated opinion on every subject. Particularly those which touched upon any given member of the family.

As the debate grew fiercer, the voices louder, and shriller from all quarters, at least one young Bouvier would begin turning a deathly shade of pale green. To Maude, the syndrome always remained a mystery.

It seemed that some mysterious ailment was striking at least one of the boys every Sunday afternoon. Always, in the midst of pandemonium, Maude would ferret out the sufferer sitting listlessly at the table; looking even greener at the mention of food, repentant face looking pale and drawn.

Maude would immediately begin voicing concern that

one of her hulking ducklings was out of sorts. Presently, she would call for the meat platter, and sitting by the sufferer's side, begin feeding him tiny teaspoonsful of the red juices of the roast. As the afflicted family member fought to swallow the liquid, Maude would be spooning out another, ready to hold it to his mouth with a cluck of approval.

If the Major had not yet turned off his hearing aid to concentrate on a poem and ignore the pitiful state of affairs at table, he would snort in disgust. Eventually, he would shake his head and shout across the table, "For God's sakes, Maude! The only thing wrong with that boy is one God-awful hangover!"

The expression on Maude's lovely face would grow purposefully vague. She would then administer another spoonful of her own brand of medicine and, ignoring the obvious cause of the malady, deliver it to one or another of her sons. In time, her grandchildren were also fitted into her regular Sunday patient routine.

Frankly, a good kick in the pants would have been a good deal more health-inducing. There are clear indications that the Major was inclined to ply that approach. But by and large, he was too busy dwelling upon his own affairs to apply the correct remedy in the proper location. The Sunday hangover ritual was unbroken from one weekend to the next.

While the conversation at Sunday dinner was always polite, no personal matters were considered out of bounds. For instance, when the discussion came around to the subject of Michelle's numerous beaux, the family ticked off their demerits one by one. In their idea of Michelle's best interests, they whittled down the field to two contestants.

As the young girl sat lost somewhere between excruciating humiliation and embarrassment, the two leading contenders went into the home stretch with Jack and the

Major furiously discussing their points, as if they were horses.

Jack proceeded directly into an honest assessment of each man's physique, beginning with the teeth. The Major, in the meantime, evaluated his background.

"Well, Bill comes from a good enough family, I suppose. His father does belong to the Cincinnati."

"Never mind," Jack cut in, "do you really think he'll ever amount to anything. I mean, how do you expect Michelle to live?"

"In point of fact, he's working for a very good firm, and of course, he did get his degree from Columbia. I would actually prefer him to be a lawyer. But if he's just a broker, I still think that . . ."

"Frankly, I'm not convinced. Take a look at the guy. Now what sort of child could you expect from a union with a man who has his looks?"

Undoubtedly, Michelle had long ago made up her mind anyway. But being used to the family say, she followed in the Bouvier tradition of either nodding politely or protesting—then doing what she wanted to in the first place.

Of course, the men would constantly be bringing up the stock market. Jack's success, combined with his outrageous risk-taking, never failed to infuriate his father.

The women would sooner or later get around to talking about the children, emphasizing the perfection of their own against everyone else's. On more than one occasion, the conversation focused upon the disgrace, or crowning triumph—depending upon how you viewed it—of Little Edie.

Edith Beale's daughter, the young lady in question, had celebrated her coming out into society slightly ahead of schedule. The young and curvaceous beauty—who was later engaged to Joseph Kennedy, Jr., some years before Jackie married his younger brother—made her splash at the Maidstone Club.

She was already quite a show-stopper as she posed on the diving board, stunning in her quite trendy and daring skin-tight rubber bathing suit, the first revealing one-piece suit made for women. As little Edie was in the middle of a perfect swan-dive, the flimsy garment burst and shrivelled like a balloon pricked by a pin—revealing the young girl in all of her natural splendor. Naked and beautiful, Edie gloriously swam the length of the pool. No man or boy was fool enough to toss a towel to her. But a solicitous matron did so soon enough, and Edie fled to the family cabana.

Some admiring gentleman shouted out *"WHAT A BODY!"*

And hard upon this incident, the blossoming teenager was crowned with the nickname "Whatabody Beale," a name she never managed to shed. But then, it was a burden no girl could be too ashamed to bear!

While everyone else was bantering and reminiscing, the Major, sitting in blessed silence with both hearing aids turned off, would concentrate on a poem for some member of the family gathering. He wrote at the head of the table, between bites of roast beef, carefully pacing himself so that his opus would be completed at the same time as the meal. Without the aid of his hearing aid, it was virtually impossible for anyone to cut into his private gambols with the Muse. The only way to reach him was to nudge him gently while shouting at the top of your lungs. Of course, if anyone really felt the need to speak with him, they didn't hesitate for one second to stretch their vocal resonance clear across the table.

While the Major was laboring furiously at the table, on the back porch the chauffeur was busy churning out home-made ice cream. He remained for years a rather nebulous figure. Presumably French, he spoke no appreciable English. He was gaunt, middle-aged, of average height and average build. Presumably, from time to time he drove Maude around in the Locomobile. But to this day, though

his name is shrouded in mystery, the memory of his peach
ice cream lives on in the Bouvier clan.

Exactly as the last spoon hit its dish, the Major would
reveal the fruit of his labors. His poetry was always florid
and pointed. At times, it was clearly jesting. At others, unintentionally funny. In the summer of 1924, one such work,
dedicated to Jack, was entitled *The Bachelor at Three and
Thirty*.

> *Not wondrous but e'er good to see*
> *The youth who's reached his thirty-three*
> *And own it.*
>
> *Unpleasant as a habit trite*
> *To take from age a solid bite*
> *And moan it.*
>
> *The bachelor may e'er contend*
> *He'll thus remain until the end*
> *Unharassed.*
>
> *Yet all the world knows him the while*
> *Politely holding back its smile*
> *Embarrassed.*
>
> *The callow youth may stoutly claim*
> *That girls to him all look the same*
> *And smoke.*
>
> *The Janes, however, fully know*
> *That every John is not the show*
> *And joke.*
>
> *He passes up the very sweetest,*
> *The best, the prettiest and the neatest*
> *He jilts.*

> *But when he really needs a wife*
> *Who can't be had for mortal life*
> *He wilts.*

> *So, Sonny, marry when you can*
> *Is my advice for everyman*
> *And you.*

> *Else, when you find the girl of grace*
> *Gaze upwards to another's face*
> *You'll stew.*

In 1924, for Jack, it was still lots of booze, girls' hearts strung like baubles on a thin golden chain—perhaps more like notches on his favorite rifle. And of course, fast, expensive cars.

EIGHT

Good Sports

After the Sunday lunch at Lasata, the family members would go their separate ways. Usually, all roads led to the Maidstone Club.

Naturally, the Maidstone figured prominently in the Bouviers' lives. Not merely because of its terribly appealing social aspects—the fact that anyone who was anyone was "Maidstone," and sure to be there on Sunday afternoon. But sports were extremely important in that universe, and the sign of good breeding in young men.

Always, they were fiercely competitive. From prep school on, the upper class was quietly fighting for that top honor and first position in life. Just as important as winning was doing it gracefully and with style. And when one could not win, it was above all important to be a wonderful loser. A good sport.

Jack and the Major—and Bud, the undisputed family champ whenever he was passing through—would play golf and argue lovingly about every stroke. The Major nearly always won.

As far as Jack was concerned, cheating had a great deal

to do with the Major's victories. No matter how far into the woods he had sliced, the ball would always turn up shining beneath his plus-fours, near the edge, with a clear chip shot onto the green. No less of a marvel were the golfing pants from which, as soon as a gap in the right pocket was sewn, would spring a new golf-ball-sized hole.

After fourteen holes—they always started at the fifth, since it lay closest to Lasata—they would continue arguing heatedly as they piled into the clubhouse, a massive new H-shaped Tudor style building. The Major always defended his honest victory, stating categorically that his success came from "playing short and steady." That comment never failed to occasion ribald remarks by erstwhile friends, concerning precisely how short, and particularly how steady, the Major was in other events.

Such kidding was always done respectably out of the Major's earshot, lest the young offender have his head handed to him. The Major, still a powerful and superbly fit man in his fifties and beyond, demanded respect at all times. It was not a good idea *not* to give it to him.

Soon, "cocktail hour," the new rage among their friends, would descend upon the weary sportsmen. For the son, the dull procedure of merely padding into the great hall and taking a seat would never suffice. For as magnificent a specimen as Jack knew himself to be, proper presentation was *de rigueur.*

Jack would straighten up his broad shoulders, tighten the corners of his perpetual half smile, stride up to the arched entry, and come to a dead halt. There he would pause against the door, giving his admirers time to take in every inch of him—plenty of time. With the same dramatic purposefulness of Babe Ruth at the plate, Jack would look around the room with the appearance of deep introspection until he zeroed in on the best-looking girl there.

Whereas the Mighty Babe would point and then smash the ball over the fence, Black Jack just delivered it personally, making a screaming bee-line toward that fortunate female. Her luck would most likely be short-lived, however, because Jack was notoriously fickle.

While Jack was swimming and soaking up the afternoon sun, the Major would head home, still full of his victory.

He was a most agreeable man at all times, and particularly when things were going his way. But even otherwise—the Major was still a good sport.

Even on such tender issues as money, the Major always lived up to his promises. Even though Maude had long ago learned to elicit them while he was still half-asleep, when the Major was particularly generous. At that point, Maude could raise the topic, explain what she needed, and have her husband groan a contented agreement, then nod as he fell asleep.

However, when the Major returned to their bedroom after winning at golf, and Maude broached the topic, he was not always so receptive. In fact, on occasion, with a leap that shook the floorboards, he would vault clear across the bed to the little Chippendale secretary which she always kept closed. Not for secrecy—Maude Sergeant Bouvier had nothing to hide. It was just that, no matter how carefully she stacked them, the bills would always spill onto the floor unless it was closed.

Naturally, when the Major threw open the desk, a landslide of paper scattered all over the floor. Seeing the sheer bulk of undone accounts, he would stare in breathless horror.

A moment later, his lungs replenished, he'd stand pointing at the bills incredulously, throw open his massive jaw and bellow, "God damn it to Hell, Maude!" Midday visitors were quite alarmed the first time they heard the agonized shrieks. But to the family, it just meant that the inevitable had come: it was time for Maude to pay the bills.

Of course, Maude had always intended to pay them promptly. It was just such an unpleasant, boring chore, she would plan on doing them all at once. As the weeks went by, and every day brought a new batch, she would plan on being efficient and spending the first rainy day writing out checks like a machine, a sort of domestic use of mass production techniques. For the meantime, she would throw them all unopened into the secretary.

With any luck, the cupboard would be bare by the time the Major was ready to find a bone to pick. If not, Maude resigned herself to torrents of fury, loud and bitter complaints about the astronomical totals, and the absurdly frivolous nature of her expenditures.

Of course, the Major was right. All of the recurrent expenses were paid by the family accountants. In point of fact, Maude's bills dealt exclusively with frills, the luxuries she lavished upon her sons and daughters and grandchildren. If she was ill-fated enough to be caught redhanded by the Major on the Day of Reckoning, then she would be forced to sit there under his ever vigilant eyes and write out each and every check. Amid his anguished groans and the perennial refrain, "God damn it to Hell, Maude!"

It was a chorus with many possible variations. Regretfully, one of the most common strains was "God damn it to Hell, Michel!" Not only was Miche the oldest and largest of the grandsons, but he was the most adept in figuring out ingenious ways of unleashing his grandfather's most wrathful explosions.

Even more than his Beale cousins, Miche was frequently within a degree or two of the Major's boiling point and a good thrashing. Since he came from a family of devoted hunters, and proud of its military heritage, it is not surprising that rifles figured on more than one occasion in Miche's less fortunate adventures.

Miche's basic training in riflery came from his father and from Jack, both of whom were quite keen on duck hunting. However, the undisputed expert on the subject was Phelan Beale, who had bought his North Shore duck blind as an economy when the price of fresh duck rocketed beyond reason. At home, the three boys practiced daily to improve their aim. Of course, they shot out all of the eyes of the statues in Maude's priceless Italian Gardens. Boys, after all, will be boys.

But soon, their targets grew more ambitious. In the absence of a duck blind at Lasata, they set up a shooting stand at the northwest corner of the property, complete with tin cans strung along the fence in front of the neighbor's bushes. Taking aim, they fired three salvoes in rapid succession.

To the washerwoman bending over a pile of clothing in the little laundry hut behind the bushes, it seemed that the Great War had begun all over again. As she dove to the floor, a bullet whizzed within inches of her nose. During a brief pause for reloading, she found the courage to bolt back to her employer's house.

One hurried telephone call later, the Major ran out to the little brick terrace above Maude's garden, cupped his hands like a megaphone, and bellowed. Fourteen acres away, the words, "GOD DAMN IT TO HELL, MICHEL!" came through loud and clear. Of course, Bouvie and young Phelan immediately vanished from sight, leaving poor Miche to take his punishment alone.

Another celebrated show of marksmanship occurred when Miche was bunking at Grey Gardens with the Beales. All morning long, they tossed and turned in the "Big Boy's" room, trying to sleep, as mourning doves cooed in the dawn's light. Incessantly.

Miche first became aware of Bouvie Beale's equally restless stirring. Then Phelan, Jr. began kicking up the sheets in annoyance. The noise seemed to grow louder, more unbearable. They thought they would be driven insane. Then Miche stood up.

"Gentlemen," he announced confidently, "the time of the doves has come."

Like church mice, they crept out of their beds, down the stairs and out of the house, pausing midway. When Phelan, Sr. wasn't at his shooting preserve, he always maintained a full panoply of weapons in his home. Selecting several light gauge shotguns, the boys were once again underway.

Lying prone on the ground in the early morning sunlight, the boys focused three sets of sleepy eyes on the nest under the eaves of the roof.

With military precision, they all raised their shotguns, then fired at the count of three.

By the count of ten, Phelan, still dressed in his nightshirt, came roaring forth from the house. This morning, there was no opening chorus of "The Battle Hymn of the Republic." Gazing upward, he saw that half of the roof had been blown to smithereens.

Behind three wide awake boys with smoking shotguns, the mourning doves sat cooing unscathed in the early morning light.

This time, the guns were locked away for a good, long time. Back at the Major's, Miche was thoroughly disarmed; his personal rifle placed in the one inviolable region of the house: his grandfather's Prohibition Closet. There, amid the sacred arsenal of fifths of Guckenheimer's rye, the rifle sat untouched for over a season.

For Jack, the high point of many days at Lasata was going "fishing." Late in the afternoon, he would set out, beginning with warming up the elegant old black Mercury, which had a removable top. Just as he was about to head off sporting, Jack found Miche and, after persuading him to change into fresh clothes and comb his hair, brought him along.

Their favorite spot was just in front of the elegant little brick-front shops on Easthampton's main street. They would cruise quietly up and down the street, watching the streams of women glide by, stopping every once in a while to admire a particularly captivating specimen.

For Jack, few things were more fun than instructing

Miche in all of the fine points of this brand of fishing, which he called "babyhunting."

With his connoisseur's eye, Jack would go over each woman's strong and weak points, explaining to Miche the benefits or disadvantages of each. When they finally found what they were looking for, Jack would gently roll the motorcar to a halt. Miche would then get out, putting on his brightest schoolboy smile, and invite the young lady to ride with him and his uncle. With the young boy's artful innocence at work, most of the young women laughed and piled in lightheartedly into the black coupe, cuddling between young Miche and his ravishing Uncle Jack.

Perhaps an hour later, the trio would be all smiles as they pulled into the driveway at Lasata, where Miche vaulted out of the car, and went running into the house to divulge his latest exploit with his uncle.

In the meantime, Jack would yell out a reminder to Miche that he would not be returning for supper. And with that, he would share a nip from his hip flask together with his sweetheart, throw a strong arm around her and head back toward uncharted regions, smiling his beautiful, supremely masculine smile, the darkness of his skin offsetting large, gleaming teeth.

For Jack Bouvier, there could never be anything to compare with the sporting life.

NINE

A Farewell to Bachelorhood

In the midst of the great upward spiral of the twenties, Jack's life abruptly took a detour. While they were by no stretch of the imagination wholesome, Jack's parties and general activities grew decidedly more family-oriented in tone. The endless flirtations grew more sporadic; the fire of passion in them seeming to flicker and almost die. More and more, he concentrated on Janet Norton Lee.

To everyone's amazement—perhaps excluding the strong-willed Janet—they made it to the altar in the summer of '28. The wedding was held at St. Philomena's church, in East Hampton. Afterwards, a sumptuous reception was held at the magnificent summer home which James T. Lee, Janet's father, had rented. People sprawled all over the great lawn, and spilled into every nook and nook and cranny of the great house.

The Bouvier clan's one fear was for Bud, once they had heard Jack say "I do." Bud's own marriage had died an unpleasant death, and his drinking problem was now advanced beyond all point of denial. It seemed that just as Jack was rising to the pinnacle of success, everything was slipping through Bud's hands. His celebrated marriage had been demolished, and his health, between the damage from the wartime gassing and the subsequent drinking, was failing fast.

Bud's divorce was a blow to the sternly religious Bouviers. Despite the fact that divorce had grown increasingly common, it alienated many members of the family forever. Particularly vehement were MC and Aunt Mary, who could scarcely suffer their nephew's presence in their Forty-sixth Street brownstone. Often, the major's caustic displeasure proved too much for Bud as well. But he could always find welcome with his grandmother, Carrie Ewing Bouvier. Her home became his *pied à terre* in New York. Miche became a more frequent visitor there as well, and was always treated to a corner of his grandfather's very own toast, together with a sip of Postum, which tasted just like the forbidden fruit of childhood—coffee.

As Bud became too ill to work on a daily basis, his millions slipped away. And although he could turn to people other than MC for shelter, there was no longer anywhere else for him to borrow money which might save the entire fortune from being dissipated.

Those were his circumstances as Bud Bouvier stood watching his brother in a great moment of glory. It would have been tough enough for anyone, let alone for the younger brother of a man who had always made fortune and women a major source of competition. Nonetheless, Bud held his head high at the wedding and remained one of the few sober men present. His beautiful comportment in the face of so much tribulation—and available booze— led everyone to hope for Bud Bouvier's rehabilitation.

After the reception, Jack and Janet sailed off for a month-long honeymoon in Europe. No sooner had they embarked on the *Aquitania,* than Jack espied Miss Doris Duke, a young Newport heiress of considerable fortune. He immediately launched into a quite serious flirtation with her, much to

Janet's dismay. The new bride immediately sent off a distress call to the twins. But despite the fact that it had gotten off to a terrible start, the rest of the honeymoon apparently passed without further incident.

After the newlyweds returned, they were offered a rent-free duplex apartment on Park Avenue, in a building owned by Janet's father, 790 Park Avenue. It was ideally situated: a block from Maude. The couple moved in and got to work setting up shop.

The first thing Jack did was to install a little gymnasium in an extra maid's room. Whatever married life would demand in the way of sacrifices, Jack was determined not to lose the great shape he had spent thirty-seven years developing. Among the items included was a massive electric hot box, in which he would regularly lock himself to melt away the excess pounds which would creep up in the midst of his enjoyment of the good life.

Jack also installed a belt vibrator, as well as a huge chrome rubbing table and a masseuse to pound away at his muscles, to make sure they kept up their tone, and his slim body stayed supple. In the absence of a terrace, he set his great easy chair in front of the bathroom window and sunbathed in the lush eastern exposure in naked bliss, oblivious to the high visibility afforded a dozen neighboring windows.

Frankly, Black Jack didn't give a damn. He had his name and reputation to live up to, and anonymous strangers could never be allowed to interfere with the process of maintaining a perfect tan. Of course, there was always a sunlamp, but Jack preferred to take those treatments at his barber's whenever the sun was recalcitrant.

Soon after their return from Europe, Jack and Janet gave the first of many lavish parties, held at the Devon Yacht Club. It was where there was always a big name band at hand, wailing in the midst of dozens of red-checkered covered tables, lit only faintly by little glass-enclosed candles.

The motif was a carefully contrived imitation of a speakeasy. The atmosphere was perfect, right down to the presence of an enormous, scar-faced man named Willy, who possessed a cauliflower ear to boot. In the heart of darkness, he added the necessary quality of furtive danger, peering sententiously through the tiny window slot in the front door as every couple submitted themselves for his admission.

Of course, the liquor was genuinely contraband, hauled on shore in a spot not too far removed from the club itself. Invitations to "Jack and Janet's," a name conspicuously like Jack and Charlie's—the real-life speakeasy which later became the "21" Club—were eagerly sought within the society whirl. During the next year, they became regular events.

Married life went on pleasantly for the newlyweds, with only minor indiscretions on Jack's part. Not only was he crazy about his bride, but he was also thoroughly involved with the Great Bull Market.

Life, to Jack, had always been one large gamble. And for the time being, he was content to have Janet as his wife and Lady Luck for a rather indulgent mistress. He was in many ways not too different from his contemporaries on Wall Street. The stock exchange, as everyone has noted at one time or another, is basically one magnificent billion-dollar crap game, and all brokers are ultimately crap shooters. An unfortunate choice of words, perhaps, but nonetheless quite descriptive.

Jack would carry around a silver piece at all times, as did all the brokers. They used it to determine which of them would take an eighth-of-a-point gain or loss (up-tick or down-tick) on a stock transaction. When the market was quiet Jack might take odds on a football or basketball game—or on whether or not the weekend would bring sailing weather—often choosing his side by a flip of the coin.

There were always many rumors to the effect that it was a two-tailed coin. However, those who were trusted to examine it maintain that it was indeed half-headed.

Regardless of whatever the coin looked like, it is certain

that it followed along as Jack was catapulted into success. In 1922, when Jack borrowed money from MC to buy a seat on the exchange, his experience was limited to three years at Henry Hentz. Since the time of his childhood, he had consistently heard his father, grandfather and uncle in running discussions about the market, debating the vagaries of innumerable stocks. Nonetheless, plunging into dealing such stocks as Kennicott Copper, Texas Gulf Sulphur, Kress Department Stores, Colorado Fuel and Power, Baldwin Locomotive and Holland Furnace, he was clearly gambling.

Jack was not merely a "two-dollar broker"—one who buys and sells at his customer's demands. By devoting himself to specialties, Jack created a much more demanding and dangerous life for himself. Since the two-dollar brokers bought from him, Jack had to maintain a certain inventory of available stocks, and also buy them up whenever interest in his specialty stocks flagged, threatening to lower the price. It was hectic, demanding work, the kind that sent so many others running for their hip flasks or searching frantically for aspirin, or drinking gallons of milk to placate aggravated ulcers.

Jack thrived under the pressure, knowing that one bad season could come close to destroying him, but trusting his gambler's instinct. In addition to steel nerves, he needed a full and accurate knowledge of what was going on at every minute of the day on the floor, and the sort of quick mind that could interpret trends as they were developing. Jack had everything it took and more. Using his own judgment, he soon established himself as one of the best in his field.

Jack made most of his fortune, as well as many other peoples', during the rampaging bull market of '27. Stocks were going for incredible prices, and trading on the floor reached fever pitch. There was no time to write out sales agreement memos, so everything was bought with a quick nod of the head across the floor, and drawn up in writing later.

A speculative fever had taken hold of America; and all at the same time, people on the streets wanted to buy into paradise. In the roaring twenties, heaven could mean only one thing—elegant town cars, a fine country mansion, and dollars by the wheelbarrowful. Everyone had stories of friends of friends who had done it, who had hopped in at the right time and been carried up to fortune by rising prices. Consequently, on the train, in the restaurant or barber shop, every set of ears was open, waiting for the Big Tip.

As for Jack, he, too was infected by the crazy buying frenzy. It was the biggest gamble that America had ever seen, and in he plunged. Against all of the traditional indicators of dangerous inflation—stock prices greater than ten times their dividend, call money interest rates above fifteen percent, high unemployment—Jack took stock in America; believing that as new technological products kept appearing, consumers would step up their pace of buying. And stocks would continue to rise.

Undoubtedly, there was a certain amount of logic to the situation. An America where there were riots at the showroom during the unveiling of Henry Ford's Model A, was a new and unexplored phenomenon. Lindbergh was the hero of the decade, and Byrd was waiting for the opportunity to fly over the South Pole. It seemed that there was nothing technology and American courage couldn't accomplish.

Coolidge Prosperity was in full force, and the president time and again expressed his full faith in the market's stability. But most important of all, the stocks kept on defying gravity. It seemed clear that with everyone investing, no small distress flag could divert the stampede of the Great Bull.

So in addition to all of his specialty stocks, Jack was trading madly for his own account. Promptly at ten o'clock each morning, he was there on the floor of the Exchange. For five hours every day, it was a constant flow of adrenaline—

turning here, running there, as quickly as possible, so that making money wouldn't take too much time and keep him from making more.

In a room full of bedlam, his clerks would be shouting at the top of their lungs while the phones rang without end, as if they had a life of their own and could fly off their black perches at any moment. All over the Exchange, in every room, the same thing was happening, as Americans bought more and more tickets to see Al Jolson in *The Jazz Singer,* more and more Fords, and more and more superheterodyne radios.

In the midst of the action, Jack plowed single-mindedly through to his purpose. While listening to thirteen different trade issues, he would also be pressing for $39^3/_4$ instead of 40 on a small block of stock with a broker across the floor nodding violently. At the height of trading Jack made a fortune in the neighborhood of $750,000.

The pressure on the floor grew unbearable at times. The only way for the men to let off steam was to tease each other unmercifully. Because he stood out from the crowd, Black Jack was the butt of a good deal of gentle harassment.

"Hey, Bouvier!" the call would echo from another corner, as Jack was in the middle of buying a block of Kennecott, selling Montgomery Ward, and haggling over the price of Standard, "How about $40^1/_2$ for Peggy?"

"Forget it, pal!" Jack would scream back while shaking on Kennecott, holding out for more on Ward, and giving in on Standard, "I'd never sell her that short. Besides, I'm still a bull on her!"

For the clerks, it was rarely a laughing matter. They were confined to quarters next to the phones, behind a brass line which they were not supposed to cross. But what really separated them from the floor brokers for whom they worked was the amount of money—from $25,000 to well over half a million—that stock exchange seats were going for at any given moment.

It was a substantial hurdle to jump, and few men had that much ready cash. In most cases, the clerk was considered beneath the dignity of the broker, until such time as he could ante up the money to buy his own seat. But in Jack's case, since he had acted like a broker from the beginning—toeing the brass line and failing to defer in the least to brokers—the heady achievement of finally obtaining his own seat did not in the least affect him.

At the height of the Bull Market, as the tickers lagged several hours behind in reporting sales and all of the communications networks were jammed, the clerks would be scurrying beyond human endurance in their struggle to keep up. One clerk, who stood well over five feet only by virtue of his top hat, always left it on his head to keep up appearances. During a heavy Bull Market trading day, it kept threatening to fall off.

After three hours, when he got a moment to spare, the man tore off his hat and pegged it. But in his hurry, he accidently spiked it on a purchase order hook in the booth, catching his thumb as well. By the time the diminutive man could be unhooked, the order under his thumb had gotten five thousand dollars more expensive. The trauma of the incident proved too much, and he retired from the Exchange the following week.

In addition to the tension of the floor, was another surprising factor of working there: the very rough edges—bordering on illiteracy—of the brokers. The "great chunks of ignorance," as Jack's contemporary on the floor of the exchange, Charles J. McDermott, observed in his "Reminiscenses of Wall Street,"—hidden beneath the cloak of the wiseguy with a sharp tongue and a furtive manner."

"Dis here place is da centa of da univoise," proclaimed a broker whose command of the English language left much to be desired. "Things is poppin', boys. So climb on and go for a ride, buy anything you can. Youse can't go wrong. Lookit my brudder-in-law. He jest bought a bungalow in Coral Gables. Don't have ta woik nomore. Jest 'cause he bought RKO.''

Competition among brokers ran the gamut from friendly to razor sharp. Not everyone on the floor had gone to Yale, or came from a prominent Social Register family. Nor did they all have Jack's fabulous looks and charm. Or his success. Even in the highest levels of brokerage, there was bitter jealousy. Hatred for those who got ahead more quickly than others was almost the rule.

Within exchange houses, there was endless one-upmanship and political jockeying: vying for the bosses' favor. Between competitors on the exchange, there were vicious mud-slinging campaigns, and sometimes outright sabotage and warfare.

Goading them all on, and held before their noses like a golden carrot, was money. Lots and lots of money. No one could be rich enough, not as long as there was anyone richer, or trying to be. And when enough of it was held out, the golden rule and good sportsmanship were thrown to the wind.

The New York Stock Exchange was a guerrilla war zone. And anyone who said otherwise had never been close enough to smell the blood flowing. Of course, it wasn't a mere matter of fisticuffs, setting down one's walking stick, removing one's wire-rimmed glasses and putting up dukes.

Wall Street vendettas were for life, the carefully engineered, slow blasting away of someone else's empire at its foundations. While he seemed to prosper and continually expand, whisper campaigns and quiet transactions of huge blocks of stock could corrode his power base. Eventually, strains would develop. Just when the magnate reached the peak of his influence, the first tremors would start.

Softly. Almost imperceptibly. Then the pecking party would begin. After five or ten years, or perhaps a generation of quietly engineered corrosion, the finale was almost anticlimactic. All at once, confidence in every sector evaporated. Buffeted about, it became merely a waiting game until the broker crashed.

In the meantime, he was robbed of everything: all of the clients it might have taken three generations to acquire. By the time the great fall occurred in the broker's life, without knowing it, he had already been stripped of power, prestige, and even self-respect.

Nowhere more than Wall Street was money a greater justification for crimes. When the oil monopoly wanted a small competitor out of the way, they had two bullets put through his head, and had his main refineries set on fire. As the work of a lifetime blazed away, a representative approached the bereft widow with a generous offer she was in no position to refuse.

The next day, 50,000 shares of privately held stock changed hands for a very reasonable price.

Money made strange bedfellows. With enough of it, you could do almost anything. As a social lubricant, it was unparalleled. There was no grating creak impervious to the greasing of a palm. In the era of Coolidge Prosperity, when the market was regularly discussed from the pulpit, nothing was a greater sign of grace than wealth. Public absolution was a question of price. Paying it off could be done on the installment plan, popularly known as philanthropy.

Of course, the seedy underbelly of the market never showed itself beyond the confines of the Exchange building. Its excitement reigned everywhere. On the New York subway trains or at any coffeeshop in any major city, four out of five newspapers would be turned to the stock prices. Everyone understood that the key to endless prosperity was increased consumption and credit. Money flooded the market and many people's lives. The more you diverted, the more took its place. With so much there, there was no reason to save.

For the man on the street, borrowing and investing were

the patriotic things to do—taking stock in America and never selling it short.

Every day, during their lunch hour, workers and professionals jammed into brokers' offices and watched mesmerized as the ticker tape tapped out fortunes in the making. Buying with ten or twenty percent down, investors owed balances they could only pay off if the market continued to skyrocket. But they could not postpone the joy of ringing up profits. Of course, because the stocks were on margin, the broker could call for additional money if the stocks declined.

So every Tom, Dick and Harry bought stocks, no matter what the forecasters cautioned, oblivious to the signs that the great journey of Coolidge Prosperity had to come to an end.

Meanwhile, Black Jack made a fortune on his own holdings, plus a hefty $75,000 in commissions a year as a broker.

Of course, he had no trouble finding ways to spend it. At the premiere of *Showboat,* he was positively splendid. Shooting a lot of diamond-studded white cuff from a seductively tailored tail coat, he sported a gold-headed cane on one arm and a beautiful girl on the other. Her silken décolletage was warmed by a luxurious swathe of white ermine. As bystanders gawked, the stunning couple was helped out of his gleaming black Lincoln, the one with scarlet leather interior.

Cameras flashing all of the time, Jack turned his head long enough for his millionaire's smile to be captured for tomorrow's tabloids.

The next moment, heads once again turned around to catch a glimpse of one of the new Arabian Sand Model A phaetons.

After theater, of course, there was dinner. Jack frequented any one of several dozen bastions of *haute cuisine,* resplendent with red velvet and shining brass on the walls, the tables set in spotless linen with double damask dinner napkins and crystal candelabra.

Before heading into the candlelit main *salle,* Jack helped his girl out of her wrap as dozens turned to stare at the beautiful couple. Casually rejecting the *maître d'*s offer of assistance, Jack paused for a moment, then threw off his opera cloak in one magnificent gesture. With all of the debonair elegance of a Douglas Fairbanks, he handed it to the checkroom attendant and followed the *maître d'* into the dining room.

It could have been clumsily melodramatic if he hadn't known how to keep up the air of excitement and mystery. Luckily, that was never a problem for the Black Orchid.

There was always somewhere to go. Tea dances and debutante parties—where Jack, in his mid-thirties, was the most desirable bachelor in the crowd. Magnificent white yachts with long thin steel hulls, like lesser luxury liners, where uniformed crews manned the helm and stewards tended the cabins, leaving the guests to sip cocktails and talk about sports and the market as they drifted from one opulent port of call to the next.

Then there were the summer mansions, city brownstones, and luxurious apartments large enough to accommodate two or three families. Together with Barney Barbin, Jack regularly flew up to New Haven in a Stinson Reliant high-wing monoplane; one weekend landing just in time to make the Yale-Princeton football game. At other times, they would fly to East Hampton, making a spectacular entrance in their goggles and aviators' jackets.

When Jack could not manage to run through all of his profits in his outrageous lifestyle, he looked for investment schemes. Always cognizant of the odds, he would calculate the risk and then, if still undecided, flip his betting coin, helping it with an extra turn of the wrist, as he saw fit.

There were immense profits to be made by jumping into bond issues floated by major investment banking houses, to finance cartels and holding companies. And Jack was in a superb position for selecting winners.

But his pet projects throughout life always involved magnificent machines. Some were as practical as the Radio Corporation, and others as visionary as the talking pictures. Some, like the Tucker car, were disastrous because they were ahead of their time.

One time, however, Jack decided to be cautious. Before he invested his money in a truly ridiculous invention, he would make sure that the thing worked.

Flying in the little Stinson Reliant, Jack began to see a great future for himself in the infant industry of aviation. The vehicle of his fortune would be something called an "autogyro," designed to take off vertically and spiral downwards like a maple seed pod if the engine failed—a crash-proof plane.

This time, Bud had gotten the jump on him. Together with a neighbor from East Hampton name Juan Tripp, Bud had briefly operated an air shuttle between New York City and the summer resort. But soon Juan got ambitious, and decided to begin a serious airline. Since Bud's capital was all tied up, he went to his family for a loan. One by one, they turned down the hare-brained scheme.

A duly crestfallen William Sergeant Bouvier returned to his partner with the message that he had to let him down. Consequently, Tripp had to go on to start Pan American Airways without the help of the Bouviers.

In the meantime Jack, not to be outdone by Bud, was going to sink some capital into the autogyro. Since he knew his family's attitude about airborne ventures, he decided to put all doubts to rest, and possibly squeeze some money out of his father, by first giving the airscrew a test flight.

Jack chose for the site a potato field. It was part of his father-in-law James T. Lee's property right off Further Lane. On the morning of the flight, the autogyro, which was basically a wingless airplane whose propeller tilted ninety degrees to face upwards—was unloaded into the field from a small trailer.

Back at Lasata, a small and early victory celebration was going at full tilt. As the hour of ten o'clock approached, Jack led a triumphal procession of automobiles down the road and toward the sea. Stopping at the potato field, they all hopped out and trailed over to the peculiar airship.

It was a glorious day, sunny and warm and crystal clear. Jack was delighted that high altitude visibility would be no problem—breathing a sigh of relief, he let it be known that it had been a serious concern. Armed with vodka in his silver flask, Jack proceeded to regale the gathering of family and friends with a wealth of facts and figures concerning the aerodynamic principles involved.

He didn't know a damn thing about it. But that was beside the point. What he didn't know, he shamelessly fabricated on the spot, while the pilot stood deadpan beside him, gulping down his vodka. The rest of the family knew less than Jack did. They listened with rapt attention, marveling at Black Jack's expertise.

Tossing off his coat with a flourish, Jack continued to build up the drama before the actual show. He looked at the assembly, lost in a search for . . . something. At last, his eyes lit upon young Miche, and Jack gestured him forward.

Singled out for some special privilege, the young nephew approached his uncle with silent awe, eyes bulging at the proximity of the great flying machine.

With a grand gesture, Jack handed Miche his gold-headed cane, proclaiming, "Here, Big Boy, you take care of this for me, please."

As Miche stood there staring with exquisite dignity, the pilot slipped into the waiting craft. Jack, his time arrived, urged Miche back to the rest of the crowd, saying, "I will now board the plane." And with that, the self-proclaimed airman put on his goggles, straightened the creases in the navy blue pinstripe suit that Alex Bussy had custom-tailored for the occasion, and made straightaway for his winged chariot.

Seated beside him, the pilot started the engine, spoiling the notion that Jack would actually be at the controls. But rising to the occasion, Jack accepted the limits of his performance. Making up for them with solemn waves to the people across the field, he bowed to the pilot, and the vehicle began to fly.

It was a fluttery, remarkably unstable machine, with an obvious tendency to prefer the earth to the sky. Nonetheless, with the engine in front groaning and the pilot gritting his teeth with determination, it continued to rise. Valiantly, inch by inch, it climbed, crab-like, into the great blue yonder.

At twenty-five feet, a great cheer went up from the crowd.

At thirty-five feet, the chorus of delight turned into incredulous shrieks as tiny bits and pieces of metal began to rain upon them. As the ladies opened their parasols to protect their heads and children, the men shouted confused and contradictory instructions.

The autogyro hovered above them, as the pops and pings continued. Then, abruptly, the noises stopped, only to be replaced a split-second later by the screech of tearing metal. Before their unbelieving eyes, the engine itself fell out and plunged to earth with a sickening thud! Black Jack's face, outlined by the tiny windowframe of the cockpit, blanched to the color of piano keys.

In eerie silence, the autogyro slithered sideways, and drifted downwards on slowly revolving rotors . . . ghostlike. Ten feet off the ground, it abandoned its aerodynamically sound and crash-proof trajectory, and plummeted the remaining distance like a boulder.

A rather mortified Jack scrambled out of the fuselage as fast as he possibly could, refusing to look back as he hightailed it back to Lasata.

As for the gold-headed cane, it was given to Miche, and

we have it still. Jack was afraid it would always remind him of that nasty first taste of death.

Never again would Black Jack Bouvier have anything to do with an autogyro. He made a big mistake there. If he had invested money in the prototype helicopter, Jack would have made more money than even he knew what to do with. Still, it was a bad gamble he felt lucky enough to live to regret.

TEN

The Turning Point

By 1929, the stock market had become the absorbing interest of every member of the Bouvier clan.

MC Bouvier was fast becoming the Dean of Wall Street, and Jack, between his grandiose lifestyle and excellence as a specialist, was no less renowned. When the Major was forced to retire from the courtroom, MC took him into the senior brokerage house, where he at first traded largely for his own account, then opened an East Hampton office.

John Davis, Maudie's husband, had his own firm of Billings, Alcott. Henry Clarkston Scott, who had married Michelle, was working as a customers' man for Bouvier, Bishop, Jack's firm. By now, Bud was relying entirely upon dividends for his income, so he kept tabs as closely as the rest of them.

Each man among the Bouviers watched the stock market with undivided interest. It was their one topic of conversation beyond family matters and politics, and each argued vehemently about his view of the market's timing and direction. Needless to say, they never agreed about anything.

The year 1929 promised even greater profit for America.

Though there had been some warning signs in June and December of 1928, the new year ushered in a sharp upward, if erratic, climb of the index. While Bud religiously followed the old adage, "Never give up your position in a good stock," Jack plunged recklessly in and out.

Worse yet, Jack's streak of luck just wouldn't break. While Bud's holdings posted modest increases as he hedged his bets, the sky was the limit for Jack.

As the older brother's fortune grew, the competition between the two grew fiercer. As far as Jack was concerned, his quarterly dividend checks were worth more than all of Bud's theoretical vacillations about the market. And every time the younger brother spoke, he would be reminded of that fact.

The bitterness between them, while it in no way diminished the deep love they had for one another, grew irrepressible. The Major felt compelled to write a poem about it, entitled, "The Difference":

> *When prices mount along the line*
> *Of stocks of yours and stocks of mine*
> *'Tis is then that brothers oft would be*
> *Craving the dizzy heights to see.*
> *When prices drop like melted snow*
> *And no one ever seems to know*
> *Exactly where the pit is deepest,*
> *Or what's the stock that is the cheapest,*
> *No longer are they brothers*
> *But mad and irritated lungers.*
> *The only wish that fits the spell*
> *Is to see the other lad in hell.*

Abruptly, both of their points of view changed. In March, then again in May, the market slipped and threatened to fall. Looking at it from the outside, Bud read the writing on the wall. He told Jack in no uncertain terms to get the hell out before it collapsed. With a wife at home and a baby on the way, Jack reluctantly agreed to consider his brother's point of view, instead of just continuing to lord it over Bud with his success.

At the same time, Bud realized that the competitive pressures of his life would soon kill him if he didn't make a break. After spending the last weeks of spring in a sanitorium, where he gave up drinking for the last time, Bud set out West in search of peace of mind.

Together with Miche, he arrived at Los Olivos, in California's spectacular Santa Ynez Valley. While Bud began working as a polo pony trainer at the ranch of a friend of Jack, Colonel McKittrick, Miche was left in the care of the Mattei's Chinese cook. There at the tavern, while Bud worked in the mountains, Wong spent the hours teaching Miche how to make flapjacks and spoonbread.

The father and son had the time of their lives. Bud bought Miche a pony, and taught him how to ride. Miche moved up to the ranch, and spent every day at his father's side. Picking up an old Flint—already a relic in the summer of 1929—Bud gave his young boy driving lessons across the endless pastures.

On Saturdays, they would devote themselves wholeheartedly to eating popcorn and drinking soda while leaning back in the seats of the Los Olivos theater. In *Plane Crazy* they met the moving picture hero who captured the heart of the nation—Mickey Mouse. Another rat who featured in their lives was Walt Disney's Steamboat Willy.

In the middle of each matinee, the Magnificent Waldo appeared with his trained dogs to perform stunts for the audience. Bud, convinced that the animals' extreme behavior could only be induced by beatings and cruelty, could not bear to watch the show. As soon as that performance was announced, the two would spring for the lobby, returning once the next feature had begun.

On July 28, a telegram dispatcher appeared at the McKittrick ranch with a message for the pair from Jack. Janet had given birth to a bouncing, glorious eight-pound infant named Jacqueline Lee!

Half a month later, it was time for Miche to return to Emmy and New York and school. Once his son had disappeared on the eastbound train, the old void once again began gnawing at the core of Bud's life. Still, he had been with his son for one glorious summer.

For Jackie's baptism, Janet's father was asked to be godfather. In truth, having had their first major row at the reception following his wedding, Jack was to share many others with "old man Lee." When James Lee was late for the event, Jack insisted that the ceremony be started without him—he would be sure to arrive any moment.

The minutes ticked by with no sign of the grandfather as the ritual continued. At last, the monsignor asked for the godfather to step forward, and there was an embarrassing lull.

With no sign of the chosen one, Jack saw his chance. With a gentle, but firm shove, he propelled young Miche forward. The next thing anyone knew, the clergyman had placed the baptized cousin into the nine-year-old's arms. By the time a chagrined grandfather came running into St. Patrick's Cathedral, the deed had been done. Miche had just become Jackie Bouvier's godfather.

In the meantime, with Miche back in New York, Bud had begun visiting the bar at Mattei's Tavern more and more frequently. Isolated in California, no one could tell he was slipping until it was far too late. The dread call came from Charles Mattei, and Jack set out to bring his brother's corpse home—for good.

It was a terrible time for the family. The strain they all felt was unbearable, filled as everyone was with feelings of guilt and self-recrimination. Maude went into a decline, to the extent that her own life was endangered. When she emerged, she lavished more affection upon the children who remained, and they became her entire life.

The twins were dazed. They just couldn't believe that their beloved brother was dead. The Major lost himself in his writing and his work, trying to escape the reality of his son's tragic demise. For Miche, it was not too hard to understand that he had somehow become the carrier of the Bouvier name, and that he would never again see his daddy. Nonetheless, for years afterwards, he would turn a corner, expecting to see Bud, or run down to the hall of his apartment building in hopes his father would be outside tapping out their secret greeting on his automobile horn.

For Jack, the blow struck too close to home. In spite of the differences between the brothers, their bond had remained unassailable. It was as though one side of Jack had died, withered from within. Bud's death shook him, then attached itself to him. He grew obsessed.

Desperately, he railed at the fate which had claimed his brother's life. Struggling to free himself of the guilt associated with their lifelong competition, he lashed out at everyone with bitter accusations, swearing that if Bud's weaknesses had been better understood and sympathized with instead of damned, he would still be alive. The family was straining to keep from crumbling altogether—the hairline cracks in its structure were beginning to show—and in many places, rifts between them grew to a point where they could never again be entirely repaired.

While the family was still in shock from Bud's death, staggering and trying valiantly to regain its equilibrium, the rug was pulled out from under it. An avalanche had begun on the stock market.

All month, stock prices had been declining. As late as October 17, some prestigious economic organizations predicted the continuation of the Great Bull Market. But with the violent decline of prices on Saturday, the nineteenth, the bubble burst.

As for the Bouviers, there was not even time to mourn their Bud's death. For sheer survival, every one of them turned his undivided attention to the Stock Exchange.

Tuesday, the 22nd, brought a brief rally in the downward spiral. But by afternoon, it had disintegrated. Wednesday saw the index sag further.

The came Black Thursday.

No one who was personally involved will ever forget it. As soon as the ten o'clock gong tolled its signal to begin trading, the brokers and their clerks knew that they could no longer pretend some miracle would drop like a skyhook from heaven and pull the market back up on its feet.

Investors had been given enough rope with the ten percent margin to hang themselves. And as they stood suspended in the noose, the bottom of the market fell out from under them. The clamor of voices shaking the great exchange hall intensified, as thousands of men tried desperately to sell stocks which were becoming more and more useless by the moment.

The atmosphere of excitement was growing into unadulterated panic. In the middle of it all, Jack struggled to forget about Bud, and salvage whatever he could for his customers—having at the last possible moment taken his brother's advice, and protected his own family by selling short.

Masses of people milled around in the streets outside the Stock Exchange, hoping that a miracle might yet save them from utter ruin. For rich and for poor, ruin amounted to the same thing. The information they received was useless, hours and dollars behind the plunge as the electronic and hand-posted systems both lagged behind schedule.

However bad it looked on the ticker tape, they knew it could only be much, much worse.

In their immediate panic, the crowds failed to notice the financiers furtively slipping into the House of Morgan at the opposite corner of the Exchange. J.P. Morgan had grown to become one of the richest and most influential

corporations in America and had been chosen as the leader
for a bankers' conference, in the hopes of achieving some
eleventh hour victory over chaos. Also present was Richard
Whitney, vice-president of the Exchange.

At roughly one-thirty that afternoon, a confident Mr.
Whitney strode conspicuously into the Exchange, his head
held high above his three-piece grey flannel suit. On behalf
of a banking consortium, he had some shopping to do. The
major houses had decided to risk a good deal of their private capital in order to encourage people to resume buying
to stem the tide.

As visibly as possible, the Stock Exchange officer began
spending his thirty million dollars.

There was an almost audible sigh of relief in the great
hall; things were finally looking up. Nonetheless, at the
day's close, the brokers recognized what a horror had tran-
spired. Men who were used to racing home with the three
o'clock gong were still bending over columns at seven, trying to glean some sense of order in the phenomenal confusion.

Orders were everywhere, hastily stashed away for future
filing. One clerk spent hours looking for papers he knew
were somewhere, only to find them jammed into a wastepa-
per basket. Some of the clerks spent the night on office
couches, knowing they had no time to go home.

It was a time when the true personal qualities of men and
women were exposed to raw reality. Friendships were cemented and fierce enmities forged. Hit broadside in their
most vulnerable region—the pocketbook—people were exposed to the core.

Everyone was suspected of violent desperation. The
streets were as dangerous during broad daylight as at night.
Those too proud or angry to face bankruptcy opted out by
jumping from high windows.

Friday and Saturday were better days. Not good, but better.

Monday came, and all hell broke loose again. This time, it went far beyond the terror of Black Thursday. Brokers, clerks, and office girls soon reached a point of total exhaustion. No one had time to answer the telephones, and from across the nation, calls to place sell orders, and panicked demands for information jammed all of the phone lines.

That night, many brokers displaced their clerks on the office couches. Many a man fell asleep sitting or standing up. The sheer volume of business was staggering, and it was all of it bad—more than the human soul could take. And Tuesday loomed ominously ahead.

With the morning gong, inevitable doom had finally arrived. Mr. Whitney and the bankers had failed to stem the tide. Now they quietly began to withdraw their capital from the market, to recoup whatever was possible.

Paper millionaires were turned to paupers that night. Everyone was selling everything, but there was no one left to buy.

Jack was surrounded by brokers with desperate orders for him to dump his specialty stocks for whatever price he could get. Of course, there were no takers. But so blind was their panic, they pressed about him as though he were a magician about to pull buyers from out of his Homburg hat. He sadly reiterated that there was nothing he could do. It looked like the end had come.

The end of an era. The end of the exuberant, opulent lives of those who lived carefree off of the Stock Exchange.

Strangely, the next day brought a rally, of sorts. Some of the large companies declared a dividend, and some pundits began to predict a restabilization of the market. When Mr. Whitney announced that the Exchange would not reopen until the following day, and would close afterwards until Monday, the news was received calmly. It would signal a return to order, to sanity, giving each man a chance to get his financial house in order. A return to normalcy all over.

The worst of the panic was over. But the bull market was dead.

With it perished the Roaring Twenties.

Across the country, families gathered in grim conclaves, sharing for the last time all of the luxuries which would vanish. Children went from Exeter and Miss Porter's to county high schools. Friends borrowed ten dollars for one last taxi ride to their yachts, then abandoned them altogether.

Houses were sold for half of their value, leaving maids and cooks and chauffeurs suddenly without work or shelter.

For those men who had not taken the easy way out, it meant facing up to lives in ruin. The seeds of destruction proliferated during the spiralling twenties had grown to a monstrous cancer. In the last weeks of 1929, with the stock market crash, the disease was radically excised. But its victim, the leisure class, had died as well.

Pampered women who had never done a stroke of work were suddenly faced with having to do everything. Men who had bought up empires were forced to sell apples or pencils. The courage of those who persevered was truly awesome. The spirit of the times was "down, but not out." As the song "Start All Over Again" expressed it, the mood was:

> *Pick yourself up*
> *Dust yourself off*
> *And start all over again.*

Throughout America, thousands of fallen families did exactly that. Starting from scratch.

Of course, there were those who escaped unscathed. Or at least with enough to resign themselves comfortably to their losses.

A handful of investors had gotten out in time. Joe Kennedy had got his millions out of harm's way. MC Bouvier had his fortune almost halved—but that still left him with close to four million dollars, plus whatever remained of his sisters' stocks.

And then there was Jack. Immediately after his brother was buried, Jack had taken Bud's last words as his legacy.

During the Crash of 1929, Jack was not unaffected.

He made $100,000.

ELEVEN

The Great Escape

When the dust cleared following the crash of '29, the real loser in the Bouvier family was the newest exchange brokerage member, Jack's father. Without much prior trading experience, the Major had lost a small fortune, with no phenomenally great holdings to begin with. Nor did he have a substantial source of income with which to recoup his losses.

Nonetheless, the Major was sixty-five years old, and had lived in luxury almost all of his life. Particularly with Maude suffering as she was from the loss of Bud, it was necessary to do everything possible to protect her from being buffeted by the changing times. No matter what else happened, they would hold onto Lasata and their house servants for the rest of their lives.

The other Bouvier seriously affected by the events of 1929 was young Miche. Not only had he lost his father, but with Bud's death, the market rapidly brought down whatever was left of his fortune. To make matters worse, Emmy's own familial holdings had been cut back seriously as well. Bud's alimony payments had always been sporadic and now were non-existent. Proud as she was, the beautiful young woman was determined to get by on her own. She pursued her career as an interior decorator, and even worked briefly in a dress boutique to make ends meet. In time, the mother and son moved from their comfortable apartment at 125 East 84th Street to a more modest one at number 119. Still, it was a far, far cry from Hooverville.

For Jack, it was one of the grimmest periods of his life. While he had escaped in full glory, Bud, his closest sibling had died and left his son Miche no inheritance. All around Jack, friends and lifetime associates had fallen upon hard times.

However, he did not have long to feel guilty about his "blood money" profits from the Crash. When an afterclap struck the market a month later, it caught Jack thoroughly unawares. He sustained a six-figure loss.

But at the time, Black Jack's thoughts were far-removed from the market. Everywhere he went, the memory of Bud haunted him. He kept moving, pushing himself to the point of exhaustion. Working out at the Yale Club every day.

Still, he couldn't shake it.

Only someone who had never before sustained the least tragedy in life could understand the hell that Jack sank into. For all of their differences, the Bouvier brothers were a matched set, or at least a complementary pair. With Jack's doppelgänger gone, part of himself seemed to be disappearing as well.

By January of 1930, there was no improvement. Reminders of Bud were everywhere. Escaping to Lasata for a weekend, Jack strolled into the front hall, only to catch sight of the missing chandelier prism. Right before leaving for Los Olivos, Bud had totalled it while practicing his chip shot into the fireplace.

It was time to get away and recuperate.

The next day, Jack made reservations aboard the ship *Augustus* bound for Europe. On the fifteenth, together with

Janet, Michelle, and her husband, Henry Clarkson Scott, Jack set out to forget. With the words, "All ashore that's going ashore," the last of their friends said goodbye and hurried down the gangplank.

Beneath the deafening blasts of the foghorn, they waved a farewell to the crowd gathered on shore. A damp chill washed over Jack and he huddled tight by Michelle's side, the two of them keenly aware of an uncanny feeling of physical loss. The beginning of their trip should have been exuberant. But the ghost of Bud still hovered sadly on their horizon.

Slowly the calm of the ocean began to dissipate the aura of depression that had clung to Jack for so long. Through great conscious effort, he began gradually to beat back his own demons, and to become himself again.

At Gibraltar, the ship made a twenty-eight-hour stop. Jack decided to hire a car so that they could tour the southern part of the Iberian Peninsula. Trusting their fates to the ancient automobile they had rented—the only one available—they braved the dusty roads and headed out to Andalucia, to Jerez, then on to Seville. Jack's special interest in that mysterious city of glistening white houses with their endless waves of red tile roofs and cascading gardens had to do with the many great horseback riders born there. Unfortunately, with so short a stay, he was unable to go out into the countryside to see any of the region's prized horses.

They had dinner on a terrace engulfed by geraniums of incredible size, in all conceivable colors. At the waiter's suggestion, they had the house specialty, tiny eels bathed in garlic. Jack loved them, and Michelle surmounted them by staring bravely at the flowers.

After dinner, the foursome found their way to a sleazy little nightclub in the heart of the city. Michelle had never been truly comfortable anywhere west of Fifth Avenue, let alone south of Forty-second Street. All of a sudden, she found herself in a cavernous foreign grotto of a nightclub, surrounded by dimly lit faces with boldly menacing stares. She was, to say the least, apprehensive.

To make matters worse, she was not alone in noticing the attention they were receiving. Scotty, on the assumption that a Spaniard's inhospitable eyes were narrowing lasciviously on the ladies' charms, was snarling at him. The vibrations started flying like bullets between the two men. All of them bad. Michelle was sure they would never get out alive.

Their troubles escalated. Somehow, Scotty and his antagonist had begun trading fierce invectives, each in his own tongue.

Jack, a few glasses of wine behind Scotty, took stock of the situation. One: it was about to come to blows. And two: while Scotty continued his assault, a hefty contingent of backers had taken up a position directly behind their countryman.

Jack was not all that fond of fighting. While swashbuckling poses were deeply ingrained in his nature, physical violence was not. Moreover, it was obvious that they were seriously outnumbered. The odds were mighty slim. There was no percentage in taking bruises with scant chance for a victory, moral or otherwise.

In a flash, after so many months of fogginess, Jack was his old self again. Immediately, he donned the almost forgotten half-mocking grin. With his best air of genteel macho, and looking quite Spanish himself, Jack stood gracefully up to his full six-foot-one height. Expanding his chest to powerful proportions which seemed to widen his very broad shoulders, he addressed the hostile crowd at the next table.

"Mis Amigos" he managed to begin—having no more knowledge of Spanish, Jack made up more sounds as he went—"we're all men here! Men should drink together. Not fight over women!"

As one, the men nodded, although whether to clear out their ears of his atrocious Spanish or in agreement—Jack

never found out. Before the moment was lost, he ushered
his entire party past the audience with one magnificent
flourish and kept smiling till they reached the street where
they made a break for the car, Jack half-dragging a con-
founded Scotty.

At six in the morning, after driving all night, they abandoned the car at the dock and made a dash for the ship,
arriving on board with not one minute to spare. Only after
she collapsed in her bunk did Michelle believe they were
really safe.

When they reached Genoa, the couples left the boat to
spend three weeks in Naples. What they did there remains
a mystery. There is not, after all, a great deal to do in that
town. Perhaps that was the implication when they coined
the old adage: "See Naples and die!"

Whatever charm the place held for them, they did stay
there the full term before deciding to take a train to Paris.

As soon as she boarded the Orient Express, Michelle was
immersed in the mystique of romance and air of adventure
that imbued that great railway train. Seduced by the dream-
like quality of the elegant decor, Michelle gave herself up
entirely to wild but lovely fantasies as the great vehicle
charge imperiously through the Pyrenees, beating its compelling rhythm on the fiery rails.

Never one to put much stock in dreaming, Jack focused
on more immediate needs. Janet had been assigned a separate sleeping compartment from his own; and it was ran-
kling him.

Somehow, he managed to convey his displeasure to the
Italian porter, explaining that he should never have been
separated from his wife. The Italian could not have agreed
more vehemently. Who, if not he, an Italian husband, could
understand the total unacceptability of the situation better!
He swore to amend it and flew off in search of a solution.

As night fell and the porter had failed in his fifth attempt
to right things, Jack threatened to explode.

Suddenly, the little man burst with enthusiasm at the simple solution: *Communicazione!*

He meant he could supply connecting rooms. Jack settled for that compromise and his respect for the subtleties of the Italian psychology was increased. As he was settled into the appointed room, his devotion to the Italian people was born.

Long before the foursome was done with Paris, Jack got an urge to gamble and dragged them all the way back to Cannes. Jack had the sort of mind for numbers that was made for baccarat, and he and Janet played that and roulette every night, leaving Michelle and Scotty to play bridge or Mah Jongg in their hotel suite at the Beau Cité.

Michelle was constantly making new friends, and it was probably through her that Jack came to meet the two Australians. If, so, she doubtlessly rued the day.

For an indecently long time, the Australians sat on either side of Jack, boasting about their great capacity for liquor, and swearing that no American could keep up with them.

"Balls!" replied Jack, a mischievous glow in his eye.

The Australians were astonished, and immediately challenged him to quaff to the death, may the best man win.

"Not I, boys," replied Jack, "but I'll lay odds that my one man will drink both of you under the table."

The Australians rose to the challenge to their national honor, giving him two-to-one odds, then doubling the wager because they were so sure of victory.

Franc notes in hand, Jack then called to Scotty. By the time the introduction was finished, Scotty almost believed the drinking distinctions Jack had claimed for him. At any rate, he was stuck with upholding the American side.

As one man to their massive two, Scotty was given the choice of weaponry. To the Australians' dismay, he chose martinis made the American way—that is, straight gin over which a bottle of white vermouth is waved. Facing off

staunchly across the small marble table, the adversaries began.

Round after round, the contestants struggled. With hor-
rified fascination, Michelle watched as each round of
straight-up martinis was ordered and downed.

The battle continued to dizzying heights.

At the ninth martini, the first Australian began to weaken,
turning a pale shade of green and slumping onto the table.
Undeterred, the other drank with renewed vengeance.

Scotty, on the verge of collapse, was about to throw in the
towel when in a last bid for glory—and with all the sobriety
he could muster—he called for another. A double.

As the crowd gathered around him and burst into applause, the last Australian whimpered—then silently collapsed, landing in a neat little pile on the floor.

Throughout the bar, Americans cheered and sang "My
Heart Stood Still," clapping the dazed victor on the back,
nearly toppling him over in the process.

The only silent figure in the midst of celebration was
Michelle. To her went the job of caring for the half-dead
victor. Brushing aside further congratulations—and glaring
across the room at Jack, who was standing at the bar basking
in reflected glory as the trainer of champions—she herded
her staggering husband out of the ring.

Once in their room, Scotty decided to take a bath. Not
only did he insist, but he locked himself up in the bathroom.
Sitting on the edge of the couch and listening for the
sounds of her beloved bubbling down for the last count,
Michelle began praying to the saints, one by one. Knowing
that she herself would have collapsed with *two* martinis,
Michelle was positive that *no one* on earth could drink ten—
and she had counted them—and survive. Trembling in apprehension, she tried without success to catch a glimpse of
Scotty through the keyhole.

After what seemed like an interminable time, a sprightly
and chipper Scotty stepped out from the bathroom, calmly

dressed himself, then escorted her regally down for dinner. As the dapper couple entered the dining room, a round of applause once more broke out from the other guests. Jack's brother-in-law had done himself proud and was the hero of the hour.

Michelle was not amused.

The next morning, Jack and Scotty decided it was time to head for England and catch the Grand National at Aintree. Janet could no longer bear to be away from her infant Jackie. And Michelle also had a baby that age to get back to. Leaving their men to their own devices, the women took the train to Cherbourg, where they booked the transatlantic passage on the *Berengaria*.

A week later, Jack and Scotty followed. By the time Jack landed at the Port of New York, his heart had healed to a certain extent. Although he would speak of Bud with a sense of tender loss until the day he died, Jack was at last ready to go on living.

He had also come to a decision. From that moment on, he would make himself responsible for Miche's welfare. It was the least he could do for his departed brother, and for the Bouvier name.

Not long after, a meeting was arranged between the Major and Emmy. According to Jack Davis in *The Bouviers*, it was at the Hotel Roosevelt that the Major offered Miche's mother "$33,000 if she would agree to let the boy stay most of the year with him." According to Emmy, the amount was $20,000 for something approaching an outright purchase.

Of course, she refused. Moreover, never again would she be on friendly terms with the Major. As for Jack, the relationship grew even more strained than it had been since she first threw him over. Ultimately, she felt that he treated most people rather poorly. But from that point on, where Miche was concerned, Jack was generous to a fault. Quite beyond reproach, his behavior toward Miche was the most valuable support that had been extended to the fatherless boy.

Jack's last memorial to Bud came in the spring. Then, despite his own shaky financial circumstances, he erected a lavish altar to his younger brother's memory at the Keyser Island Jesuit House, the last retreat where Bud had found the peace and strength to attempt one final end to drinking.

TWELVE

The Family Man

The second half of 1930 brought no relief to America. The Depression was here to stay, or at least so it seemed.

For both the Major and Jack, it was a time of using principal capital to make ends meet, while assuming that the economic picture just had to improve. Particularly for Jack, as a specialist, that was a dangerous procedure. To maintain substantial blocks of stock for trading—and to "make a market" in his stocks as necessary, required a good deal of money. And Jack's resources were rapidly dwindling.

From the start, his heart had been captured by his baby girl, Jackie. His belief in her perfection had no limits, any more than the amounts of money he lavished on her from infancy on. She was, quite simply, "the best," and Jack would brag about her to anyone who would listen, knowing no bounds in his pride.

For the time being, he settled down to a life devoted entirely to work and family. As the Depression lingered he worked harder and harder to support their luxurious lifestyle.

In addition to the maids, cooks and nannies, and to the

family stable of prize-winning horses, there was also Miche to support. Jack had paid for Miche to transfer from St. Bernard's in Manhattan to the Fay School in Southboro, Massachusetts.

Finally, his working capital supply dipped dangerously low, and it became clear that he would have to borrow money. Forsaking his pride, he sought a loan from James Lee. But not until he found himself within a year of total bankruptcy.

For Janet's banker father, it was a long-awaited opportunity. As a contemporary of the Major's, and a fellow alumnus of Columbia Law School, James T. Lee had carved out no less brilliant a career for himself than John Bouvier, Jr. He had, as a matter of fact, made far more money, becoming Chairman of the Board of the New York Central Savings Bank.

Yet, for all of his achievements, he was clearly looked upon as a social inferior by the Bouviers. He had neither their wit, nor their family name and social breeding. From Jack on up, the Bouviers had treated "old man Lee" with a touch of disdain.

In consequence of his lower social position, James Lee had more or less been embarrassed into letting the Bouviers call the shots concerning Jack and Janet's life. Thus, while the new, young family was struggling to succeed, the silken but prodding fingers of Maude Bouvier had continually manipulated and intervened.

Not a day passed when Maude didn't call Janet or stop by, offering unsolicited advice or bearing unwelcome gifts of food—consequently dictating the menu for each day. Naturally Janet objected to Maude's interference. Her mother-in-law left her no room to breathe, let alone grow and assume the running of her own household as she alone saw fit.

But now with Janet's father lending money to Jack, the balance was dramatically tipped in the other direction. Together with the cash went a rash of commandments for precisely how to make economies in his flamboyant lifestyle, as well as how to make a better husband for Janet. Living in Mr. Lee's apartment house in a duplex given them as a wedding present, and subsidized by his loan, Jack had no choice but to grit his teeth and submit to his father-in-law's dictates.

Hoover's "four more years of prosperity" drew to a close in 1933, as a downcast nation waited for Franklin Delano Roosevelt to get it back onto its feet, feeling somehow that he was the one man who could do it. Of course, they had no idea how.

Roosevelt accomplished the miracle, all right, but his method was more radical than anyone had dreamed. At the Bouvier households, the attitudes went from concerned curiosity to astonishment to rage.

Particularly indefensible behavior, from the Bouviers' point of view, was the President's appointment of Joseph P. Kennedy to a new regulatory commission called the SEC. Kennedy, a *nouveau riche* Irishman to begin with, had made his stock exchange bundle under the old system, and now was setting about to tie everyone else's hands and feet as they presume to follow in his footsteps.

Up to this point, the Bouvier men had never agreed upon anything.

Jack and his brother-in-law, John Davis in particular, had always argued bitterly about the stock market because their approach was so different. John would accuse Jack of being a gambler. Jack would tell John that his "rational and cautious" approach was meant for old widows, and that the thousand new opportunities for a fortune every day would be missed by insisting on Blue Chips.

Both arguments were essentially correct, so they would continue endlessly, engendering new ones.

Suddenly, with what they called the Roosevelt Pox, all of that changed. The agreement throughout the family, to a man, was touching. One and all, they denounced the president's base perfidy, than which there could stoop nothing lower: the New Deal was an act of betrayal to his own class!

Their conviction on that score lasted a lifetime.

Even a quarter of a century later, their censure was no less severe, At the christening of our son, John Bouvier IV, my brother-in-law Arthur Finch made the mistake of admitting to Jack that he had voted for Roosevelt in his last Presidential candidacy. Looking at him with great blue eyes both pained and sad, Jack could only shake his head. A moment later he spoke, "And I always thought you were such a nice guy."

Nineteen thirty-three brought to Jack and Janet two pleasures which would blossom as the years progressed. One was their second daughter, Carolyn Lee, who was always called "Lee." The other was the repeal of Prohibition.

Jack Bouvier was happier than he had ever been with his young family of four. He showed his delight by showering his daughters with all of the luxuries money could buy. During the Depression years, that was no small feat, but somehow they always managed.

Through his all-encompassing devotion to Maude, Jack had developed an enormous capacity for love of family. For those close to him, like his daughters, there would never be the slightest hesitation on his part to show his love. He loved his daughters deeply, and was intensely proud of them.

And when Jack loved, he expected the objects of his affection to be worthy of it. Nothing short of greatness would suffice. It was often more than a little tough on the beloved.

If by some stroke of cruel fate Jack had sired a dull or terribly ordinary child, I shudder to think of the bitter traumas it might have occasioned for both. Perhaps that is doing him an injustice, but Jack was constitutionally ill-equipped to deal with mediocrity. Fortunately, it was one problem he never did come up against.

The only boring thing about Jack was his own incessant bragging about baby Jackie. From her first breath, he was boasting about how beautiful she was, how well brought up she was, how precocious she was.

In the end, gathered around his parents' table, the entire family would be asked to admit that of all the grandchildren, Jackie was without a doubt "the best." Since each parent sitting there was convinced of his or her own children's superiority, vehement arguments would ensue. The fact that Jackie did truly have a competitive edge in beauty, talent and intelligence, only made the battles more bitter.

As Jackie and Lee advanced from their babyhood into girlhood, there was precious little that they wanted but did not receive. While Jack made sure to fulfill their every desire, Janet took very diligent care concerning their education. From the start, both girls were carefully exposed to foreign languages, and all areas of cultivation considered the bedrock of a fully-rounded education, and befitting the roles they were destined to fill.

Nothing could be more fun than to be Jack Bouvier's daughter. His love was so absolute that he went to any extreme just to please them. There was nothing he wouldn't do to make their lives as interesting and special as possible. He was a busy man, under a tremendous strain to keep his financial affluence and maintain his family in the style to which they had been born. So total was his insistence upon keeping life extraordinary that they were frequently gamboling at the brink of financial disaster.

In spite of the monetary strain, it was an exuberantly happy time for the young family. Jack and Janet were the most handsome couple around town—East Hampton or New York. They were in demand at all and any social functions, and talked about in all the society columns.

Climbing back up after the Crash of '29, things began to

look brighter every day. And as Prohibition faded into the background, there was more reason to rejoice.

Excellent judge of human nature that he was, Jack had invested substantially in the liquor industry, and held onto his stocks even during the worst days. Now they began to rise astronomically. Rocketing skywards, from thousands, to tens of thousands.

From hundreds of thousands to millions.

To celebrate his return from middle income, Jack ordered a maroon Stutz town car, designed to his own specifications. An addition to the Lincoln Zephyr, it was an incredible luxury.

In general, the town cars were built roughly along the lines of a London taxicab. Their comfort was relative. The most luxurious vehicles were tall enough for a gentleman to enter the rear without having to remove his top hat.

Since Jack mostly wore Homburgs and wouldn't be caught dead in a beaver hat, height was no object. He felt it would be far more chic to have the car built as sleek and low to the ground as possible.

The custom-ordered car arrived, complete with natural leather interior as soft and smooth as kid gloves. For Jack, it was love at first sight.

For the chauffeur, it was another matter entirely. The car was svelte and graceful and handled fantastically, but its low roofline exposed him entirely to the elements. In the rear, passengers practically had to enter crawling on their hands and knees.

But comfort was clearly a secondary concern. Despite the fact that the passenger arrangement was a deterrent to all attempts at comfort for adults, that couldn't have bothered Jack or his tiny daughters in the least. The "oohs" and "ahhs" from onlookers as they sped by made up for every ache of discomfort as Jack's princesses alternated from one side to the other and he craned his neck forward, or slumped backward with his knees doubled up, approaching his chest.

Janet was fast gaining renown as a horsewoman. With increasing frequency, she brought home blue ribbons and trophies from the East Hampton Club and from Madison Square Garden. Jackie, as well, showed talent for horsemanship from a very early age, and Jack and Janet encouraged her in every way possible, maintaining horses for her use at all times.

It was by no means her only talent. Jack's pride in her grew with her growing beauty and intelligence. She had the dramatic Bouvier eyes and Jack's irresistible smile. He took to showing her off at all available opportunities, creating them when none were presented.

From the time she was quite young, Jackie became a quite devoted reader, and showed an ability to write poetry. The Major was always swapping poems and technical pointers with the youngsters, finding endless delight in the works she presented to him, like this one:

> I love the Autumn,
> And yet I cannot say
> All the thoughts and things
> That make one feel this way.
>
> I love walking on the angry shore,
> To watch the angry sea;
> Where summer people were before,
> But now there's only me.
>
> I love wood fires at night
> That have a ruddy glow.
> I stare at the flames
> And think of long ago.

Turtle neck sweaters, autumn fires,
Swirling leaves and the sky,
Riding my horse along the hills,
To say a last goodbye.
Undressing in the cold at night,
And getting warm in bed,
Star-gazing out the window
At the cold sky overhead.

The tangy taste of apples,
The snowy mist at morn,
The wanderlust inside you
When you hear the huntsman's horn.

Nostalgia—that's Autumn,
Dreaming through September
Just a million lovely things
I always will remember.

Lee was no less talented and beautiful. In time, she developed into the first true sailor of the family.

No couple was more carefree than Mr. and Mrs. John V. Bouvier III in East Hampton. Their fortune was repaired, their future once again seemed perfectly secure—at least as far as the eye could see.

The little girls were so lovely, without being spoiled, that it was impossible not to love them. Certainly, all of the neighbors did.

Renting a substantial cottage for the summer, or staying in the Apaquogue House, there was always something of interest going on, and some special event would occur every day of their lives.

After the menace of 1929, it seemed as though nothing substantial had changed. Jack and Janet's children were free to enjoy a privileged life as unbreachable as their own had been. Ignorant of the breadlines, or the multitudes

Jack and Jackie at the South Hampton
horse show, 1934. (photo credit UPI)

Maude Sergeant
Bouvier.

The Major.

Maude and Michelle
the twins.

Emma, Uncle Miche and Bud.

Jackie, Janet, Miche and Jack

John Vernou Bouvier III

Bud Bouvier, East Hampton, 1925.

Black Jack in his prime.

Janet Lee Bouvier and baby Jacqueline.

Maude's Italian garden at Lasata

The Black Orchid
in Florida during
the roaring twenties

From Jack, to Maude, 1934

Toddler Jackie

Jackie wins first prize.

Princess Lee as
a young woman.

Happy birthday to
Marga
from Jackie

Jackie and her sister Lee.

Happy Birthday to
marga
from Lee

Jack Bouvier in uniform.

Jack, Jackie and Lee
in Central Park, 1941.

Miche and Kathleen ("Kaffy") Bouvier (top).

Jackie and John F. Kennedy—the newlyweds (bottom).

Jackie, Lee and two of their many dogs.

Black Jack Bouvier, 1948.

muttering "Brother, can you spare a dime?" Jackie and Lee spent indolent days bicycling, swimming, horseback riding, motoring, and playing with many friends and infinite cousins. Almost daily, there was somebody's birthday party or other little fête, calling for a new pink taffeta dress or a new pair of glistening patent-leather Mary Janes.

On all fronts, the honors to Jack's family just kept piling in. It seemed that nothing now could ever go wrong. He jumped onto Lady Luck's saddle and clung there, taking her for a ride no one would ever forget.

Betting on Omaha, "the greatest horse around," Jack collected a bundle, first at Belmont, then at the Preakness. He collected even more when James Braddock took the heavyweight crown away from Max Baer. In everything, he surrounded himself with other winners.

In fact, Black Jack had no idea how to lose.

THIRTEEN

A Beast For All Seasons

After their children, one of the strongest bonds between Jack and Janet was their animals. Both had limitless capabilities when it came to loving four-legged creatures, and their life together included a never-ending stream of them.

As long as Jack had anything to say about it, his animals were treated at least as well as his friends, and were always recognized as individuals with their own particular charm and personality.

An occasional cat notwithstanding, the Jack Bouviers basically ran to dogs and horses. It is not in the least surprising that Jackie's first experience in the public eye was at a dog show, at age two.

Over the years, Jack presented the girls with a variety of dogs who are still remembered with affection. There was the white bull terrier called Sister, and a Bouvier de Flandres with the lovely and fitting name Caprice. Not to be forgotten is Tally-Ho, the dalmatian purchased and so named after reading the book of that name.

But Jack's favorite was doubtlessly King Phar, the beautiful Harlequin Great Dane. "Best damn dog in the world!"

Jack would begin, praising him to anyone in the world who would listen. "You can't find a better dog anywhere!"

King Phar saw Jackie and Lee through their earliest years. He was gentle to a fault, allowing them to gnaw on him, ride him, and go to considerable lengths in teasing him. Lovingly, the King took it all in his stride.

But woeful was the fate of anyone who dared to exceed what King Phar felt to be the limits of good taste. The first to test his mettle was a rather bad-tempered Chow living down the road from Wildmoor. The Chow in question frightened everyone in East Hampton Village, to some degree, with his reputation for being dangerously unpredictable. Rumor had it that the family who owned him was equally petrified of him and at a total loss concerning what to do about it.

No such wavering ever crossed King Phar's mind. Day after day, the Chow barked challenges and obscenities at the Great Dane as he lay quietly on the front porch.

The insults escalated, and in time the Chow began to snarl and snap at King Phar. Still the victimized dog held his peace.

Until at last the Chow went one step too far. It will never be known just what the Chow did to push the great pacifist over the edge. Whatever it was, it was certainly beyond the pale.

Sedately, King Phar stood up on the porch, then strolled purposefully down the flagstone path leading to Apaquogue Road. In the middle of the street, the other animal stood snarling. In one motion, the King snatched the Chow by the scruff of the neck, shook him with one tremendous turn of the jaws, and deposited him dead on the same spot. With that, the Great Dane strode quietly back to the porch and resumed watching the day pass by, unhindered. He was publicly vindicated for his action, and there appears to have been no great mourning for the Chow.

It was also King Phar who nearly scared an old buddy of

Jack's to death. At six-thirty in the morning, at Jack's request, the friend appeared to give him a ride back to Manhattan.

Failing to rouse Jack from slumber by tooting his horn, the unsuspecting man tried the front door. As always, it was open. So he proceeded inside. Seeing his old acquaintance King Phar on the landing, Jack's friend greeted him, and didn't for an instant hesitate to enter.

Nor did King Phar hesitate. Doing what he considered his duty, he leapt straightaway down the entire flight of stairs. He bounced once, and landed legs spread, ears tautly alert, and perfect teeth glistening in the midst of a ferociously growling snout. The man, who had been a guest in the house many times, learned the hard way about the King's conviction concerning the impropriety of early morning visits. He stood there paralyzed with fear, too petrified even to scream. Eventually, King Phar's snarling awakened Jack, who gave the dog a pat on the head and the man a double scotch. "Now isn't that the best damn watchdog in the world?" he wanted to know.

Between Jack and Janet, the real medium of communication was horses. Jack was never more than a competent rider, although with the cuffs of his tweed jacket and the legs of his pants rolled up, he could cut a fairly galloping figure. Janet, on the other hand, grew to be one of the best horsewomen of her time. Jack, Miche and the Bouviers always attributed her success to Jack's round-the-clock coaching. As much as Janet insisted that she figured somehow in her own success, they would have no part of it. To them, Janet would always remain Jack's success.

Jack was also tremendously proud of Jackie's equestrian abilities. With the exception of very few women—Fanny Gardiner of the Gardiner's Island clan among them—his two lovely women could not be outclassed by any members of their respective peer groups. We have a photograph of Jackie at age four, confidently holding the reins of an exceptionally large stallion, beyond a doubt under her total control.

To the Bouviers, the hunt was no mere horsing around. Such competitions were a source of many victories for Janet, and at times, a quite serious matter.

Of all of their hunters, Janet's favorite became Ghandi, the fifty-dollar horse.

Returning from a vacation in Florida, they were motoring through back highways in the rolling Maryland hills. There in the distance was Ghandi. He was old, half-starved and gaunt, nothing but a sagging rack of ribs and hip bones. Obviously on his last legs.

Being animal lovers, they were outraged at the notion that anyone would allow a horse to die such an ignominious death. On the spot, they paid the farmer who owned him fifty dollars cash, then arranged to have him transported up to the stable in East Hampton where he could live out his life in peace—or at least with a full stomach.

As soon as the horse arrived at Lasata, he was checked thoroughly by a vet before entering his new stall. An examination of the horse's teeth and bone structure revealed that, far from being an old horse, he was just under three years old; and aside from being underweight, he was actually in good repair.

Of course, he was no show horse. In addition to all of the health problems, Ghandi was too tall and thin. Jack left instructions with his groom, Willie Woolnough, to give the animal constant grooming and feeding. Then they all sat back and waited to see what would happen.

Grooming put the shine back in Ghandi's coat. Feeding did nothing whatsoever. The horse was naturally anemic-looking, and no amount of feeding could alter that. Shrugging, and resigning himself to a long affiliation with the sad-looking beast, Jack turned the creature over to Miche.

Just for the hell of it, Miche began taking Ghandi over jumps. The horse not only had a natural talent for it, but he loved to leap. The two of them had a great time together.

After a good deal of lobbying and outright begging, Miche finally finagled permission to bring Ghandi along on a hunt. To everyone's amazement, the horse held his own in the field that spring morning.

Then Ghandi grew ambitious. Ignoring Miche's pleas, he shook his mane and, snorting, bolted into a wild gallop.

In a panic, Miche pulled hard on the reins. Ghandi just kept increasing his speed.

Miche pulled as hard as he could on the left rein, thinking that he would be able to turn Ghandi's head and slow him down. To the boy's absolute horror, Ghandi turned around and glared furiously at him, baring his large white teeth. All the while, his head grotesquely twisted, the horse proceeded to gallop blindly ahead.

One by one, Ghandi passed the other members of the party with gay abandon. Now true terror set in. Disaster was inevitable. Ghandi was drawing in upon the huntmaster. Already, just a hand's length from Ghandi's snout, the full round rump of the huntmaster's steed was bouncing.

No mere words could describe the depths of the boy's fear. From early childhood, it had been instilled him that nothing on earth could justify a rider's body passing that of the huntmaster. Knowing that he could never live with his shame, the young boy considered leaping.

But already, it was too late. While Miche deliberated, Ghandi acted, swiftly and decisively cutting off the huntmaster and galloping triumphantly on. And he kept right on galloping, until they had returned to the haven of his stall.

As Miche stood cowering in his boots, one by one the other members of the hunt, from the huntmaster to Janet, arrived. One pair of eyes after another shot humiliating and furious darts at the shamed young boy. He knew, in no uncertain terms, how far he had sunk in their estimation, to a one.

Except for Jack. With an occasional fear for his young ward's life, Jack had watched the proceedings with a good deal of amusement, noting with pride Ghandi's nonchalant ease in clearing the jumps and Miche's tenacity as he clung to the horse's back for dear life.

Nonetheless, the event signaled the end of Miche and Ghandi's pleasant summer rides. Gently, Jack eased Ghandi's care out of Miche's domain, offering him another horse, Portlight.

Ghandi was put into more experienced hands. With expert training he became a superb hunter, to the point where Janet preferred him to all other horses. Jack's fifty-dollar investment turned out to be a winner, and one more entry into his considerable stable of successes.

It is not surprising that Jackie was practically raised on horseback. As Janet's reputation rose, more and more time was devoted to her hunt class competitions. There was a lot of work to be done beforehand, and everyone pitched in. Murphy, the groom with not a tooth to his name, would braid the horse. Miche would saddle soap the tack, and make sure it was in impeccable order. Finally, when Janet was installed upon the pristine horse, Jack would come around with a rag, and wipe the traces of dust off her boots.

The competition was intense. And every minute detail brought or subtracted points from the total score. With so many vying for the blue ribbon, everything had to be perfect—or better.

For one particularly demanding show, Miche was given the additional job of checking the little leather bag attached to the saddle. Since the original hunters needed to carry some sustenance along, the tradition of carrying along a sandwich survives to the present time.

Also required is a tiny hip flask with either cognac or whiskey. However, in view of his youth, Janet took care of filling that herself, lest Miche fall prey to a desire for liquor and purloin a swig.

Miche, not nearly so interested in the sandwich, nonetheless set about his task in a slightly lazy manner. Opening the leather pouch, he determined that there was indeed a wax paper-wrapped sandwich enclosed. So he sealed it back up and helped with the final preparations.

The judges, confronted with so many top horsewomen, took out their fine-tooth combs and went over every knot of braid in the horses' tails. Then they checked every inch of boot leather and tweed on the riders. Then they went over *their* braids!

One by one, they cataloged all of Janet's details. She sat high on her hunter, nervous but obviously doing extremely well. Opening her little hip flask, the judges were impressed. It contained no ordinary liquor, and the bouquet of Armagnac '14 floated up to their nostrils. It was the first time they smiled.

It was then that one particularly zealous judge inspected Janet's food pouch. Arriving at the wax paper, his curiosity was not yet sated. Undoubtedly, he was wondering what manner of gustatory delight would go with such extraordinary cognac.

As he unrolled the wax paper, the judge stared in astonishment. The look quickly changed to abject horror. The judge's pained expression could not have been more pitiful. Until, as he remained staring and paralyzed with revulsion, the contents dropped through the wax paper and onto his immaculately spit-polished boot.

There, for all the world to see, was Janet's shame. A gelatinous green heap of mold. Whatever it might have been at the last hunt class, lo these many months, it was now clearly her ultimate humiliation!

Janet lost a crucial number of points for that moldy sandwich. She was quite near to being publicly disgraced.

Of course, she was livid. Under the circumstances, Jack's wife had every reason in the world to unload the weight of her wrath upon Miche's little head.

And by God, that's exactly what she did.

FOURTEEN

The Break

Horse shows were by no means the only times when Janet Bouvier threatened to explode. As time passed, she grew increasingly tense. Her situation would have been difficult for any girl, let alone a young and somewhat sheltered woman approaching the end of her twenties.

Miche, only thirteen years her junior, was at the height of his full-blown hell-raising adolescence. She tried to take care of him during the boy's lengthy stays with her, and to some extent to help bring him up, making sure that he brushed his teeth and washed his hands.

Although Miche was at the age when all young men have certain problems, in his teenage opinion failing to wash hands was not one of them. She was right in assuming that perhaps he needed handling, but being familiar only with little girls like Jackie and Lee, she was at a loss as to precisely *what* handling would do.

Jack, in the meantime, was treating Miche increasingly like the son he would never have. At the time, the Bouviers felt that St. Paul's in Concord, New Hampshire, was the finest preparatory school in New England—having had no particular success with the prior generation at Exeter.

So Miche transferred to that terribly grand institution in the hills of New England where he passed each form adequately, though with no true enthusiasm. He rowed, and got a solid education, but never did come to idolize the esteemed granite walls of the magnificent campus.

However, the Bouviers' guidance went well beyond placing Miche in the austere academy. The Major also feared that, in a bastion of Episcopalianism, Miche's true family religion would be lost. To avert that eventuality, the Major pleaded with Jack to see to Miche's religious training. Though Jack agreed to, he never actually did. Finally, Miche's grandfather himself undertook to write a four-page typed magnum opus on the subject, addressing it to the school rector, in Jack's name, with Jack's noncommittal acquiescence.

The letter had the desired effect. Miche and several other Catholics were taken to eight o'clock Mass in Concord; got back in time for breakfast; sang in the Episcopal choir at eleven A.M. and again at evensong. This religious schedule plus daily Episcopal morning prayers and choir practice twice a week nearly extinguished his religious feeling. While the rest of his classmates were out skiing or rowing or walking in the fall foliage, Michel Bouvier III sat entombed all day, getting his religion from all sides.

On coming down from Concord one summer, Jack determined that Miche needed a car—particularly as he was always borrowing his. So Jack bought him a sixteen-cylinder 1932 Cadillac convertible for a hundred dollars.

That was the summer when Miche, Bouvie and Phelan, Jr. perfected their techniques at "bumper tag." A favorite area for the game was the long straight road from Amagansett to the point where the rolling hills of Montauk start. The main attraction of that particular course was the "thank-you-ma'ams," bumps which sent the cars flying up into the air as they spun around blind corners, trying to tag each other's bumper in turn. While the Cadillac wasn't exactly built for that variety of high performance, it thrived on such abuse. Michel gave it plenty, but the engine was even compliant about driving on half of the sixteen cylinders when Miche was broke, and disconnected eight to save gas—a frequent occurrence.

The boys spent a good deal of time bragging to Maude about their exploits. Her concern for their safety was abiding, although in concealing things from the Major and smoothing them over with the local police force, her actions were primarily abetting.

It was exactly the sort of serious infraction where Janet might have given Miche a severe scolding to great effect. Unfortunately, the most heinous infraction she ever witnessed was a brief response to nature's call while Miche was taking the highway home.

Finding his Cadillac parked along the highway, Janet presumably expected the worst and screeched to a stop alongside. Racing headlong into the forest, she came upon Michel in the middle of urinating. "Young man," she said, quite distressed at his uncivilized behavior, "just what do you think you're doing?"

Young Michel, despite the fact that he recognized a rhetorical question, explained to her in simple English the nature of the act he was just concluding. After which he walked back to the Cadillac and drove to their house to wash his hands, while Janet stood in the middle of the forest, fuming.

If Miche was young and uncooperative, Jack was equally wild, to say the least. It was a spirit in him which could not be broken as long as he lived. And, to her great dismay, his pretty young bride soon found out how untamable he was. If she had expected a man as disciplined as the Major—whom she adored—Janet was in for a rude awakening.

It did not take long for Janet to become pregnant in their

172   *Kathleen Bouvier*

marriage. Nor did it take many more years, unfortunately, for Jack to begin playing the field again.

Women had always been a solution to the pain of Jack's anxieties, and during the thirties, they seemed to spring from issues of money and family.

For a man like Jack, accepting handouts from James T. Lee was an absolute ego grinder. Especially because of the strings attached. His liquor stock profits were reinvested disastrously, and by the second half of the decade, Jack's lifestyle was once again in jeopardy, although appearances were always maintained.

Maude was Jack's greatest fan and also his closest confidante. When he was in financial straits, she tipped him off as to which family member was in the chips at any given moment and who was therefore disposed to lend him cash, even giving him pointers on how to go about getting it. As close as the mother and son were, she was entirely blind to his indiscretions.

It had been the same all of Jack's life. His mother would cover for him as a matter of course, making up alibis as necessary. The Major, aware of it though he could never pinpoint cases in point, reacted to his wife's over-indulgence by being overly strict, particularly with Jack, and pulling no punches in criticizing him.

Even by 1934, with her children all adults, Maude persisted in denying their faults. The child who suffered the most from Maude's misguided love was Edith. She had always done exactly as she pleased, and grew to be a beautiful, talented, passionate and spoiled woman. When in that year Phelan was forced to leave her because of her flagrant infidelity, Maude just could never be made to see his side of things.

She was no different about Jack's transgressions and continued to be overly possessive and protective of him. Janet, still a young woman, was constantly under pressures from

her own father, from Jack's mother, and from her awareness
of Jack's increasing waywardness.

The pressures were no less intense for Jack. All of his life,
a war had been going on inside the Black Prince. The same
boy who broke hearts and ravished maidens with heartfelt
indifference had once been found crying as he attempted
desperately to rid himself once and for all of "that bad
French blood."

The dichotomies of his nature were getting more and
more extreme, until it seemed as though two adversaries
inhabited that strong, bronzed frame. Sensitive/indiffer-
ent, gentle/callous, caring/destructively careless—the opposing souls were tearing him apart. As his finances
fluctuated out of control, his mother courted him with endless praise, his young wife suffered out of her element, and
his father was frankly disgusted.

To escape it all, Jack spent more money, drove faster,
drank more and had more affairs, his perennial half-smile
frozen more and more like part of a mask.

In the fall of 1935, Jack flaunted one affair too many.

At the end of her rope, Janet asked for a separation. Jack
had no choice but to give it to her. The Major, siding with
the clearly wronged Janet, worked out a separation agreement which bound both parties. There was nothing left for
Jack to do but move out of their duplex and into rooms at
the Westbury Hotel.

Everything he had spent a lifetime trying to build had
crumbled. Now it was slipping through his fingers as Black
Jack tried without success to stem the flow. Jack was the
greatest family man who ever lived—in terms, at least, of
his dreams and intentions. To see his beloved Jackie and
Lee no longer under his own roof broke Jack's heart. He
was astonished at the amount of sheer pain he felt in their
absence.

If only Jack could have stopped to understand the causes
of destruction bringing down the walls around him! But

never known for his introspection, Jack was certainly particularly shy of it now. If it ever occurred to him that he and Janet Norton Lee had never been compatible Jack would never admit that simple truth, even to himself. Only in his later years, Jack was just discovering that he had never really been "of a marriageable kind."

John Vernou Bouvier III was no fool. Not by a long shot. But growing up in the fiercely competitive upper class world of the turn of the century, his rise to the top required building his strongest suit: looks and personality. The heroes of that world were beautiful, manly, powerful, flamboyant and rich.

And in that world, Black Jack was a hero in every sense of the word. Before the Great Crash, as he stepped from his magnificent limousines, escorting the *crème de la crème* of New York Society from one glorious event to the next, he was awesome indeed. "Lookit there," he would hear bystanders whisper as they pointed him out, "isn't that . . . that Hollywood actor, whatsisname?"

"You kidding?" someone was always quick to answer. "Don't you know who that is? That's Black Jack Bouvier. The Wall Street man." The admiration in their voices was unmistakable as they basked in their secret fantasies of the good life.

And Jack lived them out to the farthest stretches of his considerable ability.

Whoever would have thought that the world would change so drastically? That one day Wall Street would collapse like a house of cards and recover from the crash only to find it no longer the center of the universe. Or that the time would arrive when grace and breeding, beauty and charm, together with all of the vigor and lust for life a man could possess, would simply not be enough to go on?

Certainly not Jack.

Throughout this period, as Jack struggled with the realization that he no longer had his own daughters, he saw

them as often as possible, unscrupulously taking advantage
of every visit to compete with Janet for their affection. Because the daily care fell to his estranged wife, Jack easily
had the edge. It was much more fun to be with their zany,
laughing father who gave them everything they wanted and
let them do whatever they pleased, than with their mother
who applied the necessary doses of discipline.

Aware of that, Jack worked to make Jackie and Lee's every
visit a royal occasion, going to great lengths just to make it
interesting. It was hardly fair to Janet, placing her in the
role of drudge, but neither of Jack's beloved daughters
seemed to care about that.

To begin, of a Sunday they often accompanied their
handsome father to the Polo Bar at the Westbury for club
sandwiches. Jack always ordered them on protein bread,
which he reserved on special order at all times, since they
did not generally offer it to diners.

On days when Jack came to pick up the girls, he would
arrive in the black Mercury convertible and announce the
fact with a special honk of the horn. He had always retained
the wonderful ability to turn every little act into an exciting
adventure and the children always rushed out to hug him,
to see what new mysteries he had awaiting them. Jack never
came without something yummy up his sleeve.

As the little girls piled into the front seat and asked him
what the secret was, Jack would begin by saying, "Between
you and me and the lamppost . . ." then whisper some delicious secret into the closest available ear. Or sometimes
in the middle of speaking, he would yell "Cheese it, the
cops!" and send the daughters scurrying down for cover,
laughing hysterically with delight at his antics.

Anyone could take his beautiful young daughters for a
stroll in Central Park, but only Jack had a dog for every
occasion. One week it would be a German shepherd, the
next, a weimaraner or a Boston bull terrier. As their Sunday

strolling acquaintances looked on in wonder, the dog seemed to change its pedigree once a week.

Nor would just any dog do. He had to be the most adorable mutt in the whole world. Jack, Jackie and Lee would spend hours going from pet store to pet store looking for Mr. Right. As they stood there admiring their choice, the owner would invariably come and give them a sales pitch, winding around to dropping a price softly into Jack's ear.

Instead of arguing with the figure—no matter how exorbitant—Jack would agree wholeheartedly. "However," he always concluded, "I would have to make sure the dog is really suitable for my daughters." The only way to do this, logically, was to give it a trial walk.

With some trepidation, the pet store owner agreed.

All aglow with duplicity, the trio strolled off to the park with the dog in tow, headed for a happy romp. For the pet shop owner there was undoubtedly a certain amount of apprehension. But there was something—be it his charm or his expensive, immaculate appearance—about this particular customer that no one could say no to.

Their time alone together was precious, and no one was allowed to interfere, for any reason whatsoever. If some kindly old lady who began praising Jackie for her beauty and clothing wouldn't disappear, the girl would look mournfully at her father. "Darling," Jack would say within full earshot of the intruder, "just tell her to go take a run and jump in the lake!"

An hour or two later, the exhausted daddy would bring the pet back to the shop. Explaining that it had proved to be not quite what they had in mind, they would promptly exit—leaving the proprietor scratching his head, and trying to figure out why little girls would giggle so much when their father had decided to deprive them of a dog.

FIFTEEN

Alone Again

Once again, Jack took to staying at Lasata in East Hampton. During those weekends when Jackie and Lee were not with him, Jack especially mourned the loss of his life with the young girls.

Shella Crouse, Michelle's daughter, was the same age as Jackie, and it was only natural that a special closeness began developing between the uncle and niece. While no one could actually have taken Jackie's place, Jack did actively seek her out, and find some solace in the small girl's company.

Of course, Jack's life was still filled with older female companionships, as well. Once he had left Janet, an endless stream of telephone calls from old and new social acquaintances commenced. But while Jack never did turn down a compelling offer, he always managed his love affairs with the utmost discretion. In public, Jack would never refer to any such loves, and to a man of his sensuous bent, discussing them or bragging would have been repugnant.

In addition to Miche, Jack's one confidante was Shella.

And the stories she heard would have been admissible in any convent.

The most scandalous adventure he recounted to her was one at the Devon Yacht Club. A young debutante of their common acquaintance had been flagrantly chasing Jack for the better part of two months. He staunchly ignored all of her approaches.

Then, unexpectedly, he asked her to dance, one night at the Devon Yacht Club during a family party. The girl, who was mad about Jack, had been waiting all summer for the opportunity. As they tripped the light fantastic, she was in seventh heaven.

Jack, spurred on by the moment, was not about to pass up a good opportunity. As the band broke into a tango, Jack boldly led her into the corner. There, they slowly wound down into the familiar old one-step.

Staring at the young girl's pretty bee-stung lips pursed with excitement, Jack was moved to kiss her. He tightened his arms about her waist, drew her to him. She raised her eyes up to meet his own. He placed his hands on her lovely cheeks, and held them in place as his lips sought hers.

The young girl did more than just breathlessly submit. she fainted dead away on the spot.

On being told the story, Shella gasped with excitement, almost falling off the edge of the bathtub where she was perched, watching Jack shave. Shella was thrilled with her uncle's prowess. Her little red curls bounced up and down with excitement and her feet pounded against the side of the tub as she giggled and begged for more stories.

Time after time, Jack would oblige her, getting increasingly lyrical as he was swept away by his own imagination. Shella loved nothing more than Jack's tales, delivered in his laconic, offhand manner. In their quietly theatrical way, Jack's adventures as recounted went far beyond credulity, even given poetic license. But no one seemed to care. Jack

had a special way with children, and to a one they loved
him and the spell he cast.

Of all of her children, Jack remained closest to Maude.
With him once again living at Lasata, they renewed their
habit of long, private talks, either in her Italian Garden or
up in the boudoir. But the times Maude loved best were the
more hectic ones when Jackie and Lee, Miche, and all of
the other eleven grandchildren got together at Lasata. The
more daughters- and sons-in law there were, added to the
gathering the greater Maude's bliss.

Late into the night, the rowdy group shook the rafters
with their laughter and arguments. At the most inappropri-
ate moment possible, Edith would begin warbling, continuing through her endless repertoire until some other
member of the clan, hungry for a fair share of the center
stage, would shut her up—no easy task!

Lasata was an ideal place for Jack's weekend reunions
with his daughters. There was swimming and riding and all
of the cousins ran around getting into whatever mischief
was available when their tolerant guardians weren't around.
A chance to go out to Lasata was a hard thing to beat, and
the girls always jumped at it, waved in front of their noses
by Jack like a great big lollipop.

Jackie, Shella and the latter's younger brother, Scotty,
formed a secret club called "The Blood Brothers." Naturally, there was no blood involved beyond kinship, nor was
there any secret about it. The clubhouse consisted of a big
piece of wood propped against a tree, with their secret name
sprawled in uneven black letters across the top. Not in red,
but in black. Years later, Jackie explained that they just
couldn't find any red paint.

There were some fierce tennis games played at Maidstone. With Jack and Jackie pairing off against Michelle and
Shella, they were determined to bring home victory. But
however much of their all they gave, Jack and Jackie were
not the most coordinated pair in the world.

As it became apparent that their adversaries were once more going to solidly trounce the father and daughter, having taken the first two sets 6-0, or on an occasional off day 6-2, Jack pulled out all the stops. First, he would begin slamming shots at his younger sister for all he was worth.

Michelle, never renowned for her athletic prowess, was known as "Old Underhand Serve." It was hardly fair to pick on her, as Jack did, knowing where his opponents' weakness lay. As Michelle stood there cowering, Shella would scream, "Get it. C'mon! Get it!"—despite the fact that Michelle rarely connected.

Eventually, Shella would carry the entire game. In a last-minute stand, all other resources exhausted and sliding once more into the pit of ignominious defeat, Jack would slice the ball as close to the net as possible. Rushing in, he would contort his face horribly in an effort to scare his opponents, but only succeeded in making everyone laugh.

After Shella had won the game—and she always did—the foursome would drive down to their beach cabana, sweating and happy. There they would bask in the sun on a little deck, happy as clams, alternately exchanging greetings with the other club members and dipping into the Atlantic. In the late afternoon, they would play an equally active game of baseball. Michelle drew the line at that activity, and remained at the oceanside with Lee, while Scotty, her son, took her place in the next event.

Their baseball field south of the house was most rudimentary. It consisted of only two bases, and the sport they played was actually a mutant variety of cricket. The ball would be slammed with a bat, and as the hitter made a dash from one base to the other, bedlam would break loose as a flurry of motion sent everyone scattering. With every player doing too many things at once, it was often impossible to ascertain whether a baserunner was safe or not.

In the meantime, a more sedate activity was taking place on the brick patio overlooking the garden. There, when the Major was down from the city, he and Maude would play backgammon in a running series. They were fiercely competitive, betting recklessly, and keeping score to the penny of the amount each one won every game.

Maude was a great card player, bridge being her chosen game. But when there were no partners to be found, she acquiesced to the Major's desire to recoup some of his losses. And as the backgammon competition continued, her husband would take more and more to roaring with disgust. Maude was by far the superior player, and his losses began to accumulate.

At one point, to the Major's utter horror, he owed his wife in the incredible vicinity of two million dollars. Every time he protested the astronomical amount, he would be humiliated as Maude proceeded to document it down to the last penny, reading out her records in a quite proud voice as the years added up.

Of course, the Major never had to pay up in anything but lost pride. He was ever hopeful that someday he could win. But that day never did arrive, and he was in decidedly poor humor as the series progressed.

It was on one such sun-drenched afternoon that Maude heard an increasingly serious altercation arising from the baseball field. Jack, certain of Scotty's cheating, in an age bracket when it would not have been unusual, had declared the rascal "out," in no uncertain terms.

"In!" screamed Scotty, equally sure of himself.

There was a tense moment of silence as Maude began turning back to her own victory at hand. Then Scotty somehow passed the bounds of discretion in his defiance of Jack. The next voice to break through the hedge was Jack's, calling his young nephew, "You little bastard!"

Jack had clearly had it with the little twerp. He snatched up the baseball bat and proceeded to chase after the boy with every intention of doing him bodily harm. It must have been a funny sight, the tall, broad-shouldered, distinguished gentleman fuming as he chased the pint-sized red-headed boy.

But Jackie and Shella were convinced the result would be Scotty's murder. In an act of desperation, Shella made a mad dash straight for the source of authority. Zipping over to the patio, she screamed out, "Gran'ma Maude!" then quickly described the dangerous situation.

Just as the girl finished, Scotty plowed into view through the hedge, followed three steps later by a crimson Jack.

Sedately, Maude stood up, evaluating the latest development. Then, her diaphanous lavender gown fluttering in the breeze, she quietly breathed, "Jack, you will stop chasing that boy this instant."

With that, the bat fell from his hand. His jaw dropped as well, and for a moment, the Casanova of Wall Street looked like a chagrined little boy. He never again chased Scotty—or at least not when Maude was in the vicinity.

When all of those activities were at an end for Jackie, there was always riding Danseuse. While her baby sister was shrieking with delight at the Long Island surf, and her older cousins were raising hell in one manner or another, the quiet and sensitive little girl would spend endless hours riding or grooming her favorite steed. Without a doubt, she was the quietest member of the family—the one who thought the most and said the least.

On Monday mornings, the revels would come to an end as Jackie's father disappeared until Friday. While she waited anxiously for him to return, the girl would become thoughtful, although she was frequently enough roused from her pensiveness by her many cousins.

When Miche was staying with Jack at Lasata, it was his primary responsibility to drive his uncle to the station on time for the Cannonball Monday morning. Jack was frequently slightly bleary from the previous night's activities, and Miche was always impossible to awaken.

With ungodly speed, they would always take off for the

neat little East Hampton railroad depot. The Ladies' Village Improvement Society—a favored organization of the twins—was working diligently to beautify the station, slaving over the roses on each of the posts of the white rail fence. Into their midst, Jack's Mercury would come to a screeching halt, as he leapt out in an attempt to catch the 6:59 A.M. train.

One by one, the ladies would shake their heads disapprovingly under their flower-bedecked wide-brimmed straw bonnets. Jack's fast ways were known to all of them. To the younger members through personal experience; and to the older ones through word of mouth.

As a rule, the two men were too late to catch the train at East Hampton. But they would never give up and wait for the next one. Jack would rather have lost his bookie—or even his tan—than to miss the opening of floor trading at the market.

So, with the ladies still staring in absolute horror, Miche threw the car into reverse, lurched forward with the wheel pulled hard to the right, then shot back out of the station entrance. The two bouncing figures inside had only one object: to race the commuter train a distance of forty miles, to Speonk, Long Island.

The only road between those two stations was the old Montauk Highway, which curved in ever-tightening circles as they reached their destination. It was like driving on the Grand Corniche—or with Miche at the wheel, even more like a race track. It was also banked the wrong way at many points. So as Miche floored the gas pedal and went screaming around curves on two wheels, the car was continually threatening to flip over.

Miraculously, they never did have an accident. And even more remarkably, even out of Maude's territory, they were never once stopped by a motorcycle cop!

The summer of 1938 brought a new element to Miche's life—it was time for him to go to college. After careful consideration, he chose Brown University, and made it through their devastating battery of entrance exams.

Jack had always assumed the expense of Miche's education, and intended to pay for Miche's college as well. But when the time approached, he found himself dangerously low on cash and could not have begun further liquidating his substantially reduced stock reserves. In many matters, Jack was perversely parsimonious. He would refer to a gift of lipstick he had been cajoled into buying as "that million-dollar lipstick"; he would have his daughters' portraits done by top New York photographers for an outrageous price, then save money by limiting the number of prints he ordered, hanging studio proofs instead. But never would he hold out where Miche was concerned.

At a loss for cash, Jack relied on his wits instead. When MC died in 1935, Jack got a $25,000 debt forgiven, plus all of his great-uncle's accounts. The Major, however, had inherited over a million dollars, and he was now clearly the wealthiest family member.

Nonetheless, Jack's father had to be approached carefully. He was not generally known for his generosity. In fact, the Major maintained at all times an up-to-date folder, which listed a running tally of every cent he had spent on each of his children and grandchildren.

Once before, Jack had tried to get the Major to pitch in for Miche's education. Bringing out the ledger, the old man waved it in the supplicant's face. "Goddamn it to hell, Jack. Look at how much money I've put into that boy already," he screamed.

Not to be outdone, Jack yelled back in kind. "Goddamnit, Fa"—the nickname was reserved primarily for arguments—"take a look at how much you spent on that one!"

Poring over the pages, they began to argue viciously about each and every entry. The sound of snarling and gnashing teeth almost blew off the roof. Every member of the family—including the servants this time—listened to the bellows and began a private accounting. In time, they were fighting as well about which grandchild was getting shafted, depending upon who their *cause celèbre* of the moment was.

The Major continued arguing despite the fact that those under discussion were listening to every word. In that sense, there was nothing delicate about the old man. He would have stood up in the middle of the Union Club and shouted invectives about fellow members, if he had felt inclined to.

The episode stood out in Jack's mind. And as much as he enjoyed sparring with "Fa" he realized that Miche's future was at stake. So he played it cosy to wrest a check from the Major's fingers.

Craftily, Jack approached his father with a problem, explaining that he was upset that Miche, the carrier of the family name, seemed to be leaning in the direction of a university he didn't overly approve of.

The Major's ire was immediately aroused. Utterly devoted to Columbia, his old alma mater, he had been hurt when succeeding generations seemed to snub her, choosing instead such colleges as Yale and Harvard. Miche's choice of Brown was salting an old wound, and the Major was greatly opposed to the idea. Moreover, he instructed Jack to exert every possible influence on Miche to make him change his mind.

Shaking his head dubiously, Jack said he would give it a try.

In the meantime, the Major called up his old friend Nicholas Murray Butler, president of Columbia, who was more than willing to see to it that the distinguished lawyer's grandson was immediately accepted.

A few days later, Jack sought out his father for another college counseling session. Beyond his wildest hopes, Jack had managed to talk some sense into the boy. But now a new obstacle had arisen. Columbia was just too expensive. There was no way Jack could afford the tuition fee.

"Damn the expense!" shouted the Major. And before he knew it, he had offered to pay half of the expense for Miche's education from that point on. He suspected that he had somehow been "had," but never did manage to figure out how that was done. Semester by semester, the Major wrote out checks in a somewhat dazed manner, proud that at least one grandson had enrolled at Columbia.

To pry money in such large amounts from the old man's fingers was no mean feat. And Jack, thoroughly pleased with his subtle blackmail, told the story whenever he could.

And as for Miche, he said farewell forever to Brown University. Arriving at the gates of Columbia, he immediately joined the rowing team, and somehow became jazz reviewer for the college newspaper. Jack, a sports fanatic to the end, memorized the names and numbers of every player on the Columbia football team—in which Miche showed little interest—as well as knowing the statistics on every freshman oarsman. He spoke of his nephew and ward as "the finest oar on the Columbia freshman crew" as a matter of course, although reality did not entirely bear out that contention.

SIXTEEN

Taking Losses

For a specialty broker like Jack, the health of the market had a direct correlation to individual well-being. And from 1937 until the time war production went into full swing, it was rough going.

The autumn of 1937 had witnessed another business recession, spurred on by frantically galloping sales. Many of Jack's specialty stocks fell sharply, and kept on plummeting. Throughout the Exchange, brokers were once more seriously demoralized, with trading on October 19 reaching volumes unheard of since the Great Depression.

By March of 1938, the recession reached rock bottom. Most of the industrial indicators had sunk to half of their value in just seven months. President Roosevelt was forced to ask Congress for further appropriations to once again stimulate the business economy. They were granted under the Emergency Appropriations Act of June 21.

Jack, together with his father, and at great expense, had had Bud's remains as well as those of his grandparents and an aunt, exhumed from the Gate of Heaven Cemetery in Westchester, and reburied beneath a sapling copper beech tree in a new family plot at St. Philomena's in East Hampton.

Now, he was preparing for harder times to descend. In addition to Miche's tuition, there were support payments for his family. At the same time, Jack was supporting a groom and a stable of horses at Lasata. As his finances continued to dwindle, it became clear that his extravagant way of life had to be substantially reduced.

First to go was the Westbury Hotel. While the suite there was quite elegant, and the Polo Bar a fun place to take his daughters, it was draining too much capital while failing to provide proper accommodations for them to stay the night. Swallowing his pride, Jack moved into a two-bedroom apartment with a maid's room at 125 East 74th Street. It was a far cry from the sumptuous duplex he had shared with Janet. But it had a guest room for Jackie and Lee, and was far less expensive than the Westbury.

Next, Jack sacrificed most of his dining out, and even refrained from chartering airplanes to fly to every major sporting event at Yale. He had long since given up two of his beloved automobiles which were as costly to maintain as they were good-looking. Soon afterwards, the chauffeur followed, leaving only the Mercury convertible.

Nonetheless, Jack managed to forget the gloomy depletions in his lifestyle long enough to throw himself into the planning of a massive party in celebration of Maude and the Major's fiftieth anniversary. The arrangements were endless. Caterers, florists and musicians had to be carefully selected and followed. Every detail was going to be perfect with no care or expense barring the success of his parents' celebration.

When the party was only half a month away, the family began to notice that Maude seemed somewhat lethargic. Quite out of character, when she should should have been exuberantly organizing every last detail, the Bouvier matriarch began leaving crucial decisions to everyone else. In a flurry of phone calls from uptown to downtown Manhattan, each of the siblings came to the same conclusion: Maude seemed to be ill.

It had never occurred to any of them that the stalwart dowager was not immune to strain. Not only that of old age. But of years of living exclusively for her family. At last it had taken its toll.

Maude felt each pain in her children's lives every bit as keenly as they, and more. Also, very much a society woman, Maude had borne the brunt of dozens of scandals. In an era when divorce was a source of shame, it seemed as though each of the children of whom she was so proud was shameless. Janet had divorced Jack; Edith had divorced Phelan; and now Michelle had been forced to divorce Scotty. Not only did the Church not recognize the divorces, but most of the family, so strongly church-oriented, was clearly hostile. If Jack didn't give a damn about the dicta of Catholicism, Michelle cared deeply. She was still suffering, and Maude suffered with her.

The sorrow over Bud's divorce was greatly superseded by the painful memory of his death. In truth, Maude had never fully recovered from that terrible event. In her later years, her body swollen and in pain resulting from dropsy and phlebitis, Maude had a good deal of trouble getting about.

Throughout all of this, she continued to carry the burdens of the family on her shoulders. Particularly that of Edith. After Phelan left Edith, Maude was obliged to take over that eldest daughter's household. Far beyond just deciding and providing what food the Beales ate, Maude took full responsibility for Edith's life. Edith had grown incapable of making the least decision and was relying on her mother with such dependency that the strain was bound to grow unbearable, although it was one which she brought upon herself.

Even with his inheritance, the Major was living steadily above his means, substantially reducing his principal every year. Still, to the outside world, the Bouviers presented a united front as a glamorous and happy family, secure from care or interpersonal problems.

All of the strains and bitternesses within were for family only. To the outside world, Maude let nothing show. Years of keeping up appearances had finally taken their toll.

Now Maude was dangerously ill. She could no longer disguise the fact behind a facade of gaiety. Plans for the party were abruptly dropped, with all of the loose ends left hanging. First one doctor, then a team of specialists, were summoned up to 765 Park Avenue.

Maude collapsed, and was placed in an oxygen tent. As her immediate family stood surrounding her, the only sound they heard was that of her labored breathing. Slowly, she was fading—the great, strong mother, the rock to which the family clung had crumbled.

For four days, the household was hushed in silent prayer as Maude grew paler and more feeble. Looking out at them with pained and weary eyes, she struggled to breathe. But the bronchial pneumonia took a relentless toll on the aged woman, leaving her gasping and choking.

Then, on April 4th, in spite of all of their prayers, she succumbed.

In a state of shock and disbelief, the family made preparations for Maude's burial. For a day she lay in state at the Park Avenue apartment. There her husband and children sat in silence, as the grandchildren, one by one tiptoed in and paid their last homage, kissing the cold, blue lips. Drained of light and vitality, the familiar face could almost have been a stranger's.

After a service at the apartment, the funeral procession drove out to East Hampton. Maude was buried in the new family plot, close to Bud.

Standing under the thin and delicate branches of the copper beech tree, Jack watched as yet another person he loved was lowered into the ground.

This time he didn't fight against the inevitable fact of death. He didn't rail with grief as his father was doing. Nor did he weep and moan like his sisters. Jack wept silently, in quiet desperation.

He was too devastated to speak.

Maude's death affected Jack in a number of ways. He was never again entirely happy-go-lucky. And for the first time in his life, Black Jack began shying away from Lasata. East Hampton held too many memories of Maude.

That same year, Jack's divorce became final. At the end of the summer, Janet returned from Reno and the deed was done. Although the marriage had by no means been made in heaven, Jack's conscience tore at him over its demise. Unwilling to own up to his mistakes, Jack kept his guilt thoroughly hidden. But he was still in many ways the young boy whose hidden remorse had once led him to try to drain from himself all of "that bad French blood."

Jack was compelled to be himself even if it destroyed him. But he was also an intelligent and realistic man. While Jack never did give lip service to his responsibility in the break-up, he had always known that it was primarily his fault. Inside, he paid for his mistakes many times over. The secret ways he found to punish himself were endless.

A bachelor once more, the debonair fifty-year-old began to carry on flagrantly—in the same tradition he had begun as a very young man. Within the family now, Michelle developed a tendency to try to choose girls from among her friends for Jack. She would casually invite them out to Lasata or 765 Park—where she and Shella now resided with the Major—and hope that something would happen. As a rule, her choices left a good deal to be desired as far as her brother was concerned. But on those rare occasions when "something" did click, it was generally a good deal beyond what Michelle had intended. And infinitely shorter-lived.

Undeterred by failure, Michelle kept on trying, in the hopes that at last she would find the girl who would be just perfect for Jack. Shella, dubious about the likelihood of success, immediately discussed the matter with her uncle.

Together, they worked out a code so Shella could have a blow by blow account of this or that candidate's success in gaining Jack's affection. Shella would ask Jack what tomorrow's weather would be. Sunny would mean he approved of the girl, but rain would mean a decisive thumbs down.

In this first round of weather prediction, it was clear that there would be an increasing number of hailstorms! The prognostications were generally unfavorable whenever Michelle had had a hand in the picture. Of course, it never stopped her from trying. Anyway, Shella and Jack had great fun as her mother persisted in her fruitless matchmaking, totally unaware of what they were up to. But she was rather surprised at her daughter's sudden interest in each day's weather.

In time, Jack tapered down his associations with girls of East Hampton and Manhattan society, increasingly focusing his attention on women without his social or financial background. With the exception of some serious sexual alliances, he would never again have a meaningful relationship of substantial depth with any woman outside the family.

In 1942, Janet remarried. Hugh D. Auchincloss, known as "Hughdie," was an attractive and good natured man. He was not only from a social milieu which could match the Bouviers', but Hughdie was also, even by Jack's standards, fabulously wealthy.

Jackie and Lee entered a new stage in their lives. Janet's second marriage was a happy one. The houses in which they now lived—Merrywood, a country seat in McLean, Virginia, and Hammersmith farm, a summer mansion in exclusive Newport, Rhode Island—were both grander than Lasata. Their new lifestyle was sumptuous, and they began to develop deep bonds with Hughdie's children from two previous marriages as they had earlier with their Bouvier cousins.

With Janet and the children away from New York—Jackie was now removed from Miss Chapin's school—Jack lost many opportunities to see his girls. Incensed, he began to accuse Janet of trying to spoil their special relationship.

His resentment took other forms of expression as well. Soon after Janet's wedding, he coined the phrase "Take a loss with Auchincloss," referring to Hughdie's brokerage firm of Auchincloss, Parker and Redpath, a Washington-based company. It immediately caught on at the New York Exchange, and its echo was to plague Hughdie as long as he remained in business.

Since Jack continued to pay for his daughters' education, support and medical expenses, money became a natural way of bidding for their affection. Despite Auchincloss's apparently inexhaustible funds, Janet did not shower the girls with gifts or spending money.

With his own fortune increasingly on the decline, however, Jack did. He gave them substantial allowances, and always went shopping for clothes with them on their visits to New York, maintaining charge accounts for that purpose at Saks Fifth Avenue and at Lord & Taylor.

Just as he had spent joy-filled hours with Miche a decade before, going over the fine points of "baby-hunting," the proud father now gave himself over to lengthy lessons on how to hook the most desirable fish around, and keep them on the hook; how to dress attractively; groom properly; when to smile, and when to say no. There was no greater coach in the world than Black Jack, bringing, as he did, a lifetime of experience from the "enemy camp."

Jack's lavish gift-giving reached a point where it drained far too much from his financial resources. Refusing to lessen his outpouring of love for his girls, he nonetheless realized that something would have to be sacrificed for it.

In the end, he was forced to give up his horses, which had become an undeniable financial burden. In McLean, where his daughters now spent most of their time, every family on their own level maintained its horses, and the Auchinclosses were by no means an exception. So Jackie hardly needed the riding practice during her increasingly rare visits to East Hampton.

Miche was also no longer around to exercise or ride the horses. While rowing for Columbia, he had developed rheumatic fever. And given the precarious state of his health, the boy was forced to transfer from his grandfather's alma mater to Arizona. When he wasn't there, he was visiting his mother, who in 1932, had married a career Army officer, Carlisle Visscher Allan. Emmy and her second husband were constantly being transferred to Hawaii, or California, or Washington D.C. or Kansas or Alabama and Miche joined them wherever during vacations, rather than returning to New York.

Without enthusiastic young people around to exercise them, Jack's horses had to be kept in shape by professionals whose hourly charges amounted to a modest yearly fortune.

Jack sold three horses and boarded two with Willie Woolnough, who had hunted on Jack's team in years gone by. Knowing Woolnough's Riding Academy almost as well as his own stable, Jack could rely on him to take perfect care of the animals.

But Jack could never bear to see Jackie parted from the favorite of all steeds, Danseuse. Ignoring the obvious defeat which it represented, Jack had the animal packed in a trailer and delivered to the Auchincloss estate where Jackie could ride Danseuse daily, and where there was an excellent paddock as well as a luxurious stable.

As she grew older, Jackie was sent to Miss Porter's School in Farmington, Connecticut—better known among the daughters of New York Society as "Farmington."

With every opportunity, Jack visited his daughter there, sometimes with Miche. His arrival among the neat little white clapboard buildings would always cause a great commotion. In their efforts to see him, the girls, lined up at the windows, nearly threatened to fall out. Dozens of them would regularly profess their love.

Gone with the Wind continued to be the movie of the century, and Jack was a natural object of affection as a swarthy double for Clark Gable. Many of them swore that Black Jack was by far the more beautiful of the two, but all agreed that their mystiques were similarly overpowering.

There were no glamorous spots to take his blossoming daughter to in Farmington, Connecticut. Their most popular haunt was hardly exciting. The old country inn had a squeaky front porch, leading from worn brick steps to a boringly quaint interior. The two memorable things about those dinners were the excellent, thick steaks, and the hordes of giggling school girls who would moon at Jack, restoring his deflated pride and making his daughter miserably embarrassed.

Shella and Jackie were in the same class at Miss Porter's. There Jack's niece witnessed only sunny skies, mixed with lightning bolts of sensuality which seemed to strike every proper young lady on campus.

Shella remembers how one fall, after a particularly sun-drenched August, Jackie burst out of their house to fly into Jack's arms. A new, uninitiated arrival at the school was watching as well.

"My God," the new pupil exclaimed indignantly, "why on earth is that girl kissing that Negro?"

Shella doubled over with laughter, increasing the other girl's bewilderment.

The next time the black man appeared on campus, no words of prejudice left the young lady's lips. Instead, she was at the forefront of giggling, lovestruck swooners.

SEVENTEEN

Esther

During Jackie's years at Miss Porter's, Jack felt her slowly slipping away from him. He struggled every way he knew how, to keep her interest—even to the point of occasionally trying to create a rift between the girl and her new family in McLean.

Of course, he could not realize that what was occurring had nothing to do with Hughdie, or money, or anything of the sort. Jackie was simply growing up.

Her love for her father never diminished, but she began to have other interests as well. While she was still delighted by her handsome father's company, she was no longer content just to be with him. She began to accept invitations from young men at all of the Ivy League schools, making quite a splash in all of the society columns. By 1947, "Cholly Knickerbocker" had dubbed her "Debutante of the Year."

Jack's beautiful older daughter was still quiet, but the poise and self-confidence he had always gone to extremes to encourage were now fully apparent. Throughout her earliest years, Jackie had always been a paragon. The brightest child, the most artistic, the best rider, the most poetic. And

Jack had never referred to her in terms any less superlative than "the most beautiful daughter a man ever had."

She had always been a special child, and Black Jack had never expected anything less than greatness out of her. But now that Jackie really was coming into her own, and leading an independent life, he began to feel an acute sense of loss. Jack saw other, far younger men vying for the opportunity to become "the man in Jackie's life." And he was powerless to change it.

Miche at the time was even further removed from Jack. At the University of Arizona, he was theoretically attending a few classes while recovering from rheumatic fever. In actuality, he had deserted the campus and sought employment as a cowboy. Miraculously, the experience cured him instead of killing him. After several months, he was once again in fine health, although his heart had been weakened by the illness.

Rather than return to school, he walked into a local newspaper office and got a job as cub reporter. As the main action was on the morgue beat, Miche rapidly befriended the mortician. There, in the funeral parlor's back room—in full view of a series of corpses—a gathering of young men might be found drinking and playing poker as the mortician periodically dropped out and went about his craft in the room stinking of formaldehyde.

With World War II, Miche saw his chance to follow in the tradition of military heroes in the Bouvier clan. Volunteering as a common infantryman at Tucson, he soon entered basic training. At the first military parade, Miche was marching for inspection before a four-star general, together with ten thousand other men.

Eventually, they came to a halt. Out of nowhere, the general demanded to see "Private Bouvier." Shaking in his boots for some unknown crime, the soldier crept hesitantly forward. Saluting the general, he struggled not to faint with fright.

"Are you Michel Bouvier?" the general asked stormily.

"Y-yes sir," Miche stammered.

"Well," the senior officer whispered, "I was having diner with your mother and Carlisle last week, and they told me you were out here. Why don't you stop by tomorrow evening for dinner, and have some decent sirloin instead of ration gruel! Six o'clock sharp. I'll look forward to it."

Before the man standing before him—and ten thousand onlooking troops—could respond, the general yelled, "DISMISSED!" and turned away to finish his inspection.

As a result of that dinner, Miche was transferred from the Infantry to the Armored Force—going through basic training at Fort Knox, Kentucky. He applied for Officer Candidate School and emerged a "ninety-day wonder" with gleaming second lieutenants' bars to prove it. He had graduated first in his class of three hundred men.

All too soon after, unhappily, while on maneuvers with the Tenth Armored Division of Tennessee, his motorcycle crashed into a black-out tank on a night convoy. In spite of his leg having almost been shorn off, he eventually made a phenomenal recovery. But Michel was out of commission from the Army's point of view.

Following a rather brief and uneventful term of service in the OSS, Miche was looking for adventure and enter-prise. His mother came through for him—this time remem-bering that one of her oldest friends, Marianne Taylor had married E. Hope Norton, who was famed for having built a railroad in Ecuador from Guayaquil on the coast to the capital city of Quito, 9,500 feet above sea level and a steeper grade than even the Swiss had ever accomplished. And with-out a funicular system.

Working for E. Hope Norton was an opportunity which brought Miche the experience and adventure he always craved. It also brought me a husband.

But for Jack, it meant one less child at hand, one less child to stem the tide of loneliness he felt at the growing, if natural, distance between him and his beloved daughter. Having moved into his new apartment, Jack realized that for that reason as well as his basic distaste for housework, he needed a housekeeper.

Scouting among all of the candidates he knew, Jack managed to pick the best. Esther Lindstrom was a staff servant at Lasata who had been Maude's personal maid and then had taken care of the Major and Michelle at 765 Park Avenue.

She was just a few years older than Jack, a fiftyish woman who was slender and fast on her feet. Her slightly veiled blue eyes seemed to take in everything, weighing every detail they met as it if were some sort of evidence. Once she came to a conclusion about anything—Jack's women friends, horses to bet on, stocks to invest in—Esther held onto it for the rest of her life. She was never at a loss for strong opinions, likes and dislikes, all sooner or later revolving upon her notion of Jack's best interests.

Once having attached herself to the Bouvier family, Esther never left it. With the exception of some measure of devotion to an only sister who lived in Manhattan, Esther had lost contact with her Scandinavian family and transferred all bonds of love and loyalty to the Bouviers. She was fiercely protective and tolerant in the extreme toward all of them, although in time she began to take Jack's side as a matter of course in perennial family disagreements.

As soon as she had settled in the new apartment, Jack came to realize how badly he had needed someone like Esther. She realized it too, and at once set about building a daily routine which bound the two of them intricately in an unseverable platonic bond.

Every weekday morning, Jack would force himself out of bed—as a rule quite groggy and in not too good a mood. In anticipation of this, Esther would set out his coffee on the kitchen table, with the good sense to let a surly man have his first cup of coffee by himself.

Immediately after downing that first draft, Jack headed into the bathroom and drew a steaming hot bath while he shaved. While he never did venture one of the Major's ice water baths, Jack did take a second, cooler one, splashing about like a sea lion with the predictable growls of agony. Without fail, most of the tub water landed on the floor, so Esther always had a mop on hand.

Next, Jack selected a Brooks brothers button-down shirt and a club tie to complement it. At the dining-room table, he would appear, then, in shirtsleeves and tie—though below-table-level, he was only in baby-blue boxer shorts, socks and garters. Sitting with regal formality and cavalierly oblivious to his state of undress—Jack would read the *Herald Tribune* for the news, the *News* for the latest sporting events and his indispensable *Wall Street Journal.* But never did Jack find the slightest use for the *New York Times.*

When Jack had gone through the race results reported in the *News,* he generally realized he was running late for opening on the Exchange floor. Bolting out of his seat, Jack would struggle into his suit, while screaming for Esther to bring him a coat, or his navy blue Homburg hat or any one of a dozen other accoutrements.

Esther was soon accustomed to this last-minute crisis. Waiting at the elevator door, she held his coat in one hand and a last cup of coffee in the other while her dashing boy burst forth from the apartment.

Jack would fumble into his coat and grab up the proffered cup, complaining as usual that it was much too hot but savoring every last drop of it as he rode down to the ground floor. Only one time out of a hundred did Jack not complain that it was too hot—the rare occasion when he could complain that it was too cold! Waiting for Jack at the building's entrance, the doorman held the door open with one hand, while with the other he relieved Mr. Bouvier of his now emptied cup to be sent back up immediately to the imperious Esther.

Five mornings a week, the same taxi waited at the curb, with the same cabbie at the wheel, running the motor to get that extra head start as soon as Jack was entirely inside the vehicle. As the passenger door was slammed shut by the doorman, off they headed toward Wall Street at a healthy clip. Every day, they would argue about which route was the fastest way to get there. The hack, shouting down Jack in his best Brooklynese, would wager that his route would get Jack to the Stock Market within a given period of time— generally less than twenty minutes door to door.

Jack, always a sucker for a bet, would accept it, sweetening the driver's reward for getting to the "floor" on time. And the cabbie, a ringworthy veteran when it came to careening down Manhattan's broad avenues, had a clear advantage over Jack, knowing the city streets and traffic conditions far better.

Barring acts of God, the cabbie always won, and Jack would have to fork over the wager as well as the fare and a substantial tip. The cost of the journey was established at a fixed rate, regardless of what the meter read. Augmented by their morning bet, it was well worth the cabbie's while to be waiting for Jack on workdays.

For five hours on the floor of the Exchange, Jack alternately stood and dashed across the great hall as he bought, sold, and observed his specialty stocks, besides trading for his own account. When trading closed at 3:00 P.M., Jack brought all of his notes and trading agreements back to the office, where he and his clerk, Paul Maricondo, tallied up the final scores.

Afterwards, back aching from the strain of the hectic motion on his feet all day, Jack walked uptown to the Yale Club or the New York Athletic Club to work out. Relaxed after his exercise, sauna and massage, Jack headed back up to his apartment.

The moment Jack stepped into the apartment, he would turn on the television. While waiting for the sound to come on and the picture to appear, Jack rushed around the living room, turning on all four radios as well. Each one was set on a different station. Jack needed to keep tabs on all games going on within broadcast range, because he had bets riding on all of them.

Living with Jack, Esther began to follow all of the sporting events as avidly as Jack did. She also placed his bets for him with a variety of bookies during the day. As her own more modest wagers began to pay off, Esther's personal interest in the outcome of games and races grew to equal Jack's.

Their favorite bookie was just around the corner, on Lexington Avenue. Fritz was a big, hearty-looking German, who also happened to run a butcher store. Not wanting his more puritanical customers to know of his freelance activities, Fritz had an extra long cord installed with his wall phone. When a bet was called in, he excused himself from behind the meat counter and carried the receiver and a pen and pad into the enormous walk-in ice box.

There, among the hanging carcasses of cows and sheep on meat hooks, Fritz would transact business and settle up accounts.

The front was a perfect one, and none of his customers ever caught wind of the butcher's bookmaking activities on the side. He did, however, have one recurrent and bitter complaint about the set-up: when the butchering business was too good, his numbers and notations would often be so blood-smeared that totaling them up at the end of the month would be nigh onto impossible.

At the peak of their betting activities, Esther would find herself dashing out of the apartment every fifteen minutes, sometimes well into the evening. For Jack, the blaring of so many radios while watching television and seeing Esther come and go with her news was hardly the extent of it. As soon as he arrived home, the telephone calls would begin as Jack's women or hopefuls one by one called in and checked up on him.

Breaking off momentarily to become absorbed in developments in any one of the games, and with constant quick asides to Esther about the progress of the other events they had money riding on, Jack endlessly courted the voices on the other end of the phone. Time after time when it rang, Esther would hand him the receiver and Black Jack would go into operation.

Never did he pretend that the woman with whom he spoke was the only one in his life. That would have been an act no one would believe. But Jack did have an amazing capacity to make every caller feel that she was the only one he had really been waiting for. With the first sound of her voice, Jack's phenomenal memory would recall everything they had ever done—or hoped to do—together. As well as her likes, dislikes, measurements and family background.

After years with Jack, Esther also developed the ability to listen to a half a dozen conversations at once. However, I think that among the Bouviers themselves, this trait was present at birth, probably as a matter of survival of the fittest. So many conversations went on at once during family gatherings that it was either feast or famine—particularly when you had to defend your actions, attack someone else's, listen for stock tips and ask for another helping of prime rib in the same breath.

Talking to the continual stream of callers, Jack never once lost track of an event where he had money riding. And while he had a special talent for making each one of the ladies feel special, Jack seldom dated any who called him. In that sense he was conservative, preferring to do the chasing instead of being the prey. When Jack invited a girl out or had her to his apartment for dinner, she was someone who would never have called to seek out the invitation.

Eating dinner at home had gone from a drastic and dreaded economy move to Jack's stated preference as he settled down and began to enjoy the rare comfort of a small and cozy apartment. While breakfast was nothing more than two soft-boiled eggs on protein toast with coffee, dinner was a far more elegant observance. When a woman was invited to Jack's place for dinner she was greeted to a table set with gleaming silverware, pristine double damask linen and crystal candlelight. Fresh flowers were a *sine qua non* and, alas, so were lamb chops! The dinner menu there never changed: consommé, lamb chops, peas or lima beans and protein toast. If you didn't care for lamb chops, there was no point in discussing it with Jack. Esther, who was a gourmet cook in her own right, at first tried to sneak in the occasional soufflé, or pheasant, or even just filet mignon. But the fuss that ensued over such changes made them not worthwhile.

So Esther's desire to show off her excellence as a cook was frustrated for years. But at least the lamb chops were the best money could buy. Particularly when the bookie was ahead.

Esther's account on horses was always in better shape than Jack's, despite his thorough knowledge of the animals and the tracks. Jack was always loyal to the bluebloods. He seemed to know the sires and dames of every racing horse going back five generations. "That one," he would solemnly pronounce, "must be an unbeatable horse, coming out of . . ." And then the begats of the horse world would be recited.

Having learned her approach from Jack, Esther nonetheless also took into account the more conventional wisdom of the expert sportswriters. And unlike Jack, she generally won.

But the stockbroker's record on college football and track was unbeatable. He followed the Ivy League teams relentlessly, thinking nothing of memorizing the names, numbers and yardages of Columbia's varsity football team while Miche was there. Of course, he knew all of the details about every oar on the Hudson River.

As for track, Jack claimed that he could recognize winners

because of his years of sprinting, first at prep school, then on the track team at Yale. But many of his friends claimed that his sprinting activities were never terribly highly developed until he was discovered for the first time *in flagrante delicto* by an irate husband.

If Esther had long ago passed Jack on the horses and could not begin to keep up with his track and football system, she profited greatly from his reports on the state of the stock market. As Jack and his guests discussed various stocks and their positions, Esther's eyes narrowed and an inscrutable smile fastened on her tight little lips. Placing the lamp chops on his plate, she leaned closer, cocking her ears and blotting out all of the other sounds in the room.

She knew how to take advantage of his expertise, his observations and instinct for choosing those stocks which would make the most money.

Jack was a gambler in all senses of the word, and sitting on a stock when it was quiet was sheer torture to him, particularly since he had to stand on the Stock Exchange floor and watch so many other prices soar upwards. But Esther saw the value in a good thing, and after buying stocks according to Jack's recommendations, she then refused to give up her good position in them for anything in the world.

Balancing Jack's risks with her own caution, Esther made a bundle. Everyone borrowed money from the domestic— including her boss. She seemed to be the only family member with a constant supply of cash. Of course, that had something to do with the cash business of betting, and also with the fact that she abhorred banks and favored her mattress. Never once did Esther appear to mind handing out cash to any member of the family who needed it.

Most of Jack's women failed to appreciate how much the wiry Scandinavian woman meant in his life. He listened to her opinions and was wary of any woman who did not receive the Lindstrom seal of approval. Which is not to say that the stockbroker ceased and desisted every time Esther wrinkled her nose. But when he ignored her sixth sense and continued carrying on with a woman Esther had told him in no uncertain terms to stay clear of, Jack was generally burned.

Either way, the women Esther disapproved of were never terribly much of a concern. They never lasted long. Primarily because Esther made life miserable for them.

An undesirable evening guest would not merely be subjected to the barrage of four radios and a television. Esther would immediately double the volume of every set. Jack was so engrossed he never seemed to notice. But the candidate for his affection couldn't seem to get anywhere in her quiet conversation because the object of her attention couldn't hear a word she was saying, with all of the stations going at once.

At the least, Jack's interest in his bets always equalled his interest in any dinner partner. When Esther increased the frequency of her forays into the outer world of bookies, Jack would be further distracted from his purpose every five minutes, when she returned with a full rundown of results in each betting category. Then he would ask for the next round. If a woman who displeased Esther was staying for dinner, it would take an interminable time to serve a simple meal, giving the couple few seconds alone.

Perhaps the individual irritations were small enough, but together they would hardly fail to make anyone snappish—a trait which Jack disliked to the extreme in women. The worst possible mistake any annoyed guest could do was to glower at Esther. That would be grounds for Jack to pitch her out of the apartment.

One way or another, Esther made her will known. And got it.

If she approved of a girl, things would go graciously, and as smooth as silk. The radios were almost quiet, the dinner was delicious and served in record time. All smiles, Esther would take off to her bedroom, leaving the couple to their own devices.

EIGHTEEN

Coming Home

While Lee was growing up, Jackie was at Vassar and Jack, now in his mid-fifties, was settling down in his apartment. Miche was thousands of miles away.

Although Quito, Ecuador, is directly in line with the equator, it has a relatively cool, hospitable climate. Guayaquil, however, where I was raised and where Miche and I first met, is perennially hot as Hades! The only relief from the heat comes briefly during the torrential storms which pound the city during the rainy season.

Then there are the earthquakes, which arrive with frightening regularity. Not little seismic quakes or slow-swaying earth movements but massive earth-shaking and rumbling. Panic overshadows everything, and there is often wholesale destruction and death before the aftershocks come to an end.

The rate of exchange between the Ecuadorian sucre and the dollar was definitely on the American side. Average American wages were enough to allow Miche to live like a millionaire. Yet for him the primary attraction of the country was adventure. Working for E. Hope Norton's Ecuadorian Corporation Ltd., he was guaranteed a great deal of it.

At that point in time, the American multinational con-
glomerate held a virtual monopoly on big business in the
area. The money-making operations they did *not* own were
limited to banks, markets, and the department stores. Beyond that, from breweries to rice mills, from chocolate factories to cement factories to dairy farms to the electric light
plant and trolley car line in Quito—it was all Norton's.

Miche had a phenomenal aptitude for languages, and
within half a year, he was speaking Spanish like a native,
besides having more than a grasp of local patois. As assistant
manager to the Guayaquil operation, Miche put every skill
he could muster to work.

First off, he had to persuade the manager of the dairy
farm to introduce a new breed of disease resistant cattle
since their herds were all but decimated by vampire bats.
Next, he reworked the entire dairying program, replacing
their antiquated procedures with new ones, based on such
newfangled notions as "sanitation" and "pasteurization."

Like all Bouviers, Miche was hard-headed, insisted on his
independence at all costs and would never take no for an
answer. So much so that he seemed to be ideal cannon
fodder for a battle which the corporation had been losing
for many years. It was a territorial dispute over a piece of
land on the coast, south of Esmereldas, which they called
Salango.

Beyond priceless beauty, Salango was rich in lumber but
virtually inaccessible except by sea. As the manager explained the problem to Miche, they needed him to figure
out a cost-effective means of harvesting the tough sisal fiber
from which rope and other fabrics were made and of getting
it from there to the mills at Guayaquil. Beyond a few miles
of impassable swamp and rain forest, there seemed to be
no overbearing difficulty.

Accompanied by three Ecuadorian Indians who knew the
geography and with a smattering of the native dialect of the
primitive village located in the Salango holdings, Miche left
at once. Setting out to sea around a formidable promontory
in an alarmingly unstable—but totally unsinkable—little

balsa wood canoe, Miche pored over his topographic maps for three hours.

When the little balsa wood "bongo," as such boats are called, finally came to a rest, he was astonished. The place was fantastically beautiful. They landed on a lovely crescent of beach formed of soft, powdery white sand. The Pacific lapped at the edge of a reed hut village, almost reaching the closest of the shacks built on tall stilts which dotted the rounded stretch of land.

Deeper inland, he could make out the edge of the black rain forest, alive with the chattering of monkeys and tropical birds. The region was lush with vegetation and succulent tropical fruit. Between the beauty of the cerulean water and the brightly colored tropical wild flowers, he was mesmerized.

Exuberantly, Miche helped the Indians stow the oars and tie up the bongo. Bending over the boat, he was so enraptured that he failed to register any of the noises until he heard the loud click.

As he spun around, what met his eyes was half a dozen vicious, snarling faces. His party was widely outnumbered by a rough-looking bunch, most of them with the strong noses and dark skins of the Jivaro Indians of the mountains. Apparently, the Indian blood had trickled down from the mountains, intermingling with this sleepy ancient settlement. And the Jivaro were known and revered for one thing: their sudden bursts of uncontrolled rage.

One man, taller than the rest and far more threatening, had the barrel of his shotgun pointed casually at Miche's navel.

At once, Miche identified the click he had heard as the cocking of a rifle. He had also discovered the real problem which the sisal expedition would have to confront.

The group leader, however, was a kind man, and he did not particularly wish to blow out Miche's innards. Offering an alternative, he edged the gun upwards and pointed toward the bongo, whispering, "Go."

Hearing the man speak Spanish, Miche hesitated, stood his ground and asked for an explanation.

A burst of Spanish later, the problem became obvious. He had landed in a hornet's nest of angry squatters—men dependent upon the land and determined to hold onto what was theirs to the end. It was by no means the first time that the Ecuadorian Corporation had sought to evict them.

Over the years, several young and foolhardy men like Miche had been sent to repossess their territory. But the squatters had lived in Salango so long they considered it theirs. The company could try whatever legal remedies it wanted; now it was war.

Since his Indian interpreters were not being paid to fight, Miche had to consider the odds as six-to-one. Despite the fact that he was as big as any two of them, they possessed the weapons. Direct confrontation was ruled out. Calling up his every last reserve of charm, he convinced the leader that it was time for a tribal conference between the warring factions. For the time being, he had not the least intention of pressing his corporation's claim.

Naturally, serious conversation could not begin before a sizeable quantity of chicha was drunk. The potent alcoholic liquor, which is made from corn that has been masticated by villagers before fermentation, eased the tension. Soon the topic of conversation turned to far more agreeable subjects.

Before long, even Ecuador and America became indistinguishable. By the end of the evening, Miche and the head of the village when off arm in arm to the man's hut. The leader commanded his wife to immediately cook a meal for Miche and find him a suitable bed. She cooked superbly, and delivered a sleeping place to the best of her ability—the longest cot in the village was roughly five feet long! He spent the next six nights alternating between letting his head and neck, or fourteen inches of leg, dangle over the edge.

A week later, amid friendly good wishes from the entire

village, Miche and his translators were sent off in their bongo, back to civilization.

Not for an instant did he consider depriving the villagers of their land. Beyond the legal squatter's rights, Miche was convinced that his newfound friends had a moral title to their land.

To the Ecuadorian Corporation Limited, multinational that it was, Miche's point of view represented one more failure in their attempts to begin capitalizing on the land. They began looking to other sectors for an expedient solution. And so did Miche.

Soon after he returned from that hair-raising expedition, Miche and I got married. For our honeymoon, we bought one-way tickets to the States.

As soon as Miche caught sight of Jack, his face lit up like a little child's. "How are you, Big Boy?" his uncle called out, running to kiss him. Then came a bear hug, then a good thump on the shoulder. All this with radiant laughter and glistening eyes.

Once we had been introduced, Jack took a while to politely check me out while Miche anxiously awaited the verdict. Later that night, when Jack took him aside and whispered, "Caffy . . . she's a real peach!" Miche finally breathed a sigh of relief. Approval from the clan was hardly easily forthcoming, particularly for anyone who was not from the New York Social Register, let alone North America!

From that moment on, Jack always treated me as a daughter. He affectionately referred to me as "Caffy" and couldn't be convinced that the name was pronounced otherwise. I never did figure out why he persisted in calling me Caffy. But he did, and consequently, so did Jackie.

The next morning, as Miche and I struggled out of bed to join Jack for protein toast and soft-boiled eggs, he shook his head in disapproval. For a moment, I thought that in twelve hours I had somehow managed to violate American propriety—despite the fact that I had been sound asleep during eight of them. But looking at Miche's natty Brazilian sport coat, I realized what the problem was.

Jack was Brooks Brothers and club ties all the way. Turning to his nephew, the Wizard of Wall Street laughed out loud, "Tell you what. Let's go down to Alex Busse and see if he can't run you up a decent suit. I can't have you running around New York looking like that!" Later that afternoon, that's what they did, with stops at Florsheim, Brooks Brothers, and five other clothing stores en route. It was Jack's way of showing love, and welcoming his "son" back home.

When Jack loved someone, he expected them to be worthy of that love. Sometimes this was a little rough on the beloved. Soon after arriving in New York, we all drove down to East Hampton together. En route, Jack decided that Miche's horseback riding must be rusty, since there was not much opportunity for it in Ecuador. Consequently, it was imperative that Miche practice—and that very day.

At once, we rented horses at the Willnough Stables. Jack spent the entire afternoon instructing Miche. My poor husband must have gone over the same jump fifty times and still Jack was not satisfied.

At length, the lesson stopped—but only because Jack felt that the horse had had enough. There was no question in Jack's mind that Miche had not.

Just as all of the soldiers who had fought in World War II were returning, the market for New York apartments was gruesome. Jack turned over the spare bedroom to us until we could find something half-suitable. It was a wonderful time for all of us.

Miche and I were pretty wild in those days, and our friends were equally unpredictable. Jack insisted that the apartment be Liberty Hall to everyone, and Esther was amazingly tolerant.

One night we were fast asleep when I felt the bed shifting strangely. Opening my eyes, I noticed something lying between Miche and me. Having difficulty making out what it was, I reached for Miche and shook him awake.

A second later, Miche was sitting bolt upright in horror, and I was screaming. The thing in question was a shiny shoe and a bright argyle sock on a disembodied leg.

In the corner of the room, Phil Andrews, an old school friend of Miche who worked as a clerk on the Exchange, was grinning. "Aw, don't let it get to you," he muttered, pointing to a figure slumped in a chair across the room, "it belongs to him."

"For Godssake!" Miche shouted, "What in hell is it?"

In answer, the stranger referred to hopped over to our bed and plunked himself down on the edge. Without any attempt at introducing himself, the man said, "It's my leg. Wanna see how it works?"

"Bob always takes it off when he's loaded," Phil casually remarked. "Even in a nightclub."

"I'm *not* loaded," the other man angrily retorted. "You're the one that's tight!"

Accusations like "skunked" and "blotto" led to an argument and threatened even more than harsh words.

It was broken up by Esther, who had raced across the apartment after my scream. Seeing that we were all right, she stood there for a moment taking in the scene, offhandedly leaning against the doorpost as she watched the stranger on our bed twirling the wooden leg.

"It's all right," I squeaked. "They're friends."

She nodded. Without another word, she spun around and headed back to her bed, pausing to close the door for us. No comments, and no desire for an explanation.

As it turned out, Phil and his one-legged pal had been at a party and soaked up more than their fair share of booze. Growing sentimental, the old school chum was seized by an irresistible urge to see his old buddy Miche right that instant. Arriving at the apartment and finding the service entrance open, it was natural for them just to step in.

After the explanation, the twosome stayed around for a while to chat. Before they left, Phil's friend gave a fascinating demonstration of how to put on an artificial leg.

As they were heading off, he turned to address us once again, growing indignant. "Phil's wrong, you know. I'm *not* bombed at all. It's just that this damned thing hurts, that's all." And with that he weaved proudly out of the door.

The next morning, Esther had resumed her normal brusque manner. She didn't even tell Jack what she had witnessed. When we related the events to Jack he grinned quietly, obviously wishing he had been in on it. As for two strangers breaking into his home in the dead of night, his only comment was a terse, "Wonder who left the door open!"

Each night, when the sports and stock market statistics had been thoroughly discussed, Jack inevitably got around to talking about his daughters. With the onset of puberty, Lee was promising to become an even greater beauty than Jackie. And that was going some!

Esther adored the girls no less than Jack did. Whenever Jackie was coming down from Farmington, she would scurry about frantically—shining the already highly polished silver, waxing the impeccable floors, vacuuming the rugs, and begging Jack to give her the opportunity to cook something special—meaning, of course, anything but lamb chops!

Of course, Jack refused. Nonetheless, he was not one bit less excited. All of his previous engagements were cancelled as soon as Jackie announced she would be visiting. As long as she remained there, his soft-spoken eldest daughter became the center of his universe. Nothing that had to do with her escaped his notice. He lavished upon her dresses, stockings, make-up—anything she desired. All else faded into the background.

The morning that the teenage Jackie called up from the hairdressers' and announced that she had gotten a "poodle cut," the news was brought out to Jack on the floor of the Exchange. By one in the afternoon he had grown quite anxious. By closing time, he was a nervous wreck. He tried calming down at the Yale Club, but was just too excited to concentrate on relaxing. Giving up, he raced home.

Jack just couldn't wait to see how it would appear on her. In fact, he was really extremely worried that it wouldn't in the least suit her.

First, I explained to him what it would look like—the very

tight little curls all over her head, and how they would bush out a bit. I started to explain that she would resemble a sheepdog a bit, but caught myself in the nick of time. As it was, the hairstyle represented a radical departure for Jackie, and he was worried enough.

I found myself earnestly reassuring him, clucking like a mother hen—until it occurred to me that there was an element of the ridiculous in his exaggerated apprehension. If the poodle cut did not become Jackie it would not, after all, mean the end of the universe.

But Jack couldn't see that for a second. He was as obsessed with Jackie's poodle cut as he had ever been with the pursuit of a woman. He would not rest until he had seen it.

Worse than that, his preoccupation grew infectious. One by one, we all grew fidgety. The air seemed to grow thicker. The conversation trickled to a halt. Then, we sat in silence.

Waiting.

It must have seemed a strange tableau to the young girl as she bounced in, when we all together breathed a sigh of relief. Of course, there *was* a terribly disappointing dénouement. The poodle cut looked great, and Jackie looked radiant. The grin on Jack's face was a delight to witness, but beyond that I must confess that Miche and I felt more than a little silly about the extremes to which we had gone over such an innocuous incident.

By Saturday, Jackie was safely returned to Miss Porter's, and Jack was in top form. Arising early, he set out to go jogging, as he did every weekend he was not in the country. At a time when not one other jogger would be encountered in all of Central Park, Jack had discovered great value in that particular form of self-torture.

His suit was nothing like the cotton sweatsuits or European training outfits in such abundance today. It is best described as a cross between a diving suit and a surgical glove. The garment was a natural rubber sweat suit, very pale tan in color, and shaped like a union suit.

To get into it, Jack would strip down to the flesh, powder

it heavily, then pull it up over his skin. Of course, that was quite an operation, and he had to do it all by himself. Esther wouldn't touch the thing with a ten-foot pole!

On top of the skintight rubber suit, Jack wore a neat turtleneck, a grey flannel suit and loafers.

While the object of the suit was to encourage profuse sweating, the entire process was kept well out of view. To the interested observer—and wherever Jack ran, there were bound to be many—he just looked like a quite handsome and well-dressed man. As he jogged a good many miles around the Central Park Reservoir the sweat went unnoticed, as did the rubber torture chamber.

Trotting back from the park, Jack looked slightly out of breath but still debonair. There was a further method in his madness for some of his best dates were made on his Saturday morning expeditions. In fact, it was not at all unusual for Jack to return to his apartment escorting a beautiful young lady on his right arm.

Esther was always quite suspicious of these seemingly accidental encounters. Knowing the ways of her sex, she rarely doubted that the meeting had been carefully engineered by the girl.

Eyes narrowed as she opened the door, Esther immediately appraised the woman.

And as Jack thanked the heavens for his good luck in meeting girls, Esther was generally already switching up the volume on all of the radios, and planning an afternoon of quite heavy betting.

NINETEEN

Leaving Jack

Miche worked with Jack as his office clerk for a while, but he just didn't enjoy the work. Until three o'clock, when Jack came up from the floor, the job consisted of sitting in the broker's office and waiting. When the broker finally did arrive with the figures, Miche then had to compile them in a mad dash.

For some men, the fact that the figures represented real fortunes in dollars and cents might have been enough to commit them deeply to Wall Street. But where Miche was concerned, he could see only great sound and fury signifying little.

There were a few good aspects of Miche's stock market working day. The best of all was coming home at the end of it. Beside that, there were all those martinis at lunch with Phil Andrews, and generally a game or two of squash as well. With those being the dubious advantages of his job, and the smell of the rain forest still haunting him, it was not too long before Miche had to leave Bouvier, Bishop & Co., successors to M.C. Bouvier & Co., which had an office in John Davis's firm of Billings, Olcott & Co.

Miche's next job was in the airline industry, working out at LaGuardia Airport as a ramp agent for American Overseas Airlines. Their headquarters consisted of one large building near the marsh, where seaplanes regularly landed: The Marine Terminal. It was a lot more exciting than sitting in a Wall Street office. The planes he so longed to fly sat out on the ramp, and with every opportunity Miche would watch them land, unload their cargoes, refuel and take off again.

His big opportunity for advancement came one day when a Lockheed Constellation circled and began coming in for a landing with no one there to direct it. Having watched the hangar personnel do it endless times, Miche felt confident he could bring the plane in.

Besides, there was no one else around, which made him the best man available.

Only after he had performed the task flawlessly did Miche discover that the company's president had come in during the middle of it, and sat with his nose pressed against the hangar window, fearing the worst. However, when the disaster did not come to pass, Miche was instantly promoted.

Soon afterwards, the airline was swallowed by Pan American, and Miche moved onward and upward to Peruvian International Airways, transplanting us to Miami and then to Washington, D.C.

In the meantime, Jackie was discussing a year abroad in Paris, where she could study at the Sorbonne.

Michelle, who had been residing with the Major since her divorce from Scotty, soon found herself married to Harrington Putnam and living in Rio de Janeiro. Jack's other twin sister, Maude, was living a summer life removed from the New York scene in Ridgefield, Connecticut.

As for Edith, ever since Maude's death, she had gone into virtual seclusion at Grey Gardens, in East Hampton, gradually joined in her isolation by her beautiful daughter, Little Edie.

Throughout the years, Jack had always been bored or annoyed by the Major's constant references to the grandeur of the Bouvier family. Particularly when the orator dwelled excessively on comparisons between young and old generations, with the ancients always clearly coming out on top. Now as ever, not a family gathering passed without the Major expounding upon the magnificence of their forebears, and Jack responding from the wings with derogatory asides.

Nonetheless, Jack had never put off wearing his Tiffany gold Bouvier signet ring, and he began to pay increasing attention to his family, particularly now that he saw it scattered farther and farther afield.

The Major began failing soon after Michelle's departure. At first, his pains were not taken too seriously, and everyone was certain he would overcome them. Even during the greatest attacks, he could still dress himself perfectly, then go into his library to sit in his easy chair and read a scholarly tome, while sipping rye.

Whenever anyone asked how he was doing, the Major would reply "Poorly. Damned poorly. I'm a sick woman," then return to his reading. Occasionally, the old man would clutch his side and shout, "Goddamnit to hell!" annoyed to the extreme at the hell his body was giving him. He never did discover that he had an advanced case of terminal cancer, and even in his worst moments remained sure he would beat his illness.

The Major's main suffering was from his diminished family, particularly after Michelle had flown the coop a second time. Jack and Maude spent more time with him in an effort to stem his loneliness.

Every weekend that summer, for the first time since his mother died, Jack commuted to Lasata. On August 19, 1947, the Major celebrated his eighty-third birthday there. When asked how he felt, the old man replied, "Rotten!" But it was obvious how much it meant to him to have Maude and her family, Jack, Jackie and Lee around him.

Christmas Day of the same year, Michelle flew home from South America for a visit. Shocked to see how ill her father was, she cancelled all plans and moved in with him once again. On December 31st he took to his bed.

The Major never again had the strength to leave it. Michelle did everything possible to make the last two weeks of her father's life comfortable. But after the hell his body had put him through during the last weeks, his death on January 14, 1948 was a relief to everyone.

Services were held in St. Patrick's Cathedral, with Jack leading the funeral procession. Afterwards, the Major's body was taken out to the family burial plot at East Hampton, and laid by Maude's side. This time Jack's grief as he stood at the graveside was not unbearable. There had been too many fights with the Major over money and lifestyle, too much bitter competition. The woman whose love had held them and the rest of the family together, had been dead eight years.

All of Jack's life, the Major had played a cat-and-mouse game with him. As the years went on, Jack was always being let in or cut out of his father's will. The last testament found Jack reinstated. It was the greatest reaffirmation of love that the Major was capable of.

The Major's heirs expected their inheritances to restore their deflated standards of living to what all of the family had once enjoyed. However, the patriarch had not done nearly as well financially as he had led them to believe. Of the $1,300,000 John Bouvier, Jr. inherited from MC, all of his dividends and interest, plus an additional half million dollars, had gone into maintaining his lifestyle as a well-heeled New Yorker. Of the $800,000 which remained, a third of it went to taxes.

Michelle and Maude were the greatest beneficiaries, splitting a quarter of a million dollars and Lasata and Wildmoor. Jack got $100,000 plus release from an outstanding debt. Of the ten grandchildren, Miche received an extra inheritance because he was fatherless. Jackie and each of the other grandchildren received an even $3,000.

It was clear that the Bouvier millions were at an end.

Not long afterwards, Jack took Miche and me to Jones Beach as a special treat. He remembered the site of his childhood jaunts as a stretch of beach equal in beauty to East Hampton, serene and isolated. But that cold spring day, it was already an overcrowded and filthy stretch of sand. We didn't stay.

At the time, I was pregnant with Michel Bouvier IV. We were driving back when Jack spotted a crow. And when he saw one he had to see two, then three. It was a superstition he took terribly seriously. There was a rhyme that went with the spotting of the crows, and the last line was "And three's a boy."

In view of the fact that I was expecting a child, Jack would not be talked out of his superstition. He was convinced that otherwise something horrible would occur. That day, he spied the second easily, but we had one hell of a time coming up with crow number three. Jack would not leave the area until we succeeded, some hours later. It was a good omen and cause for celebration.

As far as Jack was concerned, when my son Michie was born in Washington, D.C., his gender proved the strength of the crow superstition. Of course, we ridiculed that idea. But ever since, I've been a bit concerned when there's only one crow in sight. And Miche has been known to go out of his way to find two more—just to be on the safe side—although he denies it.

It's a pity that the Major died before Michie's birth. It was an important day for the family, ensuring as it did the continuation of the family name in which the Major had put great, and almost exaggerated, stock. Jack had always maintained that he could not give a damn whether or not the illustrious Bouvier line was continued. Nonetheless, he was terribly overjoyed that our firstborn was a boy; and not much less when we decided to give him a name which had been in the family for so many generations.

Fortuitously, because Michie was conceived before the Major's death, he was included among the grandchildren and entitled to an equal share of the estate. While that $3,000 was a nice beginning for a nest egg, it was hardly a fortune—particularly in view of the birthrights of the three generations who had come before him.

Soon, Miche was offered a second opportunity to move to Guayaquil, Ecuador, this time for Panagra as the head of the company's five airfields and fleet of DC-3's. He was aching to return. As for me, I had been born there and had many friends to return to. I was all for it.

On Miche's decent American salary, we once again returned to life on a scale compatible with the great Bouvier tradition. With labor very cheap, we could afford to maintain several servants. The rat race of Manhattan seemed a million miles away.

Our son Michie's first birthday was celebrated in Talara, Peru, where Miche had been sent on a vacation relief job for six weeks. It was a tiny and picturesque village facing the Pacific. The wind blew constantly, scattering sand over everything. I struggled in the absence of familiar cake mixes to do my best with native flours and oils. Consequently, Michie's first birthday cake was hard as stone. The frosting had a fine, gritty consistency, the result of the persistent sand.

The news from Jack's birthday letter: Jackie was studying at the Sorbonne, and the twins had decided to give up Lasata.

For a while, Maude and Michelle had tried to keep up the estate. In a post-war recession, with diminishing capital, it soon proved a disastrously big financial burden for them. As it was, the beloved family seat in East Hampton took two years to sell. And when someone in those uncertain times did purchase the estate, it went for a fraction of its true worth.

If there was any hope for a return to the golden days of the past, it collapsed on the afternoon Lasata was sold. It was as sad a day as ever a Bouvier had known. Soon, the thick ivy growing on the main house was pulled down, and the stucco beneath painted an untempered white.

The ancient linden leading to Maude and the Major's bedroom chamber disappeared in a storm. The vegetable garden was turned into a lawn; the grape arbor grew untended. Only the Italian garden and empty stables remained; stray ghosts of the Lasata the Bouviers had known.

TWENTY

Sinking

Jackie never did return to Vassar. Upon completing her year in Paris, she enrolled at George Washington University—Auchincloss territory.

In addition to paying for her education, clothing and medical expenses, Jack was still faithfully sending his daughter her fifty-dollar allowance every month. Repeatedly, he offered to augment that sum with a salary if she would only move to New York and work as a secretary in his office.

When Jackie became engaged to a stockbroker and Yale man, John W. G. Husted, Jack began to see more of her once again. He was hopeful that she would return to New York and make her place in society there. But once the engagement was broken, so was that dream.

In 1951, Jackie won the *Vogue* magazine *Prix de Paris*, and with it an opportunity to work for that magazine for a year—half of it in New York and half in Paris. Jack wrote us ecstatically of that triumph. During her school term in Paris, freed from his jealousy of Jackie's affection for McLean, Jack's relationship with her had grown more intimate and exclusive. With Jackie half the year in Paris and half the year in New York, there would once again be nothing left to be desired. His letters were joyous and optimistic. But suddenly, we heard nothing more about it. Jack never again mentioned the matter. Rather than accepting the prize, we later learned, his eldest daughter had chosen instead to become a roving reporter for the Washington *Times-Herald*.

Lee, in the meantime, started attending Sarah Lawrence College in Bronxville, an easy commute from New York. The following year, she left school and spent six months studying art history in Florence.

In the meantime, Miche and I were going from country to country in South America, rotating between the various airports, although we were still based in Guayaquil. Jack was a sporadic correspondent and we were not terribly much better.

I can remember writing him one long letter, trying to convey the peculiarity of daily events for us in South America. About that time, for example, an Indian from the mountains descended on our airstrip with his wife, child and burro and insisted upon buying passage on a north-bound flight with a big bag of gold dust. Always one to oblige, Miche called up his central office and asked what the going price for gold was. When they sent back a cable with a price quotation per ounce, Miche took the bag of dust, placed it on his freight scale, read the ounces on the kilogram scale as best he could, and even made change in gold dust.

Another time, Miche had to arrange to fly a twenty-five foot black marlin weighing 1800 pounds to Miami for a sport fisherman named Kip Farrington. While he was agreeable in principle, the cargo section of his largest prop plane was only eighteen feet long. Nonetheless, with several fork lifts and a good deal of maneuvering, the fish was sealed into the plane's belly without a scratch.

Heading north at high altitude, the climate went from

summer to winter and the fish froze. Two days later, Miche received a brief cable from Miami, reading:

EXCELLENT WORK BOUVIER STOP FISH AR-
RIVED IN PERFECT CONDITION STOP BUT FRO-
ZEN STOP NOW HOW IN HELL DO WE GET IT
OUT?

To which Miche replied: TRY A BLOWTORCH.

Following her studies in Florence, Lee worked as assistant to the fashion editor of *Harper's Bazaar*. The next step was one which left everyone nonplussed. On April 18, 1953, she married Michael Canfield, heir to the British Canfield publishing fortune.

The wedding was performed at Janet's McLean home, where Jack had to give his youngest daughter away. Face to face with the competitors for his daughters' affections, Jack for the first time was confronted with the visible opulence of their lives as compared with his own relatively humbled circumstances. Nonetheless, he held his head high and for once rose above the pedestrian arguments with and about Janet.

Not long afterwards, we received a letter from Jack saying that he believed Jackie was in love. This time, the young recipient of her affection was Jack Kennedy who Jack referred to as "this young kid who needs a haircut." The letter said, "I think Jackie's going to marry because I saw a look on her face the other day when she was looking at that kid."

The Kennedys had long been disliked by the Bouviers. Not only because they were Irish Catholic and *nouveau riche*, and not just because of Joseph Kennedy's sell-out during the Roosevelt era, when he was named first head of the watchdog Securities Exchange Commission. As staunch Republicans, the Bouviers looked at the Kennedys as something worse than traitors to their class. They were wealthy Democrats!

Unpredictably, Jack Kennedy and Black Jack Bouvier hit it off right from the start. They were alike in many ways—healthy love of good sports and good women being only two of them. Jack Bouvier thought Kennedy was one hell of a terrific guy, and Jack Kennedy thought Jack was a riot.

The rest of the Bouvier clan could be a bit snobbish at times, and they were not overly impressed with Jack Kennedy's family background. But as far as Jackie's father was concerned, John F. Kennedy was a man with a future. He even went so far as to say he believed Kennedy had a fighting Irishman's chance for the presidency although it was hard to imagine any Catholic becoming chief executive. At any rate, the first step for the lad was clearly a decent haircut!

Soon afterwards, Jackie and Jack announced their engagement. For the first time in his life, the young senator from Massachusetts had a reasonably short head of hair.

On September 12, 1953, five months after Lee and Michael Canfield's marriage, Jackie and Jack Kennedy were wed at Hammersmith Farm, Janet and Hughdie's Newport estate. At the time, we tried to figure out a way to return for the wedding, but it was out of the question, practically speaking.

Gala affair that it was, we were not sorry, ultimately, to have missed it. While it should have been a day of joy and pride for the Bouviers, it ended up as an embarrassment—and worse.

The marriage was to be held at St. Mary's Catholic Church in Newport. Jack would walk down the long nave with Jackie, then give her away to the young man he had become quite fond of. Cardinal Cushing would be officiating, and he was going to bestow the apostolic blessing of Pope Pius XII on the bride and groom.

The animosity at that point between Jack and Janet was such that he was not invited to stay with most of the other relatives at Hammersmith Farm. He was pointedly excluded from the celebration ball the preceding evening. Janet was intransigent. She simply would not have him in her home. Instead, accompanied by a friend from the Stock Exchange for moral support, he was put up at the Viking Hotel. Jackie made certain that the Black Prince was treated regally there, but still he felt humiliated not to be with her on the night before her wedding. He was deeply hurt, and his evading self-confidence further shaken.

Because he made such a point of flaunting his masculinity, and appearing tough and even callous, few people were aware of Jack's deep-seated sensitivity and shyness. But as his fortune declined and his great good looks began to deteriorate with middle age, as his family took off for distant parts of the world, Jack's emotional fragility began to show through.

That night, as he lay in bed trying in turn to imagine then forget his own daughter's wedding party, Jack plagued himself with feelings of guilt and impotence. Never one to delve too deeply below any surface, particularly his own, all Jack could see was his own failure to be by Jackie's side; his failure to be a millionaire like Joe Kennedy or Hughdie; to command the sort of respect which they did, entitling them to a place of honor in the pre-wedding festivities.

As the sleepless night progressed into day, he suffered a severe case of the jitters. He panicked at the thought of having to walk down the aisle in front of all the people who had snubbed him. Afterwards, he would have to face the wall of hostility of Janet's family, the aloofness of the Auchinclosses, and perhaps the impudence of the Kennedys. After all, how much respect did any of them really have for him? A puppet figure who had not even been part of the official family celebration!

Normally, Jack Bouvier was not one to take an insult. But in this case, he could not fight when he was attacked. Even though they had hit him when he was down, Jack had to take it all quietly for Jackie's sake.

By dawn, his heart was pounding and his nerves, raw. He began to feel that he wanted to bolt from the altar one more time. But now there was no Maude to turn to and cry, "I just can't do it, Ma!"

In fact, there was no one.

To bolster his courage, Jack took a drink. Then another. And another.

As the ceremony approached, Michelle and her husband rushed down to the hotel desperate to find him. By the time they did, he was too far gone—drunken and incoherent.

Before Jack knew anything, the wedding was over. Hugh Auchincloss had given his daughter Jackie away, and he hadn't been there to stop him.

The Black Orchid withered.

TWENTY-ONE

Desperate Gambols

The first thing John Bouvier III did was to embark on a drinking binge.

Never before had he sunk so low. Sitting in his Manhattan apartment, with the most disgraceful failure of his life staring him in the face, Jack would not forgive himself or forget.

The most destructive episode in his life was short-lived. A few days after the wedding, while honeymooning in Acapulco, Jackie wrote him a letter which probably saved his life. She must have known just how vital it was for him to hear from her.

Jackie wrote to him sweetly, in a tone of obvious affection and deeply ingrained respect. She told him she loved him and that she understood how low he must have felt, and the incredible pressure which the wedding situation had placed on his shoulders. Most important, as far as she was concerned, although Hughdie Auchincloss had walked down the aisle with her, it was really John Vernou Bouvier III who had given her away.

Having a daughter as wonderful as Jackie, Jack wondered at once how in hell he had ever lost his dignity. At any rate, he regained it that moment, knocked off the drinking, and in a slightly less wild manner continued carrying on in the best tradition of his youth.

The sixty-two-year-old aristocrat roué continued to maintain a truly beautiful physique. Though he may not have been rich, for all that anyone could say he always looked rich and acted the part. As always, there were hundreds of calls from beautiful young women eager for his company.

But now, there were no New York Society women among them. Jack's "girls" by and large were working women who held decent jobs and were using their careers to establish themselves socially. Besides Jack's undeniable sex appeal, which carried forward unimpaired into his seventh decade, and his expensive and exquisitely tailored clothing, he had the markings of a gentleman. He was Yale and urbane New York to the core.

What woman turns down the opportunity to be courted by a true nobleman? Jack's pedigree was well known throughout the right circles in New York, and he had the family coats of arms to prove it. For women he was especially keen on, Jack had gold signet rings made up at Tiffany's. In fact, during the 1950s, he had many dozens of them ordered.

To all of those distinctions, a new one was added. Jack was now the father-in-law of one of the nation's brightest young senators. He swore that one day his daughter would be First Lady.

Not long after the sale of Lasata, a bitterness developed between Jack and his sisters. Not that he truly believed they had any choice in the matter. But he felt that something more should have been done. And as head of the Bouvier family, he had been powerless to save it.

Before his daughters were married, Jack had once more rented a cottage on the dunes for them to share with him. Under ordinary circumstances, it would have been wonderful. But with the ghost of Lasata standing around the corner, Jack was too painfully reminded of all that he had lost.

The cemetery at St. Philomena's was all too close, and those he had loved too far away. Painful memories seemed to seep up from the ground. Most of the gravestones in the little cemetery nestled in the woods bore the names of people he had known. Six bodies rested in the Bouvier plot— the remains of people who had meant a great deal to him. Bud, Maude, the Major, the first John Vernou Bouvier, his wife Carrie and his sister—all of them lay there.

All in all, there was room for an additional sixty-four bodies. He had begun lately to wonder when he would join them.

Paul Yuska, the family gardener at Lasata, had recently died and was buried just east of the Bouvier family plot.

A stone's throw from where the Major lay, old man Lee was buried in regal splendor. Certainly, no love had been lost between Jack's "Fa" and his old nemesis, Janet's father. Ironically, they had each chosen a family plot at the entrance to the cemetery; the two plots reposing parallel on either side of the path leading in.

It wasn't just the cemetery and Lasata that upset Jack about East Hampton. It seemed as though every little thing about the village in some way called to mind a happier time in his own life. Hearing the whistle of the train pulling into the East Hampton Station, he could remember springing off the same train on weekends long ago, young and virile and handsome in his gabardines, back when his life with Janet was fresh and good. Always, she would bring his beloved daughters there to meet him.

Animals walking on the street would remind Jack of King Phar, "the best damn dog in the world." Now, even Jackie's beloved Danseuse was gone. He still rented horses from the Woolnough stables down the road, but here the memories of Jack's own horses just grew stronger.

A short distance from the stables was the East Hampton

Riding Club. There, "Jack's Ladies' Hunt Team" had frequently swept off into the rolling terrain, looking svelte and lovely in their trim and immaculate boots as they galloped by their admiring host.

Seeking refuge in the Maidstone Club, Jack found it had grown larger. Less exclusive but also somehow more impersonal. He still had a million-dollar tan to show off, but there seemed to be no one who cared. The vast majority of members were now strangers to him. The few remaining old-timers really were old by then—or rapidly aging.

To the end of his days, Jack's handsome and manly appearance never failed to cause a stir. He never lost his looks, and the Maidstone women who had known him in better days recalled all of his little idiosyncrasies lovingly, exaggerating the importance they had had in his life, on occasion creating relationships that never really had occurred.

Those smiling time-worn faces brought no joy to Jack. They made it far too clear that old age was catching up with his generation.

Jack didn't give up East Hampton entirely. On occasion he would still rent a room at the Sea Spray Inn, but the visits rubbed salt on the wound of his loss. His trips to East Hampton tapered off.

Instead, Jack started making extended trips to Havana. Cuba was still in the hands of the sybaritic Batista. Of course, the man was a brutal dictator to his own people. But he understood the importance of the tourist trade and worked to make his tiny island nation the playground of the Western World.

It was just the spot for Jack! He made a lasting impression on the girls who ran the passenger service of Pan American Airways in Miami, the jumping-off place en route to Havana. He went on to become quite friendly with many of them. As a result, Jack never had any problem getting onto a Pan Am flight to or from Cuba. No king could have faulted the kind of service he received!

Havana abounded in casinos and nightclubs, and Jack made many Cuban friends who joined him night after night going from one to the next. There were some lowdown joints in Havana as well, where anything went as far as the floor shows were concerned. Few Americans failed to see at least one of those in their travels to Havana. I know Miche and I didn't miss one of them during our honeymoon there, and I doubt that Jack did either.

One of Jack's closest companions in Cuba was a young and devastatingly beautiful woman from a quite influential family there. Beyond merely giving him their blessing, the family embraced him as one of their own and provided him with entree into all of the exclusive clubs in the city.

Through them, he became accepted into Havana's extremely closed society circles. Perhaps he was never quite aware of just how great an honor that was, how rare it is for North Americans truly to break into Latin American society.

For the aging Black Prince, Havana seemed the answer to a lost dream. Beyond the universal respect he commanded, nowhere was there more fun for the asking. Day and night, he and his companions went to the race track, or to jai alai matches. The night life could easily match New York.

Perhaps to his own astonishment, Jack discovered that Cuba could never replace Long Island. He needed to be with his family. Much as he hated to admit it, Jack lived to see his children, and missed the places which held such haunting memories for him.

Being the fighter that he was, Jack refused to admit his own human needs for a long time, throwing himself more furiously into debauchery in Havana. His mad gaiety there became pretense as his homesickness grew.

Finally, Jack boarded a plane and headed back to his two-bedroom apartment and Esther. His visits to Cuba ended.

Upon returning home, Jack spent most of his time in the apartment, devoting his energy to his second occupation, betting. The finances between Jack and Esther became impossibly complex, and unravelling them also took a great deal of time. An accounting as of early 1954 read as follows:

Esther:
(1) Check for July, 1952 wages dated June 30th of '53 and which received cash from me in the amount of the check of $122 as acknowledged by you on said check.
(2) $300 paid by me to Culver Holiday for purchase of Room Number Eight.—This would take care of August '52 wages, check of $145.00, and September '52 wages check for like amount making a total of $290.00
(3) I am making out now a check to your order in the sum of $127.00 which would represent wages for October, '52 (Less $10.00 from purchase money, less $8.00 for new room rent on room eight for August '53.)
(4) That will leave me owing you a check for November and December '53 wages as well as for the first eight months of '53.
(5) Check drawn to Esther Lindstrom for $285.00 less $5.00 for my payments (This is for months November and December '52 plus incidental expenses to date, January '54.)

J. V. Bouvier III

Equally complex, but far more bitter, were Jack's accountings made to his sister Edith. At the time of the Major's death, Jack had been given responsibility of her account, plus the $65,000 which her father had left her *in trust*—a parting shot.

Of course, she called him virtually every day when he was home, just as Edith had always done. But after Maude's death Edith had become somewhat of a recluse. Living in her own little world, doing what she wanted, and believing herself happy. Perhaps she was.

But the extended withdrawal had also put her out of touch with reality. Particularly because she couldn't get her fingers on the trust fund, Edith went into long tirades against Jack on the phone, accusing him of tampering with her money. Of course, as a broker, Jack was actively trading his younger sister's stocks in her best interests. When she made a profit, she kept it. When she took a loss, Jack personally covered it out of his pocket.

"Jack, you are using my money and it's just not right!" she would shout time and again. In a thousand different ways, he would go through the transactions and her profits trade by trade—as only a broker with forty years of experience can. Still she persisted in calling him a thief.

Because Jack's brokerage was not doing all that well, the accusations seemed particularly vicious. But with staggering patience and love for his misguided sister, Jack allowed her to continue to call and heap abuse on him. Years before, when the family reluctantly admitted that Phelan Beale had good reason for leaving Edith, only Jack and Maude had stood by her, placing the blame squarely on Phelan's shoulders and going stone deaf when solid evidence of his sister's misbehavior was produced.

Now Jack once again ignored all of the reasons he had for telling her to "Get off the goddamn phone" once and for all.

He was becoming a bit of a recluse as well, and perhaps that made Jack sensitive to his sister's plight in isolation.

In the meantime, we had written Jack to inform him that we would be returning to the United States. Having spent many happy years in Ecuador, Chile and Peru, neither Miche nor I had the slightest desire to return to the States. But, as I explained in the letter, our son Michie, couldn't— or wouldn't—speak English and snubbed the company of all Americans in favor of Ecuadorians.

In addition, we felt that Michie should know something of his native land. Nonetheless, we postponed the return as long as possible. But with the pending birth of our second child—if he was a boy, we would name him "John Vernou" in honor of Jack—we could delay no longer.

In a typically laconic reply, Jack said he was thrilled that we were returning. Likewise the naming of the child. However, he would be damned if he was going to be "Jr." to a newborn.

We agreed to amend the name to "John Vernou Bouvier IV" and began packing up for the return trip.

TWENTY-TWO

Declining

After our return to the States, Miche went to work for Grumman Aircraft Engineering Corp. in Long Island, and we bought a house in Remsenburg—a half-hour drive from Lasata.

At the time of our arrival, a potential catastrophe was brewing. East Hampton is full of summer people who bring their pets and then abandon them to nature. The animals are too domesticated to survive on their own, and must depend upon kindness from strangers to eat.

Edith and Edie, living in seclusion at Grey Gardens, had begun feeding some stray cats. Unfortunately, before Edith could think to have the females spayed, barrels of kittens made their appearance and the situation got out of hand. Cats have a great proclivity for incest, and any of them that will stand still for a moment are fair game. Grey Gardens became the site of one massive feline orgy. The neighbors complained as the population continued to explode. As far as everyone in the family was concerned, Edith could not be reasoned with—so it would be left to her to have the situation and her cats altered, or face the wrath of an incensed East Hampton Village Association.

Neither the mother nor her namesake daughter saw anything wrong with having fifty or sixty cats. They intended to do nothing but have more kittens. Taking up his sister's cause, Jack declared that he didn't see anything wrong with it either. Nonetheless, he girded his loins and, dragging me and Miche along, made a trip to East Hampton to see what could be done to keep the two Ediths out of harm.

Although Edith immediately launched into an attack of her older brother's invasion of privacy on basic principles, she was clearly amenable to our interference. And more than a bit relieved.

Rounding up the dozens of cats after painful and devious hours of hunting, we managed to get an indifferent animal shelter to take them off our hands. Returning home, we shared a delightful bottle of champagne to celebrate the successful campaign.

A truly sentimental soul, Edith had kept just a few favorites hidden in an overstuffed laundry basket in one back closet. Par for the course, they were unspayed females. Within several years, she was in the same predicament she had faced before our rescue mission to the wilds of East Hampton in the dead of winter.

It would be a long time before the Bouviers once again ventured under strong community pressure to bail the Ediths out. And by the time it was accomplished, the engineers were Princess Lee Radziwill and Jacqueline Onassis.

Shortly after we removed the cats my son John was born. It was a disgracefully long time before we had "Jayvie" christened. In fact, our friends teased us that he would be walking to church if we delayed much longer. As it turned out, they weren't far from wrong!

We finally decided it had to be done and arranged for the ceremony to be held in a tiny Catholic church in Center Moriches, a village just west of Remsenburg.

Our friend and neighbor, Monsignor Charles Berming-ham, would be the officiating priest. Our good friend, Paul Divine, was to be godfather, and Jackie would be god-mother. Jack, Jackie and the twins were first to arrive in a convoy of limousines. Then Emmy drove up with Paul Di-vine from Washington.

After months of depression, Jack was looking fantastic and feeling in fine spirits. At once, all of the old bitterness was forgotten. As far as Michelle, Maude, Emmy and Jack were concerned, Lasata was still just around the corner. Just in case we didn't have any, Jack had brought along a pitcher of excellently mixed Bloody Marys.

The great uncle's namesake was brought out and Jack proposed a toast, grinning from ear to ear with pride.

Standing side by side, Jack and Emmy still made a stun-ning couple in their middle years. Nor had they grown one bit more compatible in forty years.

While Emmy had married Carlisle Allan after Bud's death, Jack never filled the void left by the divorce from Janet. At sixty-three, he appeared to have no intention of remarrying. Miche and I were worried about him, spending all of his time on the floor of the Exchange or at his apart-ment and not getting out enough.

But marriage would never have been the answer. It was a union which always petrified the most stalwart males among the Bouviers. MC, who was charming and handsome and virile, was a prime example. He never took the plunge. Years later, Maude Davis managed to corner him and ask him why. MC's answer was that every time he had consid-ered proposing to a girl, he walked once around the block. By the time he made it all the way around, he had come to his senses.

There was something of that in Jack, too. He was leery of remarrying and would "take a walk" whenever he was drawn too close to the altar. In later years, by concentrating on women who were not really up to his social or intellectual standard, he removed the potential threat.

It had never ceased to amaze me how fundamentally indifferent Jack was toward the women who flitted in and out of his life. He truly did not care about most of them, beyond their physical attributes. He would answer phone calls from other women when the date-of-the-moment was at the apartment. For any one of these women to assume that she would one day be Jack's wife would have been pure lunacy.

Now I suddenly recognized a new facet to his string of emotionless encounters. Watching Jack beside his adored and beautiful daughter, I could have no doubt that he was capable of loving very deeply. By going out with women who were valueless in his eyes, Jack had ensured that he would never again marry.

But today, as we drove out to Center Moriches, Jack's loneliness seemed a thing of the past. Monsignor Bermingham was waiting at the church, looking totally transformed from the hard laughing, easygoing man across the street we all knew. With one solemn sweep of his robed arms, he greeted us and led us into the church.

When it was time for the holy water to be poured over little Jayvie's head, I flinched, remembering the grueling time we had had with Michie when he was christened at St. Patrick's Cathedral on a bitter, freezing day. As the icy water streamed over his head, Michie screamed bloody murder, and kept right on screaming. Now, as Jackie held my secondborn in her arms, I waited for the screams.

Instead, Monsignor Bermingham spoke up once more. Turning to the party, he whispered, "In compliance with Mrs. Bouvier's wishes, the holy water in this fountain has been heated." I had told him the story of Michie's baptism, and he had listened much more attentively than I had ever intended him to!

Grinning an infectious grin, he slowly began baptizing the baby that Jackie held out to him so tenderly. John appreciated the warm water and gurgled appreciatively. And Jackie, clutching the wet little head to her bosom, looked no less enraptured by the sensation. It would be two years before Caroline was born.

All in all, it had been a wonderful ceremony. Rarely were the Bouviers united in those days. And when they were, it was generally not nearly so congenial. From that day on, Jack's interest in the boy who bore his name never diminished. He kept close tabs on his progress, called him "the brightest boy an uncle could ask for," and showered him with a deluge of terribly extravagant presents on every likely occasion.

After we all returned to the house, Jackie took off for a while to visit one of our neighbors, whose bulldog bitch had just had a litter of puppies. For a long time, Jackie had been looking for the right dog for her father. She confided to me her own fear that he needed companionship. To see a man like Black Jack unhappy in his old age was more than either of us could bear.

Since he was in the area, Jack insisted on driving home by way of East Hampton. This time, he was clearly devastated. As soon as the car pulled into the village, he caught sight of a group of old-timers in floppy hats. The East Hampton Garden Club? But now, the most spectacular garden for miles—his own beloved Maude's Italian garden—had been dug under.

He might have almost wept. The changes he had only half admitted before had now grown too obvious to deny. So many people he loved were gone—Bud, Paul Yuska, Maude . . . even little Pauline, his unquestioningly devoted nursemaid, with her Teutonic virtue and lifelong loyalty—had died.

In vain he tried to spot a reminder of their fading glory—a Locomobile, a Lincoln Zephyr, a smile of recognition from a pedestrian. Sadly, he conceded that the last traces had vanished. Lasata, the stable, the magnificent machines.

They all belonged to a bygone era. And all had passed to other hands.

Several weeks later, Jack sold his seat on the Stock Exchange. To his great disappointment, even that had lost its worth. Back in 1929, seats on the Exchange had sold for over $600,000. He received only $90,000.

It was no longer necessary to make the daily mad dash into a taxi, sweating as it swerved downtown and across toward Wall Street. In fact, there was little reason to leave the apartment at all.

The phone still rang. The girls were still in constant supply. There was no dearth of companionship to be had. But those who persisted in pursuing him had to be content to spend their dates in the apartment. There was no chance of Jack taking them out to dinner or a show. Nor even for a stroll. Having had a surplus of such companionship his entire life, it was actually becoming uncomfortable for him now, and he appreciated the rare evenings when his admirers gave him a well-earned rest.

He could not adjust to the loss of the frenetic pace he had always maintained. Without a seat to trade from on Wall Street, Jack's need to gamble took the form of intensified betting with Esther. Together, he and Esther covered every conceivable activity with their bets. The biggest winner was his domestic, who accumulated a quite sizeable wad of money, which she continued to liberally hand out to anyone in the family who needed it. Jack didn't fare nearly so well, although in actuality he had never dipped below the level where he could do whatever he wanted in life.

Their machinations over accounts receivable from one another grew even more absorbing. For days at a time, they would wrangle over pennies in an effort to keep the wagers, wages, and expenses in order. Despite the fact that they kept terribly accurate written accounts of the slightest exchange of money between them, they remained at odds over the bottom line.

In days past, the rest of us had had a million laughs about Jack and Esther's wheelings and dealings. Particularly because they could never manage to come to a mutually satisfactory resolution. But now, with nothing of true import to distract them, the way in which both parties became thoroughly engrossed in their parody banking system became cause for concern.

Soon after selling his seat on the Exchange, Jack made up a last will and testament. Like an old horse with one foot in the glue factory, Jack seemed to be giving up hope.

All through the hard times, it was hope that buoyed the Black Prince, kept him laughing, striving, winning. When the resistance grew unbearable and any other man would just have thrown in the towel, Jack never had. Screwing up his lips into that bold, almost mocking half-smile, he just never seemed to know when to quit.

Without the will to go on, he started to crumble.

Everyone who cared about Jack watched in silent horror.

He had always been concerned about his health, his appearance and his vitality. Now Jack was focusing entirely on illness. He became consumed by concern about disease, both real and imaginary. Most of his conversation was devoted to his bursitis, his excruciating sinuses, and other pains which seemed to be attacking him from all sides as the man within softened and surrendered to the onslaught.

Jack's obsession with disease reached the point where there was an element of abnormality to it. He drank heavily during the day and relied on sleeping pills to get to sleep at night. It was a routine which was poisoning him, and no one could bring him to change it.

The only light in Jack's miserable life were visits from the children—Jackie and Lee, and to some extent Miche. He wanted to be with his daughters more and felt that they were deserting him altogether.

Lee at the time was living in London and could hardly have commuted back and forth across the Atlantic. As for Jackie, she was a senator's wife to begin with—a role which demanded considerable time and energy. Besides, at that time Jack Kennedy was also ill, lying in the hospital and fighting for his life after an operation on his injured back. Jackie was with him constantly, comforting him and encouraging him in his revision of *Profiles in Courage*.

Miche and I were busy adjusting to life back in the States, and getting used to raising two sons. Although we knew that Jack needed more company, our hands were tied just holding together our own life. The rift between Jack and the twins over Lasata had once again widened till now they were no longer on speaking terms.

That left Edith as the only relative who could spend time with Jack on a regular basis. But she remained in East Hampton, needing far more than she could ever give, and Jack was left to Esther.

Nothing she could do snapped Jack out of his downward spiral. Suddenly, his physical decline was seeming very real. Mentally, Jack was deteriorating as well.

All day now, he sat inside the apartment, betting, listening to the radio, and trying to escape from the memories which were haunting him.

Now, more than ever, he listened to his favorite recording on the phonograph. It was Johnny Mercer singing "I Guess I'll Have to Change My Plans." As the muted trumpets wailed and invisible fingers swept across the piano keys, Jack would drum his tired fingers on the table, listening to the voice croon

> *. . . I think I'll crawl right back into my shell*
> *Dwelling in my personal hell . . .*
> *Oh, I guess I'll have to change my plan around,*
> *I've lost the one girl I've found . . .*

Once a day, Jack would find a detour out of his misery. The vehicle of his escape from reality was a television show. A Western.

Every week, without fail, Jack tuned in to *Gunsmoke*. Something in the character of Matt Dillon appealed to him. The bad guy always got what was coming to him and the good guy always won. There were no grey areas in that universe.

Eccentric as it might have seemed, Jack's devotion to the show was not hard to understand. The world in 1957 was a confusing and hostile place. For all of the record-breaking of the postwar decade, it had amounted to nothing more than technological advance. Impressive as it was, Sputnik's speed record did not have one iota of the courage of the Wright Brothers' first flight.

Nor did the Russian satellite have one bit of the charisma and charm with which Lindbergh had stolen the hearts of an entire nation. Maybe Lindy *was* a cardboard champion, adored by a superficial and decadent generation. But, untouched by the cares and needs of a world in distress, their lives had been filled with glamor and caprice, opulence and starry-eyed hope.

In 1957, all that remained of that world were fragments, and tired remnants like Jack. On March 11, Admiral Byrd, the last of the great explorer-adventurers, died.

Perhaps Marshal Dillon would be the last hero to go.

TWENTY-THREE

Sleep Well, Sweet Prince

After months of vegetating, Jack suddenly snapped back. Within a matter of days, he had made a total recovery.

One night, he was sitting at home with Esther, brooding over the television set and drinking his vodka. The next night, he got dressed to the teeth and escorted a beautiful friend to dinner and to the premiere of *West Side Story*.

Almost nightly from then on, he made an appearance at the Polo Club of the Westbury Hotel. Once more his favorite table at the Stork Club was reserved for his arrival in the wee hours. Jack even started commuting to Havana again, renewing close friendships and enjoying himself immensely.

No one could understand the sudden change in his lifestyle. But whatever the cause, we were all delighted! The old Jack was back, like Lazarus from the dead. And with him returned all of the charm and zest for life everyone had missed.

From one Bouvier to the next, the word went around. Everyone heaved a sigh of relief. Once again, we could discuss his life with a bit of awe mixed with amusement, instead of worrying about his sad state.

Jack and Esther's lives still centered around the sporadic visits of Jackie or Lee, but at last they seemed to have something more than that to hope for. With Jack's new vitality, his youthful looks and legendary handsomeness once more made themselves evident. His deep tan was carefully baked on as spring turned to summer, until it approached the black depths of its greatest glory.

Just when everything was going so well, Jack once again began to complain about his health. But this time, he would not let it interfere with having a good time. And seeing her employer carrying on from morning to morning, going out and laughing constantly—and most of all, once again winning bets left and right—Esther humored him and sewed more flannel pads onto the shoulders of his light cotton pajamas to ease the agony of his bursitis. Having watched him sink into hypochondria once, she refused to let him do it again.

Persisting in his belief that he was gravely ill, Jack went so far as to visit a famous cancer clinic in New York for a gruelingly thorough medical examination. It revealed exactly what Esther had thought. Jack was as healthy as a horse. His bill of health was immaculate.

A week later, it became evident to Esther that Jack was definitely not imagining it. He collapsed and she had to rush him to the hospital.

By the time Jack was admitted to the emergency room, Esther was on the phone. I was at home in Remsenburg when she called. Her voice was trembling, and in her distress she was having difficulty forming the words in English. When she finally assembled a sentence, she stumbled over the words, garbling them incomprehensibly.

"I don't understand!" I shouted, trying to calm her down. "Now tell me slowly what's the matter. What's wrong?"

"It's Mr. Jack," she answered breathlessly. "I had to take him. To the hospital. Mr. Michel must come quick. I think he's really sick!"

I hung up and called Miche at work, while Esther called Jackie and sent a telegram to Lee. Miche dropped everything and raced home to pick me up. Esther, with her terribly practical mind, would never dream of crying wolf.

Generally, the drive to New York takes two hours. That day, we virtually cut the time in half. We rode in comparative silence, both Miche and I too frightened about what we might find at the hospital to risk talking about it. We did not doubt for a second that Esther was right. Jack had to be very, very ill.

Arriving at the hospital in record time, we parked the car and ran into the lobby. There we stood for what seemed an interminable length of time while a yawning and self-important grey-haired woman took her time finding the number of Jack's room. Having located it, she fielded several calls, chatted with a nurse or two, then offhandedly divulged the information we wanted.

The deadly silence, the antiseptic smell, the nauseating green—all of them hit me as we stood at the elevator bank, waiting. Beyond hating hospitals, I had always been terrified of them. The thousand doctors and nurses who stare at you with knowing eyes out of a sea of white uniforms.

But most awful of all, there is the attitude that says they somehow really do play God, putting themselves into the postures of giving life or taking it away. I had seen them out of their spotless uniforms too many times to be impressed by their stance of infallibility.

Upstairs, Jack was lying in a narrow bed. Lying against the bleached linens, his skin no longer looked black. Instead, it seemed clouded by a sickly, greyish film.

Although he heard us come in, Jack seemed unable to locate the source of the noise, turning his head with difficulty until he found us in front of him. Breaking into a shy grin, he whispered, "Miche . . ."

For a moment there was silence as Jack put out his hand and Miche grabbed onto it tightly, fighting back tears. Then Jack caught sight of me and, with all of the relief of a frightened child when it spots a familiar face in a sea of strangers, he said, "Caffy?"

I held out my hand to him and he grabbed it in turn. He held it tentatively, a confused look on his face. Then he began to clutch and unclutch my small offer of comfort. He searched my face, looking for something that wasn't there. He looked into my eyes and asked, "Jackie?" asking me if that's who I was.

Before I could answer, he softly let go my hand, smiled a little and died.

For a moment I just stared. I think I whispered, "Jack is dead." It seemed inconceivable, wrong. He was far too vital a human being to just die before our eyes. Gay, happy-go-lucky Jack. The source of so much love . . . *and* so much resentment.

Through a blur of tears, I looked up and saw Jackie standing there, her face as pale as fine parchment. Behind her stood Jack Kennedy, his tall frame outlined by the deadly white walls of the room.

They had missed being at Jack's side the moment before he died. Esther's message had reached them in Boston just a few seconds too late.

Too aggrieved for words, the four of us huddled around him. At length a nurse came and motioned us out of the room. Glancing back one last time, I saw Jack lying peacefully propped up against the pillow. Still smiling quietly out of the corner of his mouth. The old familiar smile, but without the half-mocking quality this time.

It was as though he were sleeping, dreaming happily, waiting to awaken. Refreshed and full of hope, ready to spring into one more glorious day.

Reluctantly, I trailed after the others as they headed for the elevators. There were five of us in the elevator, as the doors closed and shut us all out of Jack's life. In addition to the Kennedys, Miche and myself, was the emergency ward doctor who had admitted Jack earlier.

He explained that Jack had died of cancer of the liver. He said the words matter-of-factly and seemed not to realize the effect they would have on us. As a doctor dealing with sudden death on a daily basis, perhaps the horror of its impact no longer affected him. But all I could think of was the week of agony Jack must have gone through between the time he first went to a clinic because he felt the cancer rampaging through his body, and his final minutes in the hospital bed.

For Miche and Jackie, the shock and sudden loss of him were almost unbearable.

Pausing to catch his breath, the high-strung doctor then went on to ask if he could whisk Jack down for an autopsy, to study his skin, because the pigmentation was so fascinating!

I stood there gaping in horror as the man discussed the procedure—as if Black Jack Bouvier were some guinea pig in a biology lab.

Jackie did not even dignify him with a reply.

We rode down in stony silence.

TWENTY-FOUR

The Last Rite

For Miche, the worst part of all was going to inspect Jack's body once the morticians had gotten through with him. Instead of heightening his beautiful black tan, they had tried to disguise it with flesh-colored make-up. They forced his mouth into the kind of sickly sweet smile Jack would never have been caught dead in. They hadn't even bothered to trim his pencil-thin moustache.

Anything was better than seeing the man who was almost a father to him, disgraced like that. Years before, when he had spent time with his friend, the mortician at his working place in Arizona, Miche had learned something about the gruesome art. Now, erasing the New York morticians' hideous handicraft, Michel devoted himself to restoring Jack to his beautiful self so that he could be buried right.

Miche was disconsolate to the point where no one could help him. Neither could he abandon himself to his mourning: the next few days had to be devoted entirely to funeral arrangements.

First of all, there was the matter of the will. Jack's estate amounted to roughly a quarter of a million dollars. As far as he was concerned, he died a virtual pauper.

While that was obviously not the case by anyone else's standards, his obituary in the *Times*, impressive as it should have been, led people to think he was at least as wealthy as his uncle MC had been. And no poorer than Joseph Kennedy.

Together with Maude's husband, John Davis, Miche set out to buy Jack's coffin. As head of the Bouvier family, it was a duty he could not relegate to anyone else. Arriving at a store on Manhattan's East Side, they were greeted at the door by a mousey little man in a dark suit and an insincere look of solicitude on his round face.

Upon hearing the name John Vernou Bouvier III, he remarked that he had read the obituary and had known the name. Shaking his head sadly, the little man led them into a special display room where the most expensive coffins reposed. Pointing out one constructed of rosewood, with ostentatious gold handles decorating the sides, he showed them all of its features. Of course, as he explained, they would also need a lead container for the coffin to protect it, covered in turn by a concrete outer box.

Beyond a doubt, Miche realized that the unattractive little man was taking advantage of their grief. To get right to the point, he asked how much the entire thing would cost.

The salesman didn't bat an eyelash as he looked Miche in the eye and casually mentioned a price in the vicinity of $10,000.

Calmly but firmly, Miche asked to see less expensive models.

In response the salesman shot him a look which was clearly intended to shame him for stooping to question price at a time like that, when nothing but the best should have been considered.

Backed by John Davis, Miche stood his ground. No one was going to exploit the fact of Jack's death. He had personally attended to the body to see that it was done right. He would do no less for the coffin. The Black Orchid would go out in style, all right! But not by virtue of some shoddy funeral parlor notion of class.

By the time of Jack's funeral there remained only a few dozen friends and associates to attend it, some of whom we recognized from the floor of the Exchange, others by their college ties. For all of his vanity and pride, Jack never had been a snob, and intermingled with the wealthy Social Register mourners was a crowd of everyday acquaintances there to pay their last respects.

And then there was the row of ladies in mourning, sitting side by side in the rear of the church.

After the funeral ceremony, we drove down to East Hampton in a limousine with the twins and Esther. The ride seemed endless, and the conversation was thin. Although Jackie had decided that we should make it as joyous as possible—which was the way Jack would have wanted to go—there was not a trace of gaiety among us.

From time to time, the twins would alternate quick, disjointed phrases about anything but what was on our minds. But they could not succeed in banishing the reality of Jack's death.

In silence, Esther sat clutching her gnarled hands in her lap. Beneath her veiled eyes, I saw one tear slip down onto her cheek. Ever since I had known her, I had always thought of Esther as ageless. At once she seemed old and brittle, many years showing in the network of lines carved into her face.

I touched her hand and she struggled to give me a tiny and brave smile. The next moment, her face once again registered a blank demeanor. Jack and Esther had grown so dependent on one another that it was impossible to imagine her without him. I wondered if she had been able to think of how life would be now—where it could lead now that Jack was dead and she was alone.

From that day on, Jackie looked after Esther's well-being and provided for her comfort as much as possible. Naturally, the most valuable things she could never give her. Later, when Esther was struck and killed by a car while crossing a street, I had to wonder if she had seen it coming and decided not to move out of the way.

Jackie, Lee and Jack Kennedy were already at the cemetery, having flown down in a helicopter. Jackie had a controlled, almost remote look of tightly restrained emotion. Only her mouth would not be reined in. It was drawn up with a vulnerable, hurt look. Constantly on the verge of crying, she never once did. Not in public.

It was a hot August day. The sun danced on the leaves of the copper beech—grown old and full now—and played between the deep shadows it cast on the Bouvier headstones.

As we stood there with its rays pouring down on us, everyone suddenly seemed to brighten. It was a day for playing in the surf. The type of day made for Jack. To lie under the sun's scorching rays—looking great and knowing it. It simply was not a day for sadness.

A gentle breeze stirred the bachelor buttons mingled with bright yellow daisies. They had been ordered by Jackie to transform her father's coffin into a miniature spring garden.

There would be no drabness at Black Jack Bouvier's funeral. Jackie's glamorous, debonair father was buried in such a way that you had to smile, remembering above all the life-loving and colorful man that he had been.

A small gust of wind rustled in the tree limbs above the grave. One rich-hued red leaf fluttered down and landed on the coffin as if it were an emissary of the tree, welcoming Jack to its shelter.

As the sun beat down, the stark demarcations on the headstones seemed to stand out in its glare. Maude, the

Major, his young sister, Bud, Jack's grandparents. All of them were waiting for him in that familiar spot.

A horse's hoofs beat down on the dirt of the country road flanking the graveyard. Then the sound disappeared, receding in the direction of Lasata. The whistle of a Long Island Railroad train moaned with melancholy yearning. Out of habit, I checked my watch. It was late, as usual.

Far away, a group of children were howling with laughter. Jack would have liked that happy sound touching the air. If he could have been anything in the world but Jack Bouvier, then it would have been the god Pan—a free spirit—a satyr gamboling to the tunes of his pipe—taking his full share of the pleasure and denying harsh realities that often enough intruded upon his careless joys.

The bachelor buttons and daisies were removed from Jack's coffin as it was lowered into the ground. In the breeze, their petals waved a chorus of goodbyes, as the greatest bachelor there ever was sank out of sight.

We turned and left, scattering each in his own direction.

TWENTY-FIVE

First Lady

Dear Jack! How I wish he had lived a little longer. Long enough to see his beautiful grandchildren born, and to share some of the glamor which his daughters brought to his name.

Not long after Jack's burial, Caroline Kennedy was born. By the time she came of college age—if it was not too great a shock—she might even have chosen to go to his old alma mater, Yale.

It was only a matter of months before Lee's marriage to Michael Canfield was annulled. When she remarried, it was to Prince Stanislaus Radziwill, the son of Prince Janusz of Poland, who in his time had been one of that nation's first citizens before being deposed by the communists. While Stas, whose name was pronounced like the Bouvier's "Stache," was born into a title only—all of his hereditary lands having been confiscated—it was enough.

Moving to England, Prince Stanislaus entered the construction and real estate trades. He made a greater than considerable fortune. Besides being a superlative human being, decent in every sense of the word, Stas brought Lee into the realm of the super-rich, as well as into the aristocracy.

Jack did not live to learn that Jack Kennedy was going to enter the primaries for the 1960 presidential election. As far as he was concerned, Jackie had always been First Lady. In January of 1961, I could just imagine him standing near Jackie on the official platform as Jack Kennedy—with close-cropped hair—took the oath of office and became the 35th President of the United States.

Now that Jackie was officially First Lady, all of his faith and years of bragging were justified before the eyes of the world. Moreover, from that point on, he could have boasted about his daughter's accomplishments to his heart's content. Not a soul would ever have been bored.

If Jack had lived, I am certain he would have become nearly as famous as Jackie. He could never have been a run-of-the-mill father of a First Lady, secreted obscurely somewhere in the background. Jack always stood out. Perhaps he would have caused difficulties, but never could he have been ignored.

A personality as distinguished as Jack's was certain to provide good copy for the news hounds. In the style of the dashing figure spotted at the White House, at the Stork Club or "21," I can imagine hopeful thousands of older men sitting under sunlamps until they were toasted to a deep golden brown. Pin stripe suits might have come back into vogue that much sooner. Likewise striped club ties and gabardine suits with the cuffs rolled up.

You could not put it past Black Jack Bouvier to single-handedly engineer the return of gambling, horse races and the pursuit of women in a romantic manner as the order of the day.

With Jack in the papers, there is no question that laughter and fun would have sliced into the deadly serious mood of the early sixties. Anyone who tried to tame the old boy down in order to enhance the image of the First Family would have found it rough going. Particularly if he was a Democrat!

Mavericks across the nation would have rejoiced in their relief, knowing that there was one of *them* out there, dedicated to enjoying life, appreciating its seriousness with a good sense of humor. Jack would have taken a lot of abuse from the added notoriety, but then again, he always had. And carried on without the least hesitation!

The day of Jack Kennedy's inauguration, Jack Bouvier wasn't there. With a touch of pride to be among those who *had* survived to witness it, I watched President Eisenhower and President-elect Kennedy and their families seated in their allotted chairs, snugly warm on the platform specially erected for this occasion.

No man would ever have been prouder to sit there than Jack Bouvier. For a second, I caught a glimpse of his familiar form, strutting proud as a peacock across the stage. Then I realized that it was just one more suntanned dignitary.

For days before the ceremony, the city of Washington had been pelted with snow. Par for the course in the nation's capital, the streets had not been cleared. The icy slush was piled so high that people wearing short boots—as I was—got it down the neck of the boot. It was like walking around barefoot on a soft carpet of wet ice.

The night before the inauguration, some member of the government had woken up to the fact that something had to be done. The procession from the Capitol to the White House could not take place, because Pennsylvania Avenue was covered with snow.

Despite the fact that Washington does have severe winter weather, there was virtually no useable snow removal equipment on hand.

With eleventh-hour desperation, army troops equipped with flame throwers were dispatched to the rescue. Taking arms against the sea of snow, they drove it back. At last, Pennsylvania Avenue was clear. The other intersecting streets, however, which had been close to impassable before the advance of the troops, were now coated with a solid layer of ice beneath the snow—run-off from the flames.

In spite of a great deal of trouble, Miche and I did manage

to arrive at the stands, just in the nick of time. The rest of the invited family members were already there in Section C, facing the official stand. Side by side, we huddled under our fur and woolen coats and fought a losing battle to stay half warm.

The Capitol dome looked terribly impressive shrouded in the snow. But the austerity of that stern white building rising in the background only seemed to add to the chilly atmosphere. A winter wind blew up from the north, penetrating even the many layers of clothing we were wearing.

A number of invocations by representatives of many religious denominations started the ceremony. The men of God not only had their eyes and hearts tuned to heaven; they were also aware that the earthbound before them were freezing their blessed bottoms off.

The sermons were mercifully short.

Then Robert Frost read a poem he had written in celebration of the occasion. Perhaps it was not the most memorable work he created in his lifetime, but the delicate white-haired man read it with such feeling that it was deeply moving.

We were so spellbound by his voice that it was some time before we noticed the little plume of smoke curling up from the dais where he stood. At first, we thought it was just his breath smoking. Then someone noticed that it was coming from behind the orator. A short circuit had caused an electrical fire on the platform. Seconds after it erupted into flame, a security guard yanked out the microphone plug and the wire stopped sizzling.

Robert Frost hesitated only briefly, then valiantly continued his poem to the end. Appreciative of the verse as they were, the Bouviers were no less engrossed by the flame, irreverently whispering remarks about how nice it would be to warm their hands by.

Marian Anderson sang gloriously. Her beautiful voice filled the space around us, so that for a moment even the numbing cold seemed to vanish.

Her magnificent performance was a hard act to follow.

Nonetheless, it was time for the President-elect to be sworn in. He stood there coatless, his thick hair tossed dramatically by the wind, his blue eyes laughing with the joy of hard-earned victory. The waves of inner confidence he radiated were astounding, like electric sparks arcing out from his body.

The oath of office was administered to Jack as he stood surrounded by the family, friends and countrymen whose lives were being brought under his leadership. As he became President, he showed self-assurance in his own ability.

His famous inaugural address was delivered slowly, with every sentence stressed, to make sure his every word would be understood by all.

The words, "Ask not what your country can do for you . . ." rang out clearly on that bitter cold afternoon. He was giving notice that his administration would not be a clubby institution resting on its laurels. Everyone would be put to the test. The demand for action however small, was universal. It was a great speech, inspiring and reassuring.

Not many of the Bouviers had voted for Jack Kennedy despite the love they all bore him. But Republican as they were, I doubt anyone there had any qualms about the man the nation had chosen.

The impressive ceremony really seemed to be remarkably short, in spite of the frostbite we were all facing. Suddenly the girl I had first met when she was a sixteen-year-old at Farmington had become the wife of the President of the United States. So much responsibility rested on those two slim shoulders!

Looking at her widespread eyes, the defiant jut of her chin and her dark, thick hair, there could be no doubt that Jackie was Jack Bouvier's daughter to the core. Her sweet but firm smile had the same upturned corners which made Black Jack's so very captivating.

But now the disarming young woman wasn't just Jack Bouvier's daughter. She was the wife of the most powerful man in the world. Without her father there to see her take that long stride forward, her bridge to the past and the people in it seemed to fade before our eyes.

She wasn't just Jackie anymore. And never again would she fit into the family as if she were merely one more member.

The United States Marine Corps Band played "The Star-Spangled Banner." By a prearranged announcement, it signalled that the ceremony was over. And time for the Bouviers to dash over to the designated busses which would carry us to the Mayflower Hotel for a special luncheon for the President and First Lady's families, thrown by Joseph Kennedy.

We scurried around in the slush like a collection of beheaded chickens, searching amid the armada of vehicles for the one dedicated to our service. As we rushed forward in the wrong direction, trespassing on a heavily guarded section of the grounds, I found myself at the fore.

Staring ahead, I found my eyes locked in the sights of a row of soldiers, their rifles drawn. They meant business. Zealously defending his President, one young marine was zeroing in on my mid-section.

In a flash, Miche had vaulted over to the guard and straightened the matter out. A moment later, we were escorted to the bus which joined a parade to the Mayflower.

Due to the condition of the roads, many of the guests were late in arriving there. The lunch had been intended as a short affair to begin with. Now we were forced from a slow trot into galloping through the meal. With no time to say "Hello," the two families, like enemy camps, occupied two halves of the room with an aisle proclaimed as "no-man's land" in between. Finding the time to meet any of the Kennedys would have been nigh on to impossible.

The luncheon passed so quickly that not even the Bouviers could make their presence known. As soon as we were seated, the luncheon became an obstacle course to pass through in time for the Inaugural Parade.

We got back into the bus—which was increasingly feeling like home—and were driven to the White House. People were already lined several shoulders deep on Pennsylvania Avenue in anticipation. Spotting our bus, and assuming that we were riding at its vanguard, they began to break out in a cheer. The proudest members of the family nodded quietly and arched their backs, presenting a perfect profile. The more theatrical members bowed graciously to the herd below, deigning to wave back at anyone who saluted them.

We were just about thawed out from the earlier part of the program when it was once again time to face the elements. We found our way to the reserved section of seats beside the Presidential reviewing stand.

As the parade began, we rose every half minute to applaud. Not only because it was marvelous, but because it was probably standing up so frequently that kept us from freezing to death. Every other minute we were also required to stand and salute the flag—another godsend!

The magnificent procession came to a merciful end, and we ducked into the state dining room of the White House. A small reception for some two hundred relatives, family members and political allies was being held. It was strange to see the faces of dozens of people we knew by name, and had just dined with, though remaining perfect strangers.

Again the Bouvier family was isolated in one half of the beautiful dining hall. This time, they had chosen the half which contained the only three tables in the room: one laden with Beluga caviar; one with champagne; and the third with mixed *hors d'oeuvres*.

It was a brilliant strategic maneuver. The hermetic Kennedy clan, leery as they were of mixing, were drawn ineluctably toward the tables. Sporadic incidents of intermingling began to occur.

It was a good while before Jack and Jackie arrived. The minute they swept into the room, everyone surged over toward them. Maude's husband, John Davis, burst into laughter, saying to Miche, "Bet you never saw so many Republicans chasing after one Democrat!"

The President and First Lady didn't stay long. After shaking hands with everyone in the room, they had to leave us

once again. It was time to change into a new wardrobe for
the first of the Inaugural Balls that would go on all evening
and well into the morning.

We had brought twelve-year-old Michie along to share
the unforgettable experience. With a start, I remembered
that, given the chance, he might well be getting into a small
variety of hell. Looking over to where he stood beside Lynda
Byrd Johnson, I was relieved. She had taken him over the
second we entered the room.

One look at them told me he was still totally enthralled
with her. And she was evidently getting terrific pleasure out
of solidly spoiling him. I breathed a sigh of relief and
headed back to the tables to further enjoy the champagne
and caviar.

Moving away from the crowd, I stood at the massive windows with their elegant satin drapes flowing down on either
side. Outside, below the window, the expansive lawn of the
White House was covered by a shifting blanket of ice and
snow. For a moment, gazing out at the sparse isolation, my
thoughts fell once more on the Bouvier family plot. I
thought about Jackie's beloved father, buried there beneath
the freezing elements.

It was not merely morbidity which kept dragging my
thoughts back to Jackie's father, nor even the realization
that it should have been the crowning experience of his
lifetime. The other members of the Bouvier family had
grown up with her, or spent a good deal of time watching
her grow. But for me, Jackie had been seen first through
Jack's adoring, uncritical eyes. Perhaps it colored my own
perception.

The people outside who had waited hours for a glimpse
of her might think of Jackie as the wife of Jack Kennedy.
Or as a vivacious, soft-spoken yet powerful First Lady. To
me, her every motion and word will always recall the father
she loved so much, and who called her "the most beautiful
daughter a man ever had."

Turning away from the window, I caught a glimpse of
Miche on the far side of the hall, talking with a small, pretty

woman. Although she was no longer in her prime, one look
at those bright, inquiring eyes told me who she was. I had
never met Janet Auchincloss, since she and Jack were divorced before I married Miche. After so many years, she
and Miche had a good deal to talk about.

I walked over and was introduced, then stood there as
they rolled back the past. As for me, I was alternating between listening to their words of fond remembrance, and
watching Bouvier Beale with awe. Crystal bowl in hand, the
gourmet was turning gourmand as he attempted to drain
it of its contents—certainly no less than five pounds of beluga!

Coming over to Miche and identifying himself as the
White House housekeeper, a smallish man in a dark suit
said Jackie wanted to see Miche in the private quarters of
the White House. We took our leave of Janet and followed
the scurrying figure through the White House.

In one of the downstairs rooms, the little man insisted
that I be dumped—rather unceremoniously, I thought—
while Miche was whisked upstairs.

I sat at the base of a magnificent carved spiral staircase,
feeling a little miffed. Not only at being prevented from
accompanying Miche upstairs, but for being taken away
from the dining hall and all of the fascinating people there,
only to be left alone in solitary splendor at the gate. Having
had at least one rifle barrel aimed in my direction that day,
I was not about to test my luck by coursing through the
private quarters of the White House unescorted.

However, I did not have long to be annoyed. Spouting
apologies, the same little man reappeared and begged for
forgiveness, explaining that there had been a misunder-
standing. He then asked if I would please allow him to escort
me upstairs, to join Miche and Jackie.

I said certainly.

Once again, Jackie had demonstrated her sensitivity to
my emotional needs, then gone the extra step to have the
housekeeper set things aright. With a smile as he escorted

me upstairs now, I remembered the first time I was at a public function of Jackie's.

It was not long after Miche and I had moved back to the States. Jackie invited us to a Wild West dinner party for some charity which I have forgotten.

I do remember that we were fairly broke at the time. Having worked as a cowboy in Arizona, Miche was able, ultimately, to produce a rather credible outfit. He wore a straw hat, not a Stetson; and his cowboy boots were neither lizard skin nor anteater. But with a bit of saddle soap, they looked fairly authentic.

Unfortunately, having grown up as an English banker's daughter in South America, I was not so well apparelled. Far beyond missing the requisite pearl-handled derringer, my entire cowgirl wardrobe consisted of a bandana!

I knew better than to go out and buy an elaborate costume which I would wear only once. I went in a black velvet dress and a cowboy hat. Although I knew I was doing the sensible thing, I felt increasingly uncomfortable as one after another beautiful lady passed by me with a carefully researched costume, authentically representing some frontier woman of yore.

Sooner or later, it was bound to happen! A terribly well-heeled cowgirl, eyeing me on the other side of Jackie, looked puzzled. At length, introducing herself as Annie Oakley, she asked me pointedly, "And *who* are *you?*"

Certainly I had no specific American woman in mind, and was at a loss for an answer. Seeing me begin to sink through the floor, Jackie immediately spoke up. "Kathy, you're really so clever. Why, that's exactly what Texas Guinan would have worn!"

Whoever Texas Guinan might have been, it was my alter ego for the rest of the night. Sammy Davis, Jr. put on a great show that evening. So full of vitality and showmanship that, if Jackie hadn't told me, I would never have known he had been forced to fly in direct from Europe with a fever and chills. Secure in my identity, I sat back and enjoyed the show, instead of being embarrassed!

We all agreed in the family that Jackie had a rare understanding of people.

By now, the White House housekeeper and I had arrived at a bank of elevators. Immediately before us, Jack Kennedy appeared in the center of a living wall of Secret Service men. For a moment, I assumed we would share the elevator, but the doors closed immediately behind him, and another set opened for us. The Secret Service was not taking any chances with the new president.

Jackie looked truly radiant, and more excited than I had ever seen her before. After kissing her hello, we settled down for a few minutes of conversation. Her private quarters were like Grand Central Terminal. Like bees in a hive, people kept darting in and out.

With constant interruption, it was almost useless to try to keep up either end of a serious discussion. Jack Kennedy then appeared with a towel draped around his neck. The subtle device instantly cleared the room, but by then it was time for Jackie to be getting ready as well, so we said goodbye and joined the departing crowd.

Miche had always been Jackie's favorite cousin. Besides being her godfather, he was so close to Jack that they had been virtually raised as brother and sister. Yet, in her insistence in seeing him in the midst of all of the insanity, I thought I recognized a desire to remember her father. Like Jackie, Miche had the distinctive eyes and chin which were Jack's trademark, as well as a pencil-line moustache and physique that recalled Jack's almost exactly.

We then drove to Emmy's townhouse in Georgetown and collapsed on our warm, comfortable bed. It seemed like a matter of seconds before it was time to get up and get dressed once more, this time for the Inaugural Ball.

For me, dressing was not too difficult a feat. But Miche's suitcase had been stolen two days before in New York when the car was parked on the street for fifteen minutes.

It was the height of the formal celebration season in

Washington, and every six-foot-two man in the town was out renting a tuxedo. In the middle of all of our other preoccupations, Miche had to rent a set of tails in a hurry, and it is doubtful that without Carlisle Allan's popularity he would have succeeded. As it was, the tails arrived at the last possible minute.

Emmy had arranged a dinner party for us before the ball. We had a dinner which I'm certain was excellent. But at the time, I was far too excited to really taste anything. I do remember that we ate our salad from crystal plates which had been "liberated" from Adolf Hitler's private collection at Berchtesgaden when Carlisle's 15th Army Corps took that edifice.

When the hour arrived, we were picked up in a Cadillac limousine and driven to the Armory, I in a glorious mink borrowed from Emmy, and Miche in his rented evening clothes. The limousine had no snow tires, and there was one hill we were sure it could never negotiate. To our surprise, we did make it over the crest, but only after sliding backwards halfway down the street a few times.

The crush at the Armory was amazing! We strained and pushed our way to our seats one tier up from the dance floor. For the first time in years, Miche, Bouvie, Phelan Beale, Jr. and Jack Davis were reunited. Phelan, Jr.'s wife Rosella, as well as Shella and her husband, Bill Crouse, Jr., were there as well. As soon as we had all exchanged greetings, there was a small commotion to our left.

With difficulty, we made out the figure of Rose Kennedy. The section beside ours had been allotted to the Kennedy clan, and she was trying without success to get to her seat. As one, the men in our party lifted her bodily over the railing, dropping her gently into the waiting chair.

"Ruffles and Flourishes" burst forth from the orchestra. Looking like two dolls from a wedding cake, or perhaps like something out of a fairy tale, the President and his First Lady appeared out of nowhere on the dance floor, where they waltzed in long, flawless circles around the room. Then, with the entire hall roaring with applause, they vanished as magically as they had appeared, leaving the dance floor to the rest of the celebrants.

It was too crowded to be really enjoyable, and the combined noise of thousands of conversations was growing deafening. After a conference, the cousins and their spouses and guests decided to head for wider spaces, a place that would be more comfortable, less crowded, and with slightly less starched music.

We got home from the jazz club sometime in the morning, wonderfully exhausted.

The next day, as we drove back north, Miche and I were happily reminiscing about Jack. We laughed at the sensation he would have caused at the ball. Particularly if he had followed his usual custom and danced the "Why Dance?"

The old "plenty of hip motion and very little footwork" was an item some enquiring photographer would have been sure to use.

TWENTY-SIX

Versailles

The spring following Jack Kennedy's inauguration, Miche was named Assistant European Director of Grumman International. It was an altogether hectic time for us.

Everything seemed to be happening at once. Miche arrived right at the start of the Paris Air Show, one of the most important events in the aviation world. Every two years at Le Bourget Airport, north of Paris, the gigantic affairs are put on and the city is turned absolutely upside down by the influx of airmen.

To find any hotel room (which we had been forced to do) is nearly impossible. Every spare bed in the city seems to be invaded by the military representatives of any nation in the world big enough to own an air force. In addition, there are an equal number of hordes of shadowy grey men slinking around in an attempt to ferret out the secrets of all of the new classified aircraft of every nation represented.

Then there was one other set of conspicuous visitors. M. le President Kennedy, and his wife, La Jolie Jacqui. The airshow as enough to turn Paris into one enormous French traffic jam. But the French flocked by the hundreds of thousands to see Jackie. She had made quite an impression on a very select group while living at the home of the Countess de Renty and studying at the Sorbonne. She spoke French fluently and was instantly recognized as a woman who could match the snobbish Parisians when it came to elegance and class.

Moreover, Jackie was one hell of a beautiful woman. All told, it brought the citizens to the streets in record numbers.

While all of this was going on, we were still living out of a hotel, searching for an apartment. Miche battled the chaos to the best of his ability, balancing the demands of settling our family in a foreign country, running an air show, and at the same time arranging to get from point A to point B so that we could accept our invitations to some of the social functions Charles de Gaulle was giving in honor of the Kennedys. With all transportation routes snarled, travelling in Paris had grown virtually impossible.

To begin with, the Grumman show meant flying the aircraft, which in turn meant getting the proper air clearance; babying the pilots and keeping them sober the night before; somehow managing to secure prime flying time so that the maximum number of foreign military men would be there to see it; and constantly attending to the myriad vice-presidents who use the show as a good boondoggle. How Miche managed that and got us in to see Jack and Jackie I'll never know. Although his exhaustion at the end was a partial answer.

In the meantime, I was struggling to get our children enrolled in new schools, find a new apartment, and do the thousand other things necessary to become established in a new city. My schoolgirl French had always been fine at cocktail parties, where manners dictated that my stumbling efforts be at least tolerated. But the Parisians have never been noted for patience where mutilation of their language was at issue, and the disdain I felt subjected to at every contact did not help out at all.

The only clothing I had with me was whatever my suitcase could hold. While the rest was on its way over from America, I had to somehow get appropriate clothing for all of the parties we would be attending. The first step was scurrying around finding a baby sitter. My two bored-to-death and neglected sons, plus our dog, were all stranded in a hotel room while I searched for clothes that would not be entirely ridiculed at the greatest event of the year in the fashion capital of the world.

Under those circumstances, buying an armload of designer clothes was somehow not half as much fun as it ought to have been.

First on the calendar of social events was a formal reception given by General de Gaulle at the Elysée Palace. At the entry to the palace, we were given a thorough going over by the guard. In Paris, the name Bouvier did not in the least imply Jackie.

Unfortunately, as the glorious arrival of Jackie brought a new vogue to the common name, everyone was suddenly a relative. The instant kin multiplied, going to crass extents to cash in on their newfound heritage and crash the reception. The name Bouvier was fast becoming a thorn in de Gaulle's side.

Being quite new in Paris, we were appreciative of all of the recognition we received on the streets as true American Bouviers. But when a young girl with that last name raced her car to Paris to see her "aunt" Jackie and was killed, it seemed like half of the *arrondissement* called up with condolences. It was certainly a tragic accident, but the girl, apart from being a total stranger, was not even a distant cousin to us!

When the guard at the Elysée Palace discovered that our invitations were genuine, he cheerfully saluted us through. Once inside, we approached a greeting line and were announced by the major-domo. General de Gaulle was standing at the head of the line. At once, he turned toward us with a tortured expression of outraged anger which would have sent a boa constrictor running for cover. He had us pegged for impostors and whispered something to the honor guard beside him.

Involuntarily frightened by the malevolent leer in de Gaulle's eyes, I had instinctively drawn back. Now the man beside him began walking toward us with a purposeful, determined stride. With no questions asked, he was going to throw us out on our heels.

Jackie, standing concealed on the other side of the general, peeked around his chest and immediately apprehended the disaster he had caused. Despite the tight fit of her stunning formal evening gown, Jackie somehow managed to leap across the floor, cut off the official bouncer in his tracks, embrace us both, and lead us to the welcoming line.

Approaching de Gaulle, she raised her voice from the normal whisper to a sufficiently emphatic level and said in her perfect French, "General de Gaulle, please permit me to introduce you to my *cousin* Michel and his wife," emphasizing the relationship. We relaxed and shook his hand. If he was not convinced, the French leader was at least begrudgingly willing to let us stay.

I thanked God that the incident was over. For a few seconds, it had been quite touch and go.

We made our way down the line to Lee, and spent the rest of the night chatting with her, particularly since Miche had not seen very much of Lee since the marriage to Michael Canfield. Married to Stas, Lee had quickly become accustomed to being the toast of Europe. She was absolutely thriving, looking young and happy and beautiful and terribly successful.

The highlight of Jackie's visit to Paris came the following evening. June 1st, 1961 was to be one of the most thrilling evenings in Jackie's life. Jack Bouvier's pride would have known no bounds on Inauguration Day. But nothing could have held a candle to Jackie at the Palace of Versailles.

In Washington, Jack Kennedy had naturally been the true star. But this night belonged to Jackie and to her alone!

The chateau itself is spectacular. At the height of the grandeur of the Kingdom of France, it took fifty years to build. Beyond that, Louis XIV, the Sun King, spent most of his life improving it. In fact, it is said that he never saw the outer facade without some sort of scaffolding attached, since the work went on continually!

On either side of the chateau, two entire hillsides were entirely cleared by hand, then replanted with the trees geometrically placed on a grid stretching as far as the eye can see. Below the palace, a garden complete with shade trees, diagonal paths, canals, statues and magnificent fountains vies for the beauty of the chateau itself.

Of the fifteen hundred original fountains, only three hundred remain intact. This night, all three hundred of them lit by soft lights as we passed was dizzying enough. As we walked past the *Garde Républicain* in their intricate and colorful sixteenth-century costumes, the insistent patter of the water in fountains seemed like chanting. Like some ancient song of history, bearing witness to a chain of kings and queens and mistresses, and to their sad tales of disappointment, cruelty and death.

General de Gaulle could not have found a more perfect site for the banquet than the "Galerie des Glaces," or Hall of Mirrors. On one side of the vast reception room an unbroken expanse of glass looks out onto the fountains and the garden below them. The opposing wall of the hall is composed entirely of mirrors, one per window. Seated around a central long table, every guest is therefore afforded a view of the magnificent rear grounds of the palace.

Between the reflections of the lighted fountains caught in the mirrored glass, pillars of marble decorated with gold thrust upwards to the ceiling, dividing the mirrors on the inside, and the windows on the outer wall. Works of art dotted the heavy carved mouldings touching the ceiling. Above our heads, a universe of figures spread out in an endless series of ceiling frescoes, lit indirectly so that the wonderful blending of color was apparent.

One incredibly long, thin oval table ran the length of the room. Upon its surface, the reflection from hundreds of candelabra danced, shimmering across the glistening surface of the silver and the priceless French china.

White-gloved waiters in cutaway black jackets stood behind the chairs throughout the meal, one per guest. There they remained and effortlessly kept a constant flow of wine in the glasses and food on the table, their faces as immobile and as expressionless as those of robots. It was a six-course dinner, and the sheer bulk of gourmet food served was staggering. It's a wonder that people could get up out of their seats!

When they finally did exit, it's amazing that they didn't stagger out of the room. We drank a Riesling 1955, a Chateau Cheval Blanc '53 and then a Corton-Grancey Lanson '52. Throughout the meal, the waiters replenished my wineglass regularly—virtually after every sip!

The dinner was a thing of wonder. But the *pièce de resistance* was seated next to de Gaulle. Jackie had on a soft, creamy satin dress designed by Givenchy. Her bare shoulders looked exquisitely soft and feminine in the flickering light of the candelabra. Set in her stunning Alexandre *coiffure*, was a tiny and delicate diamond tiara.

General de Gaulle was more than delighted to find himself seated beside the radiant woman of French blood. That night, Jackie's southern French heritage was startlingly evident. She looked like one of the more beautiful portraits of Madame Récamier.

Later, we were led to the Theater of Louis XV. An exquisite eighteenth century room, decorated in gold and pale robin's egg blue, sparkling in the reflection of the light from chandeliers which were hung by long blue cords from the domed ceiling. Above our heads, the balconies were adorned with still more chandeliers, so that the great room was blazing with a million lights.

It was then that the two presidents and their ladies appeared on one of the balconies. Surging up out of our seats, we all rose to our feet and saluted them.

Perhaps no woman had ever before looked as radiant and as electrifying as Jackie. That night, she stood up and became the "greatest woman in the world" before our eyes.

Jackie stood there calmly, confidently. It was evident now that, as Jack had always asserted, she was born to be there, applauded by countless millions.

There are those who will point to another's success and trace it back to the influence of a parent throughout childhood. With all due respect to Freud, Jackie's achievements must be laid at her own feet. To say that she had succeeded in fulfilling her father's greatest fantasy would be to rob her of her own crowning moment.

Yet that night of palaces and nobility, of opulence and fine wines, powerful and handsome men and women of global importance was a salute to Jack as clearly as it was to his daughter.

It might have been the greatest night in Jack's entire life. He never made it to see Jackie in Versailles. For that I nearly wept.

But looking at her standing beside Jack Kennedy, no less dazzling or enchanting than a Helen of Troy, sadness was impossible. Across the great theater, I could just make out the faint outlines of her smile, the corners of her mouth ever so slightly upturned.

Perhaps Jack was there, after all.

TWENTY-SEVEN

November, 1963

It was a chilly, damp evening in France two years later.

Miche was at a distinguished restaurant in Metz, wining and dining an important business associate. All of their conversation was devoted to one thing, the Mohawk OV-1, a Grumman army reconnaissance plane which had been tested at a French air force base that afternoon. The tests had gone superbly. One after one, the two men exchanged data, growing more excited with every result.

There were excellent prospects for a major sale in the air. Perhaps dozens of the aircraft would be ordered. It was an evening for celebration, and it deserved an excellent dinner plus a healthy sampling of the region's famous *blanc de blanc*.

After the meal, they leaned back in the chairs making small talk as they sipped a mellow cognac. A waiter came over to the table and asked softly if they were American or British.

When Miche replied, the old man shook his head sadly. His tone was formal, almost diplomatic as he announced, "Gentlemen, I am desolated to have to inform you . . . but we have just heard on the radio that your President has been assassinated."

There were tears in the old man's eyes, as though he had just lost his son.

Throughout Paris, the news spread with the speed of lightning. It crackled along the streets and burned along the telephone lines. Some Frenchmen said that losing the husband of "La Jolie Jacqui" was like losing a brother. Others wept in the streets. There was an atmosphere of terror.

I was at the apartment on Rue Adolph Yvonne with our two children. Exactly how the news first reached me, I have since banished from memory. But I do remember sitting before the radio with Jayvie on my lap, clinging to me as we listened to the reports filtering in. Above the anxiety and the grief, the senseless brutality of the assassination tore at my insides. The descriptions of Jackie seemed surreal; macabre little snippets which exploded in my ears: *Mrs. Kennedy's pink suit splattered with blood . . . Mrs. Kennedy crawled onto the back seat of the limousine. . . .*

Things I never wanted to hear and would rather not remember. Images which will continue to haunt me forever.

That day, the phone never stopped ringing. Countless people, mainly strangers from the quarter where we lived, were calling to express their sympathies. Those who knew us understood that Miche had been raised virtually as Jackie's older brother. Their condolences were deeply motivated.

But as to the hundreds of other callers, we were merely Bouviers they had found in the *annuaire.* The French national grief was so strong and the personal grieving of every citizen so intense that they had to express it somehow.

There was no way that Miche could reach Jackie. All of the international telephone and telegraph lines were held open for news reports.

Miche could think of nothing but of some way he might possibly get a message to Jackie. Speak with her for a moment and see if she wanted him there.

Never before had I seen so much frustration and rage in my husband. Scattered and divided as they were, he was still the head of the Bouvier family. He felt that he might be letting Jackie down—that Jack would have wanted him to join her in those dreadful hours of her life. But unable to reach her, he could not presume it was what he should do even if he *could* get a flight out of Orly. Which was dubious.

Instead, we went to the memorial service for Jack Kennedy at the Cathedral of Notre Dame. It would be a good long time before we could get through to Jackie.

In the photographs of Jack Kennedy's funeral, Jackie's mouth was once again drawn up tightly, looking hurt and vulnerable. As I knelt on the cold stone floor of Notre Dame, I remembered the same expression when she buried her first love, the Black Prince.

I thought not of heaven, but of Jackie, Jack Kennedy and Jack Bouvier.

In his last years, Black Jack Bouvier had lived for his daughter. He laughed when she was happy, and wept when she was sad. If he had missed her crowning moment of glory, he had also missed these darkest moments of her life.

For that, at least, I was thankful.

TWENTY-EIGHT

East Hampton Revisited

Ten years later, Jackie Onassis drove into the driveway of our Remsenburg home.

First to greet her were our three dogs. Of course, like her father, Jackie always enjoyed animals, adoring horses, dogs and cats. But I was surprised to see the feeling was reciprocated by the two large labradors and the long-haired dachshund, all of whom take guarding the property behind our massive hedge quite seriously.

Normally, they don't bite. But it would be a hard thing to convince a stranger of, considering their barks and occasional snarls. When Jackie arrived, not one of them as much as whimpered. They just sniffed at her inquisitively, wagged their tails, then returned to their stations on the porch, carefree and prone.

We soon headed out to pay a visit to the family graveyard. It had always bothered Miche that only initials and numbers had been used to mark out each of the graves; particularly that of his father. He felt strongly that the full name of every Bouvier should appear on the headstone so that future generations, made forgetful by time, could know exactly where each ancestor lay and exactly what their names had been.

By this time, Miche had decided that new headstones were needed. Jackie agreed. They also decided upon a few different kinds of bushes and flowers, to give the family plot more of the sense of lively beauty which Maude's Italian garden had brought to Lasata.

It was a sunny but frigid late fall afternoon. Leaving the graveyard we searched for a place to eat. On an off-season Monday, everything that could pass for a restaurant in civilized parts of the world was closed. Finally, we gave up on trying to find a good place and settled for a place that Miche called a tried and true "eat-it-and-beat-it."

Jackie was dressed in black slacks and a black turtleneck sweater. As always, she was wearing very big sunglasses.

We walked into the main dining area, and past the bar to a little pine table without placemats. Crowded into the front, a group of local clam diggers were on their lunch break, loading themselves against the bitter cold. They all turned to greet us, then returned to their drinks, oblivious to the fact that the most famous woman in the world was among them.

I watched Jackie arch her back and lean forward on the hard pine bench, lighting into some horrible concoction with terribly greasy-looking chicken. She looked happy and at ease with a ketchup bottle at one elbow and a paper napkin dispenser at the other. Just as happy and at ease as she had looked at Versailles, with all of the world marvelling at her feet.

As we were eating, a woman at the bar began staring. After doing a double take in Jackie's direction, she slid off the bar stool and came tottering over for a better look. Five feet from our table, she sloppily came to a halt and took in our little group.

Miche smiled and took another bite of his hamburger. Jackie shook a bit more salt onto her plate.

The woman shook her head with disgust. "Naw, it *couldn't* be!" she mumbled, and went reeling out of the bar.

After lunch, we proceeded to an appointment with the new head of St. Philomena's church. He had been alerted that we were coming, and now stood taking in our approach. As Miche's small blue Toyota—slightly in need of a new tailpipe—swept into the driveway, he plainly looked annoyed, thinking we were intruders who would interfere with the grand entrance that Jackie Onassis was about to make at any minute.

But as we drove closer, his anger turned into bewilderment. This *was* the grand entrance!

After the introductions and handshakes all around, he asked where the rest of the retinue was. The limousines, the police sirens, the Secret Service men. We had to explain to him that there weren't any. He seemed terribly disappointed.

We discussed our plans for improving the landscaping in the little family plot, and discussed how to arrange for the new boxwood shrubs and flowers to be planted and maintained. The priest sat and listened, nodding his head absent-mindedly.

But what should have been a glorious event in his mind turned out to be awfully mundane, I could tell. From start to finish, the petty little details seemed all too boring. With one ear, he might still be listening for the wail of the sirens, and I am not certain that he ever quite forgave us for letting him down.

So close to the site of so many childhood memories, Jackie and Miche gave in to the temptation to sneak a peak at Lasata. Driving up before the long horseshoe driveway, they looked at the great house with a sense of shock. The tangle of ivy which had encased the stucco walls was now entirely removed. By now, even the stump of the linen tree which led to Maude's bedroom had been dug up by a windstorm without leaving a trace!

East of the house, and back on the road which had once led to the stables, a massive modern swimming pool complex had been erected at great expense. Of course, there was not a trace of Maude's mighty vegetable garden, or of Jackie and Jack's ancient baseball field.

Once there, they had to satisfy their nostalgic longing and curiosity and sneak an unauthorized peek at the stables. There was a strong possibility that no one was home. At any rate, there weren't any cars around. So Miche drove down Further Lane, circled around and came up on the tiny road leading to the back of the property.

Parking the car in a ditch, we jumped out. Nervously, we scanned all four directions. Seeing that the coast was clear, we walked past the bushes where Miche and the Beale brothers had once set up a shooting stand and headed for the paddock.

Without the lush summer foliage, there was something very blatant about our little foray into Lasata. For the two Bouviers, there was a moment of absolute ecstasy.

For once, there were no photographers or reporters. Except Miche and myself, no one was there to witness the event. Jackie looked for all the world like a guilty little child engaging in some delicious forbidden luxury. She was engrossed in the past, and a sort of childish, naughty little girl grin reached her lips.

I can't imagine what they would have done if the stables, too, had been removed. Luckily, they still stood in place, albeit more than a little worse for wear. At the time, you could still make out faint traces of the horses' names above some of the stalls.

Jackie was looking very hard for Danseuse, the favorite horse who had followed her down to the Auchincloss estate. She had no luck there, but we did manage to discover Ghandi's nameplate.

A moment later, we walked back to the car and headed back to Remsenburg.

* * *

When Edith Bouvier Beale died, most of her relatives attended the funeral at St. Philomena's Church.

It was a terribly cold day, one of the coldest in New York's history. The ground was so solidly frozen that it had taken the gravediggers hours to pickax a spot in the Bouvier family plot for her.

We shivered, pulling our coats tightly around us as the priest continued his benediction at the graveside. Above us, the old copper beech tree drooped sadly. Its leaves, which in the summer were a glorious reddish color, lay scattered and crumbling beneath our feet. The boughs stood starkly bare against the grey sky.

Aside from the members of the family, who had gathered from all over the globe, there were very few people there. In her last years, Edith had not once stepped out of Grey Gardens.

The house, which had not been one of the loveliest and liveliest in all of East Hampton, was now a pale shadow of its former glory. With quiet generosity, Jackie had poured many thousands of dollars into it, while Lee oversaw the work done to restore it. With Edith's death, the only inhabitant besides their cats would be her daughter, Little Edie.

Years ago as "Whatabody Beale," Little Edie had been the belle of East Hampton, parading through the village at the head of a string of beaux a mile long. Like her mother, Little Edie had retreated more and more into her own little fantasy world at Grey Gardens as she grew older . . . instead of marrying and settling into a life of her own.

The twenty young boxwood shrubs which Miche and Jackie had planted less than a year before, were starting to give shelter to the site. Two tall trees bearing sharp thorns, like those seen in the crown of thorns in paintings of Christ's crucifixion, helped the copper beech keep vigil.

In accordance with Edith's last request, a scratchy old 78

rpm recording of her own voice singing "Together" was played. It sounded beautiful ringing out proudly in the eaves of the small church.

As the body of my husband's aunt was lowered slowly into the ground, my eyes turned automatically to the simple marble slab rising modestly out of the snow-covered earth. The writing on it was only half-discernible, but I knew it by heart. "J.V.B. III, 1891-1957," it tersely announced.

After discussing the matter with Lee, Jackie had decided not to alter her father's original headstone. Today, only Jack is represented by his initials, rather than by his full name.

Even in death, Jack is different.

Laconic though he was, I have wondered many times about the separateness of Jack's tombstone. He was a funny man, all of his life making light of ancestor-worship, ignoring the dictates of the class to which he was born, devoting himself to temporary pleasures.

Black Jack Bouvier lived high and fast. Throughout New York and the Hamptons, his notorious seductions, his cars and his horses left an indelible impression. Twenty years after his death, they are like fingerprints in the dust, the lingering last notes of a sonata.

John Vernou Bouvier III was the father of Jackie and of Princess Lee. But the time will come when that claim to fame will be obscured by time.

I can only imagine what Jack would think if some casual visitor to the gravesite read the initials and did not know whose they were. He'd probably say "Look, I don't give a damn!" But he would. He would want to be remembered.

TWENTY-NINE

Vestiges

Last spring, we went to East Hampton to visit Jack and Bud.

The old copper beech was in full bloom. The sun was shining as it had been on the day that Jack was buried. All around, tiny spring flowers were just coming into blossom above the new blades of grass.

A pair of birds swooped overhead, getting a nest ready for their family to be hatched. They chattered angrily, annoyed that we were disturbing them in the midst of their labors.

The boxwood planted by Miche and Jackie had grown quite tall. Already, it was time to begin cutting it back.

Someone had placed a bouquet of bachelor buttons on Jack's grave. I held one of them in my hand, then showed it to Miche. The purplish flower was as fresh and strong as our memories of the man who lay near to those he loved in the little cemetery.

Afterwards, we drove down to the shore. The pounding waves on the beach beat back the sand again and again, forever chanting reminders of the past.

By now, the traces of Jack's world have all but disap-

peared. Several years ago, the Canoe Place Inn on the Shin-
necock Canal, Jack's beloved hunting retreat, was repainted
orange, covered with massive drawings of fruit, and re-
named "Peaches." This year, even that has been replaced
by a discotheque named "OBI East."

Even Merrywood and Hammersmith Farm, the opulent
and thorny symbols of his failures, have passed into new
hands.

The sand was hot that day, and I watched it caress the
prancing feet of other people, an untried generation, busy
building their own lives, their own sand castles. Dreaming
as the generation before dreamed of comfort and stability
in the world. That it would be theirs forever, and that the
sands of time might not float their castles into the sea.

Rightly so, for what would be the purpose of dreams if
we always saw the shadow of the future, mocking our struggle to build for the future. Oblivious to threats of destruction we still build our beautiful houses in the dunes, where
the storms in the past have destroyed many before them.

The wisest ones buy the land when the hurricane has just
done its job, and swept away all remnants of the old. Land
comes cheap then. Later, it will be sold to dreamers to build
upon once again. Once the memory of the terrifying wind
is gone.

In truth, it is better to build shelters less vulnerable to
the winds of chance.

But watching the wind tear across the sand, heralding
the onset of the approaching squall, I understood the promise of a howling wind. When the hurricane is over, the air
is filled with a rare violet light which casts a hopeful glow
over the soul. It makes one want to turn cartwheels in the
sand.

We ran to the car as the rain came crashing down. As we
raced across the dunes, the faint strains of dance music
drifted out toward us. Someone was having a party.

Life was going on as usual in East Hampton. But it would

never be the same without the glamorous likes of Jack Bouvier.

Harvesting his autumn crops to be stored safely in his cellar, the wise man may win in the long run. But it is the fool who reaps the incomparable first bite of the stolen apple.

Knocked about by the hurricanes of life, Jack still had taken what to him was the best of all.

That first bite of the apple tasted wondrously good.